THE CITY OF THE
SACRED WELL

"A last forward swing and the bride of Yum Chac hurtles far out over the well."

THE CITY OF THE SACRED WELL

BEING A NARRATIVE OF THE DISCOVERIES AND
EXCAVATIONS OF EDWARD HERBERT THOMP-
SON IN THE ANCIENT CITY OF CHI-CHEN
ITZA WITH SOME DISCOURSE ON THE
CULTURE AND DEVELOPMENT OF
THE MAYAN CIVILIZATION AS
REVEALED BY THEIR ART
AND ARCHITECTURE, HERE
SET DOWN AND ILLUS-
TRATED FROM
PHOTOGRAPHS

BY

T. A. WILLARD

GROSSET & DUNLAP ~ Publishers
by arrangement with The Century Company

Printed in U. S. A.

PREFACE

This book is primarily an attempt to recount the many thrilling experiences of Edward Herbert Thompson in his lifelong quest for archæological treasures in the ancient and abandoned city of Chi-chen Itza, for centuries buried beneath the jungle of Yucatan.

As a boy Mr. Thompson—or Don Eduardo, as he is affectionately known to the natives about the Sacred City—sat in his snug New England home and read of the adventures of Stephens in Yucatan, descriptions of the old Maya civilization, and the legends concerning the Sacred Well at Chi-chen Itza. Then and there he determined that his life-work should be the uncovering of the age-old secrets of the ancient city.

When still a mere youth he was appointed by the President of the United States as the first American Consul to Yucatan, the appointment having been urged by the American Antiquarian Society and the Peabody Museum of Harvard University, both of which were anxious to have a trained investigator on the peninsula.

Enthusiastically Mr. Thompson undertook his double mission. For over twenty-five years he remained at his post as consul. During this long period, sometimes at the head of regularly organized expeditions under the auspices of American archæological institutions, at other times with only his faithful native followers, he discovered ruined cities until then unknown to the world and carried on exhaustive researches among those already discovered.

At last Mr. Thompson resigned the consular office, in order to carry on the various scientific undertakings that required all his time and energy. Chief among these was the search for relics that for hundreds of years had lain buried in the mud at the bottom of the Sacred Well.

Many and many a night, under the gorgeous moonlight of Yucatan or by some cozy fireside in the States, I have listened entranced, as the hours glided by, to the true tales Don Eduardo tells of his experiences or of the customs and the folk-lore of the country. I know intimately this lovable, modest, blue-eyed six-footer, this dreamer and adventurer, gray-haired now but still with the heart of a boy. I know him better, perhaps, than does any other man, and if I do not write down the things he has told me they will never be written, for Don Eduardo will not do it. Therefore I have asked and received his permission to write, from memory and from his notes and my own, this book, which he has read and corrected.

It is a faithful account of the many valuable archæological finds he has made, but, though written as if Don Eduardo himself were speaking, it inevitably lacks the color and fire of his word-of-mouth narrative. It contains, further, such description of the Maya culture and history as may help the reader to understand this ancient civilization. The writer hopes that it may be acceptable to the avid reader of travel and adventure, and there is also the timid hope that it may be of some little educational value to the serious-minded reader, to the end that he may feel that he has not wasted time on a mere "yarn."

T. A. WILLARD.

ACKNOWLEDGMENT

The author is indebted, for information and assistance, to many good friends in Yucatan, but chiefly to Señor Juan Martinez H., to the late Teoberto Maler, and to Mr. and Mrs. William James for their timely hospitality.

The books and writings of the old priests, as well as current books on the Maya era, also have been of much aid.

T. A. W.

CONTENTS

LIST OF ILLUSTRATIONS

THE CITY OF THE
SACRED WELL

THE CITY OF THE SACRED WELL

CHAPTER I

YUCATAN, THE LAND OF THE MAYAS

IMAGINE yourself the sole owner of a plantation within which lies a city more than twelve square miles in area; a city of palaces and temples and mausoleums; a city of untold treasures, rich in sculptures and paintings. Would you not feel shamefully wealthy? And does it not seem strange that Don Eduardo, the master of such a plantation, takes the fact of his ownership with apparent calmness?

But, before your fancy carries you too far, let me tell you a little more about this remarkable city, which may dampen your ardor for ownership, but which only increases its value in Don Eduardo's eyes. It is a dead city. Its thousands of inhabitants perished or abandoned it nobody knows how long ago—probably before Columbus first saw the shores of America. And it is in the heart of Yucatan, where Mexico, ending like the upflung tail of a huge fish, juts into the gulf, while Cuba serves as a sentinel a hundred and fifty miles to the eastward.

The Treasure City, the City of the Sacred Well, with the queer-sounding name of the Chi-chen Itza (pronounce it Chee'chen Eet-za'), is for the most part overgrown with tropical jungle. Its treasures are valuable only to the antiquarian.

Early in our conversations about the City of the Sacred Well, Don Eduardo told me that because at the time of his purchase the plantation was well within the territory dominated by the dreaded Sublevados, the re-

THE ANCIENT CITY OF CHI-CHEN ITZA IS AT NO GREAT DISTANCE FROM THE UNITED STATES.

bellious Maya Indians, no planter dared live in or even visit the region for long, and so he was able to secure the land from its absentee owners cheap, as plantation prices run in Yucatan.

"My life-interest has been American archæology," he said, "and I came first to Yucatan, thirty years ago, to explore its ruins and relics of an ancient civilization. Even before that I had read of the immense Sacred Well at Chi-chen Itza—a well as wide as a small lake and deep enough to hold a fifteen-story building—and had made up my mind that I would be the man who some day made it yield up its secrets. For a long time I tried to persuade various wealthy Americans to finance the undertaking, but organizing a stock company to raise sunken galleons along the Spanish Main would be a simple task as compared with my difficulties in promoting what seemed a will-o'-the-wisp project. At last, however, I did succeed."

But I am ahead of my story.

The trip from New York to the City of the Sacred Well requires but a week and may now be accomplished luxuriously, whereas my earlier journeys over the same route were anything but comfortable. Mr. John L. Stephens, who was sent to Yucatan by the United States Government in 1841, describes, in his interesting book "Incidents of Travel in Yucatan," the difficulties of travel which he met. They might have daunted any spirit less courageous than his. His four volumes, although written nearly eighty years ago, retain their pristine freshness and are still authoritative. I recommend them heartily to the reader.

On any Thursday the traveler destined for the City of the Sacred Well may board at New York a Ward Line steamer bound for Progreso, the only port of Yucatan. The liner stops over at Havana, and a day and a night after leaving that hectic city one awakes in the early dawn to the deep-chanted tones of a sailor who is casting the lead. "Four fathoms," he cries; then, "Three fathoms," and finally the engines are hushed and out goes the anchor. Through the port-hole is seen a lighthouse and behind it a faint, foggy vista of low-lying sandy shore.

By the time the unhurried ritual of arising has been performed and one appears on deck all is flooded with brilliant sunshine. The sky above is a cloudless cobalt blue. The day is hot, but the sea-breeze keeps it from being uncomfortably so. One senses, nevertheless, in some subtle way, that he is actually in the tropics. So shallow is the water that ocean-going vessels may not safely approach to within less than five miles of the rather uninspiring port of Progreso, marked by several long piers jutting into the sea and the aforementioned lighthouse. Passengers and goods must be taken off in lighters or in small boats. On approaching the shore one sees rows of pelicans sitting alongside the wharves—the most serious and sad-looking birds imaginable. They remind one of the rows of Glooms frequently portrayed by one of our cartoonists in the daily newspaper comic strip.

There is little reason for tarrying in Progreso, even though it is the third most important seaport in Mexico. It is from here that the henequen of Yucatan is shipped, and the cultivation of this cactus-like plant, from whose fiber rope and twine are made, constitutes the chief enterprise of the province. Two railroads, one narrow-gauge, the other standard, cover the twenty-four miles between Progreso and the lovely city of Mérida, capital of Yucatan. Oddly enough, the fare is higher on the narrower, longer, and poorer road than on the road of standard gauge. The latter is modern in every respect and provided with coaches and locomotives imported from the

United States. The daily Peniche Express starts on time and arrives in the same fashion.

The Grand Hotel at Mérida is the customary stopping-place for all foreigners and is a very good and well-operated institution. It faces the beautiful tree-lined Plaza Hidalgo, but is, unfortunately, located close to a number of churches and a cathedral whose cracked bells are rung mightily at various hours and particularly when one wishes to sleep. As a result, persons not yet hardened to this venerable Spanish-American custom are likely to have a broken night's slumber.

Mérida is a city of 63,000 people and is modern in many respects. It is hot there in the sun but cool in the shade, for there is always a breeze from the perpetually blowing trade-wind. The city is healthful, well paved, electrically lighted, and excellently served with street cars, and it has many handsome buildings and residences. Its population varies all the way from the pure Castilian, through the Mestizos, to the Mayas or full-blooded Indians. Almost every night a band plays in one of the several plazas or parks. North-American airs are favored and I have heard them much more badly played by musicians in our own land than here under the tropical moonlight, in a setting of rarely beautiful and fragrant flowers. During the band concert daintily clean Indian girls, in their voluminous embroidered dresses or *huipiles* and embroidered sandals, circle about. In another circle stroll their Indian beaux in high-heeled sandals and starched white cotton suits. The ladies of the upper class, dressed in the Spanish or European manner, are driven slowly about the plaza in their automobiles.

Formerly carriages—the sort we call, or did call, landeaus—were used, but the automobile has displaced these and in so doing has destroyed half the charm of the scene. Nevertheless it is still charming. The romance of it may be guaranteed to put a thrill into the cold heart of the loan shark from Chicago. It alone is worth the trip to Yucatan and it cannot be described; it has to be experienced at first hand.

During the month of February there is a carnival in Mérida, ending with a fancy-dress ball for the four hundred socially elect. The carnival rivals the Mardi Gras of New Orleans and is enthusiastically celebrated by the whole populace. The floats and decorations are quite as costly and tasteful as any seen in the New Orleans celebration. One year I happened to be in Mérida at the time of the carnival and through the kindly assistance of my good friends Mr. and Mrs. James I received an invitation to the ball. This gorgeous affair would have compared creditably to any similar festivity in New York.

The ball took place at the palatial home of a wealthy Yucateco. This house is built in the usual Yucatan fashion. In front is a large doorway guarded by a heavy wrought-iron grill or gate. On each side of the doorway are the living-quarters, consisting of a dining-room and what we should call a living-room. These rooms form the front of a quadrangular structure surrounding a patio in which are flower beds, fountains, and tiled walks. Around the inner wall of the quadrangle is a promenade wide enough for several people to walk abreast and this is roofed over, the tile roof being supported by pillars and arches of Moorish type. The wings and rear section of the house contain the chambers for the family and guests, the kitchen, and the servants' quarters. I imagine that this particular residence had cost not much less than a million dollars. The interior is finished in Italian marble and luxuriously furnished in the Parisian manner.

And this is by no means the most palatial residence in the capital. The wealthy people of Yucatan spend much of their time in Europe and their homes show the effect. The houses have beautiful tiled floors and the walls are frequently frescoed or covered with excellent paintings; yet as a rule the rooms are somewhat bare of furniture. One building particularly worthy of mention is the most ancient in Mérida, erected in 1549 by Don Francisco Montejo, the Spanish conqueror of Yucatan. On its façade is a grotesque Indian-Moorish representation of two armored knights trampling on prostrate Indians, while below is a stone tablet bearing the name of Montejo and the date of building.

Recently an American club was started in the city, with a membership of several Americans, three or four Britons, and the remainder Yucatecos who speak English; and some do speak it fluently. The club is predominantly masculine, as the only ladies who attend are those who have lived at some time or other in the States and have acquired our customs. As a rule the women of Yucatan observe the old Spanish custom of seclusion. Girls are not permitted to go out with young men. A girl's lover may spend the evening standing before the barred window of his inamorata's home, conversing with her and strumming upon his mandolin or guitar for her edification. If he is finally accredited as a suitor, he is permitted to enter the house and sit in a stiff-backed chair across the room from his sweetheart, but Mamma and

Auntie and all the other ladies of the family are there, too, to insure decorous behavior.

The population of Yucatan is chiefly composed of the native Indians or Mayas. They are simple, kindly people and capable of development, for they are highly intelligent. To the best of our knowledge they are the direct descendants of the early Mayas, who in culture and achievements compare favorably to the people of ancient Egypt. Some of the wealthy Yucatecos are descendants of the old Maya nobility and still retain the original names denoting noble birth. But many descendants of Maya kings of old are now sunk in poverty.

Most of the present-day Mayas speak a language which has developed little from its primitive syllabic form. The Japanese, many of whom are found in Yucatan nowadays, learn the Maya tongue easily. In fact, many Japanese and Maya words are identical in sound, but as far as I know they have absolutely no kindred meaning. Some theorists have even advanced the idea that the similarity in form and construction of the Japanese and Maya languages indicates a common prehistoric origin. But there is scant proof of this, inasmuch as all primitive languages are syllabic in form.

The Maya is short in stature but surprisingly sturdy. A native will carry a load of a hundred pounds for fifteen miles without showing signs of undue fatigue. The carrier supports the load on his back and it is held in place with a band or strap passed around the forehead. Occasionally the carriers stop and let down the loads, but never for more than a few moments. An Indian porter will trot upstairs with a trunk which an ordinary mortal could hardly budge and which, alone, he contrives somehow to lift upon his back. I remember seeing two Indians carry a piano, supported on poles, for a distance of two blocks, with their customary gliding shuffle when carrying a burden. Had they at any time fallen out of step the piano must surely have been wrecked. This shuffle or trot is half-way between a walk and a run and it eats up distance.

Not uncommonly the Mayas are handsome, with regular, delicate features. Some of the young women are very beautiful, even judged by North-American standards. They are mature at twelve years of age and, like the women of so many races of the tropics, they wither or grow fat at a comparatively early age. The color of the skin is about that of a good summer coat of tan, though possibly a bit more reddish in hue. Dress the average Maya in our mode and put him on any street in our country and he would pass without comment. On closer inspection he might be said to be of foreign ancestry, but certainly he would not be mistaken for a negro.

These people, descendants of a truly great race, are decidedly superior to all other native American peoples. Their mentality is of a fairly high order. At first, in my visits to Yucatan, I had no knowledge of either the Spanish or the Maya tongue and when I had only natives for companions I was compelled to communicate with them by sign language made up on the spur of the moment. Even in the jungle my companions always understood my directions easily and carried them out correctly.

The ordinary, every-day dress of the native men is a pair of white-cotton trousers ending half-way between knee and ankle. We should have difficulty in defining them either as long or as short. The upper garment is a short-sleeved undershirt, and the ensemble is topped off with almost any kind of straw hat. Usually they also wear a short blue-and-white-striped apron fastened about the waist. Wide belts are popular—the wider the better. Frequently the men go barefoot, but more often wear sandals, fastened with twine about the ankle, a string passing from the front of the sole and between the first and second toes. When working in the fields the men sometimes discard apron and trousers, wearing only a breech-clout and hat. Sometimes they let their hair grow long so that it falls over their faces and then even the hat is discarded. On Sundays and feast-days the more affluent, at least, blossom out in starched white trousers and jacket and high-heeled wooden sandals.

The women customarily wear a *huipile,* which garment is neither a Mother-Hubbard nor a nightgown, but belongs, evidently, to the same genus or species. At any rate, it is sufficiently modest. It has a slightly low neck and short sleeves and reaches half-way from the knee to the ground. Beneath this is the *pic,* a white underskirt tied about the waist with a draw-string. Over all is worn the rebozo, a kind of shawl, and the native woman feels much ashamed if seen without this useless garment. Sandals may or may not be worn. The costume is always essentially the same. Sometimes the *huipile* is ornately and beautifully embroidered at the neck and on the sleeves. I am told that a girl will spend a year in embroidering a single *huipile* for her hope-chest. The garment is of ancient origin and I have seen murals in the ruined temples, painted centuries ago, which show women in just such embroidered garments, and at work making tortillas, which are still the main article of food in this land.

Many of the Maya women wear gorgeously embroidered sandals or slippers. The hair is done up in a knot at the nape of the neck and tastefully fastened with a ribbon. Gold chains with various sorts of pendants, such as medallions of the Virgin Mary or crosses, are very popular. Frequently the Maya belle wears several of these chains. And they *must* be solid gold; plated stuff or alloy may not be worn. It simply is n't done. In her native costume the Maya girl is very pretty and picturesque, but in European dress she resembles only a shapeless bundle tied in the middle.

The Mayas are all very clean; the daily bath for men, women, and children is universal. A sort of wooden trough serves as a bath-tub as well as the family wash-tub. The bather pours the water over his body and makes a little water go a long way, because water must be carried by hand, usually from a distant well. For a man, even the humblest, to come home at the end of the day and find his bath unprepared is just cause for a rumpus with his wife. Clean bodies and clean clothes are characteristic of the Maya and much of the generally considered more civilized world might well take a lesson from him in this respect.

The women stay at home and attend to their household tasks and take care of their numerous children while the men work in the fields. This custom is universal even among the laboring people, and it is noteworthy because nearly everywhere else in the world both women and men work in the fields. In fact, in many countries the man does the most resting.

The Maya men are exceptionally fond of children and a widow with children stands an excellent chance of finding a stepfather for her brood. It is not uncommon for a man of twenty to marry a widow twice his age, chiefly for the sake of a ready-made family. Incidentally, the unmarried Maya maiden with a child or two, especially if the children are boys, is somewhat more likely to find a husband than her virgin sister. The fact that there may be some question as to the paternity of her offspring is of small consequence in the eyes of her prospective husband. But once married, she may accept no attentions from men other than her spouse. The husband may and does shoot on sight any cavalier found hanging around her. It used to be the custom to suspend a string of shells near the door, and one did not enter a house without giving due warning by shaking the string. A man did not enter at all unless the men of the family were present.

Maya nature is that same human nature found the world over. If abused, these people can be ugly and vengeful. Treated in a reasonably decent manner, they are kindly, generous, hospitable, and scrupulously honest. Personally, I have never been cheated nor overcharged by a native. I suppose that as more and more tourists come to Yucatan the invidious custom of fleecing the traveler will be established here as it has been everywhere else.

As has been said, water is scarce in this land, and frequently the women have to go long distances for even a jugful; yet they are always willing to share their supply with any one. The wayfarer is never turned away from their doors thirsty or hungry, even though he consume the last drop of water or bit of food in the house.

The Indian met anywhere, in the woods or on the trail, invariably removes his hat and voices a polite greeting. There were employed at Chi-chen Itza, during much of Don Eduardo's work, about one hundred Indians. It was their pleasant habit each evening about sunset to pass in line before the hacienda and bid us good night. The ceremony took place as they were returning from the little near-by church,—for all the natives at that time were good Catholics,—and we saw no more of them until dawn, which was our hour for beginning work.

The modern Maya is devout, but he takes his religion placidly, leaving it to his spiritual adviser to tell him what to do or believe. In nearly every native hut is a shrine before which are dutifully observed the articles of faith— the faith of his conquerors who took away his galaxy of gods and substituted Catholicism.

The Maya home is built much as it was in ancient times. It usually consists of but one large rectangular room. The foundation is of stone held together with plaster called *zac-cab,* which means "white earth." The walls are of poles or of stone plastered with *zac-cab.* The roof is peaked and thatched with straw or with stiff palm-like leaves. The door is of wood and there is sometimes a window, barred but without glass. A wooden cover may be inserted from within to close this opening when desired. No matter how poor the Maya family, there is always a flower garden in the rear of the house. If his domain is very limited, the garden of the Maya may be reduced to what may be grown in a large-sized Standard-Oil can.

Within, the Maya home is very simple. There are no beds as in ancient times; the native has adopted a Spanish innovation, seeking his rest in a hammock suspended from wooden pegs set in the wall. The hammocks are taken down when not in use. A simple stool or two, a bench or a chest, possibly a table, and the ever-present shrine constitute the furniture. Not infrequently there is an American-made sewing-machine. The kitchen is outside, in another smaller building, and the stove consists merely of a crude stone oven or heap of stones. The bath-room and laundry, where there is a wooden trough to hold water, also is outdoors. At meal-times the family sits on stools about a pot or vessel containing the pièce de résistance, and the use of fingers is not frowned upon.

The natives not resident in the towns or cities are for the most part employed on the haciendas, the majority of which are engaged in the raising of henequen. A few years ago there appeared a series of magazine articles, under some such heading as "Barbarous Mexico," describing in the most approved yellow-journal style the cruelty and tyranny of the Mexican planters. I suppose there really are some isolated cases of cruelty, but in general the treatment of native workers by the plantation-owners leaves little to criticize. The native is free to leave one employer to seek another. His pay is good and he certainly is not overworked. On nearly every hacienda ample provision is made for entertainment and the fiestas and dances so dear to his heart. Many native families have lived and labored on one plantation for several generations—a fair indication that they are not ill-treated. One of the atrocities recited in the magazine articles just mentioned was the tying of an Indian to a post, where he was whipped severely. The whipping-post has existed, but its use was fostered by the Indians themselves and was reserved for the habitual drunkard or him who repeatedly abused his wife and children. Possibly a similar course of treatment might be beneficial to some citizens of the United States.

There was one unfortunate event, however, which reflected no credit on the natives, but for which they were far less to blame than a certain class of whites. Not long ago the creed of bolshevism was spread among these poor credulous people by a Rumanian fanatic, resulting in the murder of several plantation-owners and the burning of several estates. A few Indians at Don Eduardo's hacienda, who had for some time failed to pay the slight rental required of them, became unruly and the master ordered them to pay up or leave. In reprisal they set fire to his house, Casa Real, and all the out-buildings, destroying many priceless antiquities intended for an American museum of archæology. The house has been rebuilt, but the lost treasures can never be replaced. The Indians also drove off all Don Eduardo's stock and took everything in the way of valuables that was portable.

Don Eduardo, in relating his experiences as a plantation-owner, once said:

"A certain residue of Indians were never conquered by the Spaniards, nor have they ever been subdued by the Mexican Government; and they pay no taxes. They are called Sublevados and I have been warned ever since I came to Chi-chen Itza that some day the Sublevados would go on the war-path and wipe me and my hacienda clean off the map.

"Eventually I became tired of waiting for them to visit me and enjoy the friendly reception I had prepared for them, which included, among other things, the fortifying of the Great Pyramid. So I decided to make a little reconnaissance. Traveling south into their own country, I lived for some time in their villages, where they still practise the ancient Maya rites and incantations, even though there is a slight veneer of Catholicism among them. Since then I have traveled many times into the Sublevado territory; in fact, have been made a chief of the tribe by solemn bond and ritual. I have found them a peaceful, friendly lot of ignorant Indians, unlikely to do any harm as long as they are left to their own devices and in their present habitat."

The Maya is happy-go-lucky, improvident, and usually lazy. He dearly loves a good time, a good story, and a good joke, especially if it is of the practical variety in which the other fellow is the butt. He is very fond of fiestas and dances.

The native dances are quite different from ours. The men and women sit close to the walls of the hut or inclosure, sometimes on chairs but more often on stools. On important occasions, the music is furnished by violins, guitars, and perhaps some wind-instruments. But always there is one musician with a long gourd containing stones, which is shaken in time to the music, producing a hollow *chuck-a-chuck, chuck-a-chuck* sound. Sometimes the only instrument is a flageolet. The music is always in a minor key and is without pause or period or end. A girl—any girl—gets up and proceeds to the center of the floor, where she shuffles about for perhaps a minute. Then from the other end of the room some man, who may be a stranger to the girl, comes forth and shuffles about in front of her. They do not touch each other. They gyrate rather slowly and move in circles, always facing

each other. When either becomes weary, he or she re-
tires and another takes up the dance. If the room is sufficiently large there may be as many as three couples dancing continuously in this manner. The dancers do not
smile nor appear to be enjoying the occasion; yet they
must derive pleasure from it, for throughout the country
dances are held frequently.

Knowing the Mayas of to-day, and their customs, it is
interesting to follow their history back to the earliest
times of which there is authentic record, and from there,
through legends and scraps of knowledge, into their most
ancient past. For four centuries we may trace them backward through well-known history. For still another century the record is fairly clear. Back of that is only
legend, with here and there some startling, incontrovertible fact to prove their antiquity. The flickering light of
our knowledge becomes dimmer and dimmer. We know
a date in their history about one hundred years before
Christ, but on what preceded that no feeblest ray falls to
enlighten our ignorance.

To one man, long since departed, we owe a great debt.
But for him, our knowledge of the ancient Mayas would
be almost nil, and it is only by a lucky chance that what
he wrote was not lost to us. This man, Diego de Landa,
was Bishop of Yucatan (1573-79), and he came to America on the heels of the Spanish conquerors. His manuscript,—almost our only guide to Maya antiquity and
known as "Relacion de las Cosas de Yucatan,"—lay hidden in Madrid for nearly three hundred years ere it was
discovered and published.

To show how little the Mayas have changed in four
centuries I am going to quote from Landa, using a very

free translation but endeavoring to preserve his meaning.
I hope the reader will bear in mind that the following is
a description of the Mayas of the sixteenth century and is
chiefly interesting when compared with the Mayas of
to-day:

The Indians of Yucatan are well built, tall and robust. They
are generally bow-legged, because mothers customarily carry infants astride their hips. It is considered a mark of beauty to be
cross-eyed. The heads and foreheads are flat, having been bound
in infancy. Their ears are pierced for ear-rings and are torn by
the sacrifices. The men do not have beards and it is said the
mothers burns their boys' faces with hot cloths so that hair does
not grow. Some do have beards, but these are very stiff, like the
bristles of a pig. The men permit the hair of the head to grow
long except on top, where they burn it off. Thus the hair of the
crown is short, but the remainder is long and is braided and
wound like a wreath around the head, leaving a small tail in
the back as tassels or tufts.

Their dress is a strip of cloth about as wide as a hand and
wound several times about the waist, with one end hanging in
front and the other in the back. The women adorn these ends
curiously with feathers. They wear large square blankets, which
they fasten to their shoulders, and sandals of hemp or deerskin.

They bathe a great deal and do not try to hide their nudity
from the women, except with their hands. The men use mirrors
and the women do not. The expression for cuckoldom is that the
wife has put the mirror in her husband's hair above the occiput.

Their houses are roofed with straw or palm-leaves and the roof
has a considerable slant. They put a wall lengthwise through the
middle of the house and in it some doors. In the back half are
the beds and the other section is whitewashed and is the reception
room for guests. This room is like a porch, the whole front being
open and without a door. The roof over this part of the house

extends well down over the walls, to keep out sun and rain. The common people build the houses of the chiefs and house-breaking is considered a grave crime. Beds are made of small rods with a mat and cotton blankets on top. In summer the men especially sleep in the open room or porch, on mats.

All the people unite in cultivating the fields of the chief and supplying food to his household. In hunting, fishing, or bringing salt, a share is always given to the chief. If the chief dies he is succeeded by his eldest son, but his other descendants are respected and helped. The subordinate chiefs help in all things, according to their stations. The priests live from their offices and from the offerings given to them. The chiefs rule the town, settle disputes, and govern all affairs. The principal chiefs travel a great deal and take much company with them. They visit rich people, where they arrange the affairs of the villages, transacting their principal business at night.

The Indians tattoo their bodies, believing that they become more valiant thereby. The process is painful, as the designs are painted on the body and then pricked in with a small poniard. Because of the pain the tattooing is done only a little at a time, and also because the tattooed part becomes inflamed and matter-ated, causing sickness. Those who are not tattooed are ridiculed. The natives like to be flattered and they like to imitate the Castilian graces and customs and to eat and drink as we do. They are fond of sweet odors and employ bouquets of flowers and sweet-smelling herbs. They are accustomed to paint their faces and bodies red, which does not improve their appearance but which they consider beautifying.

They are very dissolute in getting drunk, from which follow many evils such as murder, arson, rape and incest. . . . They are fond of recreation, especially of dances and of plays containing many jokes and witticisms. They sometimes become servants for a time in a Spanish household just to absorb the conversation and customs and these are later artfully represented in native plays.

Their musical instruments are small kettle-drums played with the hand and another drum made of hollow wood, played with a wooden stick containing on the end a ball made of the milk of a certain tree [rubber]. They have long, slender trumpets fashioned from hollow sticks with gourds fastened at one end. Another instrument is made from a whole turtle-shell, which is played with the palm of the hand and emits a melancholy sound. They have whistles and flutes of reed or bones of the deer and from large snail-shells. These instruments are played for their war-dances. One of these dances is called *co-lom-che,* meaning reed. A large circle of men is formed. Two go into the center. One has a handful of darts and while dancing in an upright position he casts the darts with all his strength at the second dancer, who dances in a squatting position, from which he deftly catches each dart with a small stick. After the darts are all thrown, these two dancers return to their original places in the circle and two new dancers advance to the center and repeat the dart-throwing. There is another war-dance in which about eight hundred men take part. They carry flags and the tempo is slow. They dance the whole day without stopping and during the whole day not one man gets out of step. In no case do the men dance with the women.

There are many occupations but the people most incline toward trading, taking salt, clothing, and slaves to the lands of Ulna and Tabasco, where they exchange for cocoa and counters of stone which are their money. With these coins they buy slaves, or the chiefs wear them as jewels at feasts. They have other counters and jewelry made of certain shells. These are carried in purses made of network. In the markets are all manner of goods. They loan money without usury and pay their debts with good-will. Some Indians are potters and carpenters who are well paid for the idols of wood and clay which they make. There are surgeons —or, rather, wizards—who cure with herbs and incantations. Above all, there are laborers and those who plant and gather the corn and other produce which they store in granaries to be sold in season. They have no mules or oxen.

The Indians have the good custom of helping one another in

all their work. In working the land they do nothing from the middle of January to April except gather manure and burn it. Then come the rains and they plant the fields, using a small pointed stick to poke holes into the ground in each of which they deposit five or six seeds which grow very rapidly in this rainy season. They also congregate in groups of about fifty for hunting or fishing.

When going on a visit, the Indian takes a present to his host and the host gives the guest a present of proportionate value. They are generous and hospitable. They give food and drink to all who come to their houses.

They take much pride in their lineage, especially if they are descendants of some ancient family of Mayapan and they boast of the distinguished men who have been of their family. The whole name of the father is always borne by his sons, but not by his daughters. But the children, both sons and daughters, are called by the compound names of father and mother, in which the name of the father is the given name and that of the mother the surname. Thus the son of Chel and Chan would be Na-Chan-Chel, which means son of Chel by his wife Chan. A stranger coming to a village, especially if he be poor, will be received in all kindness by any family of his name. Men and women of the same name do not marry, for this is considered very wrong.

CHAPTER II

ONE particularly lovely Sunday morning, some time after taking up my abode at Chi-chen Itza," says Don Eduardo, "I was awakened, as on other occasions, by the softly melodious chiming of the bells in my little church on the hill. As I lay in my hammock, idly listening to the pleasant sound, I could distinguish the different tones of the several bells and it was a pleasant thought to me to know that I had equipped the little church with bells having a superior quality of tone. The sound of them was indeed delightful because while church bells in Yucatan are as plentiful as millionaires in Pittsburgh, they are usually cracked and raucous.

"It was still early when I stood before my manor and turned my gaze eastward toward the little stone church perched cozily on a near-by gently sloping hillside. Both my manor and the little church had for many years been in ruins, unused. Extensive repairs had just been completed on both, to make them habitable. Here and there one of my Indians, or a whole family, dressed in their Sunday best, were already churchward bound, and the chimes continued softly to remind the laggard of his duty. The red rim of the sun was just peeping over the horizon behind the church, while the birds in every tree and thicket were voicing their welcome to this glorious new day. A lazy, blissful breeze laden with the mingled scents of a

24

thousand tropic blossoms ruffled the tree-tops. Before
me stretched a vista of wildly beautiful country-side with
no sign of the handiwork of man other than the little
church. No towering peaks, no gushing streams, no bot-
tomless cañons greeted my eye; merely a terrain that is
just saved from being flat. Yet it is all divinely lovely—
a study in green and blue with here and there a spot of
flaming color. The cloudless sky was of so clear and
vivid a blue that I was tempted to stand on tiptoe and
take down a handful. Foliage of some sort covered every
inch of ground and was of every imaginable shade of
green, from the shadowed purple-green where the rising
sun had not penetrated, to the pale green of some of the
tree-tops, turned golden in the first slanting rays. A gorgeous parrot flashed from tree to tree and disappeared
and by his flight brought my eye to rest on a riot of
flame-flower high up in a distant tree.

"The sudden silence of the bells warned me that if I
too intended to go to church there was no time to lose.
My little stone church is not without fame, for in its then-
abandoned sacristy that remarkable traveler and historian
John L. Stephens made his abode when he visited my City
of the Sacred Well. It was here that he wrote his notes
on 'The Ruined City of Chi-chen Itza.' Though it has
been repaired, it looks almost as he left it one cloudy
Sunday morning nearly eighty years ago. Its cut-stone
walls and bell-tower are the same, but its old roof, bowed
with age, has been replaced with a fine new thatch of
palm.

"San Isidro is the patron saint of the plantation—for
no well-organized plantation is without its patron saint,
whose image is venerated by all the natives there em-

ployed. The image of San Isidro in this little church on the hill at Chi-chen Itza is of unknown antiquity and is believed to be possessed of miraculous powers which are constantly manifested. Veneration for the image, together with the attraction of the three-belled chimes swinging in their places in the tiny tower, makes the little church a sacred spot not only to the people of my hacienda but likewise to the inhabitants of the near-by village of Pisté and the region for many miles around. Has not the sacred image and the big stone baptismal font been used by the archbishop himself? Was not Mat-Ek healed, who was blinded for many months by the vapor from the *ikeban* plant, blown into his eyes by the wind while he was gathering his crops? Was he not given back his sight in less than a week after he had prayed for aid and kissed the feet of San Isidro? And did not Mat-Ek, in token of his gratitude, have made an eye of pure silver and give it to the sainted image—an eye which now hangs over the altar for all to see? What more can you ask?

"The church was filled to overflowing in token of a great and special day, for it is only occasionally that the regularly ordained priest comes all the way from Valladolid, and confessions, christenings, and marriage bans await his coming.

"As the congregation slowly drifts into place, the gentle rustling of the unstarched *huipiles* and *pics* of the women and the louder rustling of the stiffly starched trousers and jackets of the men sound remarkably like the lapping of summer wavelets upon a sandy beach. The soft laughter of the children outside the building, mingled with the restrained voices of admonishing Indian elders, all combine to create an atmosphere in perfect accord with the surroundings and the low-toned service. Within the chapel many candles of wild beeswax give forth soft lights and heavy odors which, mingling with the fragrant smoke of incense, fall with pleasant, soporific effect upon the congregation.

"The chimes ring their tuneful, familiar message—a message come down the centuries since the Child of Bethlehem was born in a manger; a message brought across the seas to this little stone church, by some unknown, long-departed padre. The solemn peals roll out and up to those gray old temples of another faith, wherein the sacred music of the ancient Mayas, the sound of *tunkul,* or priestly drum, and *dzacatan,* once beat in pulsing chorus. These sound symbols of the Sacred Cross are wafted to the altars, still standing, of the Sacred Serpent, whose creed once reigned supreme over this land.

"The beloved priest begins the age-old intoned creed and as the service lengthens through the chants, singing, and sermon, there comes a penetrating, strangely sweet odor. Stronger and stronger it grows, filling the church and floating out into the morning air. The worshipers nod their heads. 'The *xmehen macales* have blossomed; God is good to us,' they murmur. Six graceful, big-leafed plants like large calla-lilies had been placed upon the altar, among other flowering plants. And as I look, the six white buds of these lilies, each slenderly sheathed in green, open slowly to the light, revealing blooms of creamy white. They open in unison, as if at the bidding of an unheard voice. To me it is startling, uncanny. And here is the story about them that met my eager questions at the close of the service:

"Francisco Tata de las Fuentas, caballero of Castile, blue-eyed and yellow-haired, was fair of skin as a Saxon. In his youth he was as hot of blood and of head as a Gascon and traveled the pace with the best and worst of Castile and all the adjoining provinces. His offerings to Venus, to Bacchus, and to the little gods of chance were so fervid and frequent that they soon caused his real castle in Castile to become as those common ones of the air. And his broad lands on the banks of the Guadiana passed to more careful guardians. When nothing remained to him but his horse, Selim, he betook himself with Hernan Cortes to New Spain. Here, under Cortes, he learned discretion bought by hard experience, so that he acquired some wealth. With Francisco de Montejo, trusted friend and lieutenant of Cortes, he came to Yucatan, received a royal grant of land with many natives, and took to himself a wife, the lovely and virtuous daughter of a native chief or *batab*.

"Time passed and he was gathered to his fathers, leaving an only child, a son named for him. The second Francisco Fuentes inherited the father's fair skin and bold blue eyes, as well as the gorgeous gold-and-silver trappings of the once fiery Selim, not to mention half a dozen big plantations, houses and lands in Valladolid and Mérida, and scores of minor holdings in several other towns and villages.

"This Francisco Fuentes, or Pancho as his friends called him, had two sons and a daughter. The sons were stalwart, upstanding fellows, recalling in their stature and temper their Spanish ancestry, but showing in their brown skins the admixture of native blood of mother and grandmother.

"Maria, the one beloved daughter, had the plump figure and the sweet temper of her mother, but her proud little head was covered with a wealth of yellow hair and her eyes were of clearest blue, the dauntless eyes of the first Francisco. And now Maria, the idol of her father and worshiped by her brothers, darling of the whole village, was slowly dying; wasting away with a strange fever that could not be abated. By day her body was cool and her brain clear, but with the setting sun came the fever that defied all skill of physicians and nurses. At midnight her frail, fair form was shaken with ague and burned with a fever almost to sear the hands of those who ministered to her as she tossed in delirium. Wasted to a shadow, Maria seemed beckoned by the Grim Reaper.

"The sun again touched the western horizon. The sorrowing family, father and brothers, were at her bedside. Friends and neighbors gathered to watch over the last hours of the helpless little sufferer, for there seemed no hope. A knock sounded at the door, hesitant, timid, as of supplication.

"'It is but one of the beggars who constantly impose on Maria,' said a sharp-tongued watcher, peering through the window into the dusk.

"Maria, restlessly turning in her hammock in an inner room, heard the knocking and the words of the watcher.

"'I think,' whispered she, 'it is old X-Euan, come for some milk I promised her for her orphan grandchild. Fill with milk the clean flask which is on the shelf behind the door and give it to her.'

"Old X-Euan took the flask of milk, but from her lips did not come the whining thanks of the mendicant. Instead, from beneath the tattered folds of her shawl, she brought forth a vase of strange antique make, in which was growing a broad-leafed plant with a single swelling bud at it center. Handing the plant to the watcher, the old Maya woman said:

" 'Take this to Maria; place it close by her with the blessing of one to whom she has done as her kind heart, guided by God, has told her to do.' In her voice was a note of command which brought obedience from those who heard. Old X-Euan departed, but some—those who were nearest and so should have seen clearest—insisted that a faint glow like a halo enveloped her head.

"The hour of twilight had passed. The dreaded time of the quickened pulse and panting delirium had come. Maria lay tossing in her hammock. Close by her the virgin petals of the flower began slowly to unfold. A fragrance, at first almost imperceptible, was wafted through the room. As the blossom opened to full bloom and its perfume permeated the sick-room, the restless turnings, the feverish mutterings grew less and less and at last ceased altogether. A dewy moisture appeared on Maria's pallid forehead and she sank into deep, refreshing slumber.

"Amid the rejoicing there was a note of awed wonder, for in the very center of the flower the beautiful calyx seemed to have taken the fever heat that was Maria's, and as her fever abated the heat in the heart of the flower increased, until at midnight it was almost incandescent.

"A week passed. Each night, so the watchers told, the flower took to itself the heat of the fever, while Maria, feverless, slept soundly. And on the morning of the eighth day she was convalescent. But the beautiful blossom was but a withered, brown, shapeless nothing.

" '*La flor de la calentura* has performed its task,' exclaimed the joyful natives, but Maria, lovely once more with returning strength, said, 'Alas! *La flor de la calentura,* the flower that saved my life, is dead.'

"And thus it was told by Maria to her grandchildren and retold by them to their grandchildren and is now known by every one in the region. Surely it must be true! Why should n't it be? At any rate, it is accepted as literally by my Indians as the less pleasing story of Jonah and the whale."

CHAPTER III

THE FIRST AMERICANS

IT has been said that civilization is but a layer-cake of eras—a building up of strata, with the brute state at the bottom. Layer upon layer, each succeeding generation adds its small bit of culture or knowledge, until a golden age is finally reached. And, sadly enough, from that age of enlightenment, the hope of the world, there has always been a rapid decline, until centuries later, perhaps, again begins the tedious gradual uplift.

And the story of man's rise and fall, in the passing of the ages, usually is buried in the earth, to be laid bare to our eyes if we have but the patience to find and the ability to understand. Just as a good woodsman can read from a scratch on a tree or a faint footprint on the ground things not obvious to the untrained observer, our men of science have developed remarkable expertness in divining the history of bygone eras from the scanty traces that remain. From a skull, centuries buried in a cave, they reconstruct the Neanderthal man. The fragments of an earthen pot tell them the degree of culture and the period of him who once supped from the vessel.

Wherever there are caves there is the likelihood of uncovering vestiges of aboriginal life, for primitive men everywhere used caverns, either as temporary shelters or as permanent abodes. Beneath the cave floor may be the

evidence of many generations of men—the relics buried
in layers one upon another as the discarded and broken
implements of one generation were trampled underfoot
and submerged under the charred embers and rubbish of
the succeeding one.

The written record of the Mayas gives but little clue
to their origin and no indication at all of their descent
from more barbarous ancestors. Did these people, already of a high state of culture, immigrate from some
other land? If so, were they the first comers or did they
find the country even then inhabited? Or were their
ancestors natives of this region for hundreds of centuries
before them?

Yucatan is a land of caverns, veritably a honeycomb
of caves, and eagerly the paleontologist rolled up his
sleeves, shouldered his shovel, and set out to find the
answer to these vexing questions. The answer was found
and is conclusive but disappointing. Beyond the question
of a doubt, the Mayas brought with them their culture,
and they were the first inhabitants of this country.
Whence they came, or how, or why; from what race they
sprang, we know not and probably never shall know. A
few conflicting legends of their arrival as recorded in
some old Maya writings constitute the sum total of our
knowledge on this point.

Many intricately derived meanings of the name *Maya*
have been offered. The most obvious, however, is the
direct translation. *Ma* means "not" and *ya* means "emotion," "grief," "tiresome," or "difficult." The combination means, "not arduous," "not severe." We know that
the Mayas frequently alluded to their country as the
Land of the Deer and the Land of the Wild Turkey—

U-Lumil-Ceh, U-Lumil-Cutz. "Maya," therefore, may quite likely have been descriptive of the region as a pleasant, comfortable place of residence. Juan Martinez, who knows the Indian and the language, present and past, as no one else, once said to me: "Work and grief are synonymous to the native mind. Work is grief to the Indian; therefore a land of no grief and no sorrow may well mean a land of no work." However, any explanation of the derivation of so ancient a name is little more than surmise.

According to one myth, the Mayas came over the sea from the east, under the leadership of a hero-deity, Itzamna; hence the name "Itzas" as applied to a part, at least, of the Mayas. In the Maya books Itzamna is represented as an old man with one tooth and a sunken jaw. His glyph or sign is his pictured profile, together with a sign of night, the sign of food, and two or three feathers.

The more credible legend refers to an immigration from the west or north, under a chieftain named Kukul Can. There are reasons for believing that this legend may be founded upon fact. It is mentioned in several of the most ancient of the surviving Maya records and in the testimony of a number of well-versed natives at the time of the Conquest. Farther up the coast, north of Vera Cruz, is another branch of the Maya family called the Huastecs, while in Central America, through Honduras, Guatemala, and even in Costa Rica, are present-day Maya tribes and ruins of ancient Maya civilization. Also, there is a close similarity between the Kukul Can legend and the Aztec annals, indicating a common origin.

Everything points to the probability of a remote great migration of their common ancestors from the north.

The Aztec tradition is particularly interesting and describes the arrival by boat of several different tribes at the mouth of the Panuco River, which spot the Aztecs called Panatolan, meaning "where one arrives by sea." The expedition was headed by the supreme leader, Mexitl, chief of the Mexicans, with whom were other chieftains and their followers. They traveled on down the coast as far as Guatemala, and some turned back and settled at various places along the shore. On this journey an intoxicating drink was originated by one Mayanel, whose name means "clever woman." [1] There is a possibility that "Maya" is derived from her name. At any rate, one tribal chief, Huastecatl, imbibed too freely and cast aside his garments while intoxicated. His shame was so great when he realized what he had done that he gathered his tribe, the Huastecas, and returned with them to 'Panatolan and settled there.

Landa says in his book that some old men of Yucatan related to him the story, handed down for many generations, that the first settlers had come from the east by water. These voyagers were ones "whom God had freed, opening for them twelve roads to the sea." If there is any truth in this tradition, these progenitors may have been one of the lost tribes of Israel. An interesting side light on this hypothesis is the distinctly Semitic cast of countenance of some of the ancient sculptures and murals

[1] The suffix "el" added to any Maya word denotes action. In the glyph sign this often was indicated by adding the wing of a bird to the main hieroglyph; therefore "Mayanel" was an active woman, hence very clever.—*Author.*

found at Chi-chen Itza and in other old Maya cities. The dignity of face and serene poise of these carved or painted likenesses is strikingly Hebraic.[1]

While we are in the field of conjecture, we may as well consider the old Greek myth of the lost continent of Atlantis. From the geological point of view, it is not impossible. The whole of Yucatan is low and was once the bottom of the sea, as is indicated by its surface rock and sand. Furthermore, the stretching out of the Antilles as though to form a bridge with the Azores, and the shallowness of the intervening Atlantic Ocean, lends plausibility to the idea that there may have been a cataclysmic upheaval of the ocean-bed during some past era, and not long ago, geologically speaking—an upheaval which created the land of Yucatan and caused what was land to the eastward to sink beneath the level of the Atlantic. What is more natural to suppose than that in some prehistoric period the lost continent of Atlantis did exist and proved an easy means of passage between Europe and America?

The mist-enshrouded history of the migrations of ancient people, the crossing and recrossing of their pilgrimages and of their blood, is a fascinating study, but one which tells us comparatively little that may be crystallized into fact. And so, in these various speculations as to the origin of the Mayas, no theory contains enough weight of evidence to warrant the assumption that it is the right one. It is, however, pretty clearly established

[1] In an article written for "Harper's Magazine," by Mr. Edward Huntington, reference is made to the Jewish cast of features of the modern Mayas, and I have often noticed the similarity. One prominent writer on Yucatan considers the possibility of Jewish origin for the Mayas as being the most substantial of the several theories I have mentioned.—*Author.*

from the ancient Maya writings and legends that there were two main immigrations, the greater one coming from the west or north and the lesser one from the east.

Emerging at last from the purely legendary, we reach the middle ground where the history of the Mayas is still unrecorded but where the word of mouth, as handed down from father to son, is more precise and has some relation to definite dates. Then we suddenly step over the threshold into the historical era.

The first recorded date, which corresponds to 113 B. C., is on a statuette from the ancient city of Tuxtla, and there is some doubt as to whether our reading of this date is correct. The next inscription corresponds to 47 A. D., and here we are on sure ground. A monument in northern Guatemala contains a date prior to 160 A. D., at which point the ancient Maya Codices take up the history of the race and carry it on to the time of the Conquest. And even at this early time, the Mayas had hieroglyphic writings and were skilled in stone-carving and the erection of massive works of architecture. With the written Chronicles, the many hieroglyphed stones,— "precious stones," I like to call them,—and the history of progress as indicated by the different periods of architecture and sculpture, we are able to verify and correlate most of the subsequent dates.

The written Maya records, without which our task of piecing together anything of their history would be almost impossible, are among the most interesting and valuable remains of this bygone civilization. The records are of two kinds. The first, the Codices, are the original texts, written in hieroglyphics. The second, the Chilan Balam, are written in the Maya language but with Spanish characters, and are chiefly transcripts from the more ancient records.

Only three hieroglyphic Codices have survived, and they are known respectively as the Dresden Codex, the Perez Codex, and the Tro-Cortesianus. All are in European museums and many facsimile reproductions have been made of them for use in other museums and libraries. These manuscripts are painstakingly illuminated by hand, in colors, and were done with some sort of brush, possibly of hair or feathers. They are done on paper or, rather, a sort of cardboard which has been given a smooth white surface through the application of a coating of fine lime. The body of the paper is made of the fiber of the maguey plant. The manuscript is folded like a Japanese screen or a railway time-table. According to early accounts, some of these records were also made on tanned or otherwise prepared deerskin and upon bark. None of the hide or bark records has ever been found by present-day explorations. It is known that the Mayas had many records concerning religious history, religious rites and ceremonies, medicine, and astronomy. The Spanish priests caused all of the Maya writings they could find to be gathered together and burned, in the fanatical belief that they were serving the church by so doing.

If only their bigotry had vented itself in some other way, how much these old manuscripts might have told us! Apropos of the burning of the priceless documents Landa says, "We collected all the native books we could find and burned them, much to the sorrow of the people, and caused them pain."

The group of books called the Chilan Balam, which are chiefly ideographic transcripts of the more ancient works,

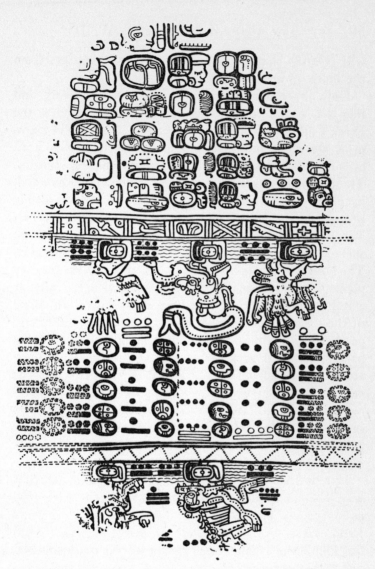

A PAGE FROM THE PEREZ CODEX, DESCRIBING AN ECLIPSE OF THE SUN. THIS
ANCIENT MANUSCRIPT ILLUMINATED IN COLOR IS NOW
IN THE LIBRARY OF PARIS

written in the Maya tongue but in Spanish characters, probably were made surreptitiously by some of the educated natives soon after the Conquest. There are sixteen of these books still extant. The meaning of this Maya name, *Chilan Balam,* is interesting. *Chi* means "mouth"; *lan* indicates action. Therefore *Chilan* is "mouth action," or "speech." *Balam* is synonymous for either "tiger" or "ferocity." But the tiger was worshiped as a deity and the combination of the words, *Chilan Balam,* means "Speech of the Gods." The Maya priests were sometimes called by the name, indicating that they were the mouthpieces of the gods, and doubtless these records took their name from the priestly appellation.

The individual books of the Chilan Balam are known by the names of the villages in which they were found, and in a few cases the name of the village may have been derived from the presence of the book. The most important of these books are Nabula, Chun-may-el (which means "something of the first" or "original"), Kua, Man, X-kutz-cab, Ixil, Tihosuco, and Tixcocob.

Just when these books were written is not known, but there is evidence that the book of Mani was written prior to 1595 and the book of Nabula tells of an epidemic which occurred in 1663. While teaching the natives to write the Maya language in Spanish characters, Bishop Landa employed a rather original method, which is our only key to reading these writings and which serves as our only clue to the more ancient hieroglyphs. The ancient Maya writings were purely picture writings, but to some extent the hieroglyphs had lost their original picture significance and had come to have a somewhat symbolic meaning.

In arranging the so-called Maya alphabet (which was first used by the priests in writing out the prayers for the Mayas), Landa employed a very ingenious method and one that was practical at the time. He took the Spanish alphabet and beginning with "A" he asked the educated Indian to draw the character for him in which the sound of "A" was predominant. Naturally, after many attempts by the Indian to furnish such a character he finally selected the hieroglyph *ac*, which is a picture of a turtle's head and which in Maya means "turtle" or "dwarf" or something having a slow movement. Next he took the letter "B" and eventually chose the character *be*, which means "road," "walk," "run," and consists of the picture of a footprint. Therefore—not to go into a lengthy description of the system—he had "A" from *ac*, "B" from *be*, etc. With this extemporized alphabet the priests were able to write out the Catholic prayers in such a way that the Indian could repeat them in Spanish by using the sound of the first part of his hieroglyph for the sound of each Spanish letter.

It may be seen from the foregoing that Landa's alphabet cannot be used for translating Maya, for when the hieroglyphs are made to represent the sounds of the Spanish alphabet the result does not indicate the original connection of a Maya word with its glyph. This fact was a great disappointment among archæologists, who at first expected to translate the Maya Codices by the use of the Landa alphabet. Their hopes, however, were short-lived and they even pronounced Landa an impostor. On the contrary, he has unintentionally given us what is almost a Rosetta Stone.

The Codices, I fear, will never yield a connected story, as they are written in a stenographic or shorthand style consisting of disconnected sentences.

Many of the stones, or *stelæ*, may contain history, and as soon as we know the meanings of, possibly, a thousand glyphs we shall be able to make a decided advance in the art of reading the books. Landa in his book explains not the Maya glyphs but the way the priests used these Maya characters for religious purposes. For example, he says *Ma-in-kati* means "I do not want," represented in the ancient Maya by three simple glyphs. Written as the priests had arranged, with a glyph for each sound of a Spanish letter, the result is a combination of five glyphs, which, if given their original Maya pictured meanings, leads to the rather surprising knowledge that "no dead animal was seen at this place," or, literally, "not see tail [animal] death place."

Besides the Codices and the Chilan Balam, which together are frequently alluded to as the Maya Chronicles, there are some other documents such as titles to land, records of surveys, etc. There is a unique history of the Conquest, written by a contemporary native chief called Na Kuk Pech, whose name means "house of the feathered wood-tick." The story was written in the native language, by means of Spanish characters, and has been translated recently by Señor Juan Martinez, whose profound knowledge of the Maya language has eminently fitted him for this task.

The history of Chi-chen Itza is of especial interest because this was the Holy City, the Mecca of all the ancient Maya people. According to the Maya Chronicles, one or several tribes set out from a place called Nonual, in 160 A. D., and apparently spent many years in aimless wandering, arriving finally, in 241 A. D., at a place they named Chac Nouitan. Then follows a gap in our knowledge and the next we learn of these people is that in 445 A. D., while they were residing at a place called Bak-Halal, they heard of Chi-chen Itza. It is clear that Chi-chen Itza was already an inhabited city at that time. Soon after this, these tribes moved to Chi-chen Itza, where they lived until about 600 A. D., when, for some unaccountable reason, they abandoned it utterly and migrated to the land of Chan Kan Putun. And this residence was in turn abandoned two hundred and sixty years later, because of some calamity; one Chronicle speaks of a great fire.

For nearly a hundred years, to quote from the Chronicles, "the Itzas lived in exile and great distress under the trees and under the branches." Then, some of them reëstablished Chi-chen Itza in 950 A. D., while others founded the city of Uxmal or went to Mayapan. The second residence lasted for some two hundred years. About 1200 A. D., the Itzas, under the ruler Ulumil, invaded the city of Mayapan and at about this same time Chi-chen Itza was attacked and depopulated by foreigners—in all probability the Nahuas (Mexicans), who came down from the north. The last event alluded to in the Chronicles is the coming of the Spaniards under Montejo, who found the Mayas already decadent and their cities long ruined and abandoned.

We have no authentic description of the actual condition of Chi-chen Itza when the Spaniards came, but it is known with certainty that Tiho (place of the five temples), one of the ancient cities, the site of the modern city of Mérida, was in ruins. The temples were dilapidated and overgrown with vegetation and great trees were rooted in the walls. The few inhabitants living around these ruins knew virtually nothing of the founders of the city, nor of those who had lived there when it was in its prime.

At the coming of the Spaniards to Chi-chen Itza, about 1541, the city was inhabited by a few people who were, I think, nothing more than campers—inferior people using as shelters the buildings which they had found there and of whose history they were quite ignorant.

While it has no place in this book, the last known migration of some of the Mayas is interesting and it is certain that a considerable number emigrated between the years 1450 and 1451 southward to Lake Peten,[1] where they built a city on an island and there they survived, together with their ancient culture, until conquered in 1697 by the Spaniards, who destroyed all their temples and books and perforce made either good Christians or "good Indians" of all the inhabitants.

Landa says, under the heading, "Various Misfortunes Experienced in Yucatan in the Century before the Conquest":

These people had over twenty years of abundance and health and multiplied greatly. All of the land looked like one town and they built many temples which can be seen to-day in all parts; and crossing the mountains, one can see through the leaves of the trees sides of houses and buildings wonderfully constructed. After all this happiness, one evening in the winter a wind arose about

[1] Peten: "Something surrounding an island."

six o'clock and increased until it became a hurricane of the Four Winds.[1] This wind tore out the large trees, made a great slaughter of all kinds of game, tore down all the high houses, which, as they were thatched with straw and had fire inside against the cold, caught fire. Great numbers of people were burned and those that escaped were torn to pieces by falling trees.

This hurricane lasted until noon of the next day. Some who lived in small houses escaped—the young people who were just married, who were accustomed to build small houses in front of those of their parents or parents-in-law, where they lived the first years.

Thus this land then lost its name, which was U-Lumil-Ceh, U-Lumil-Cutz, Land of the Deer, Land of the Wild Turkey, and was without trees. The trees now seen all appear to have been planted at the same time, as they are all of the same height, and, looking at this land from some spot, it seems as though it had been trimmed off with shears.

Those who escaped felt encouraged to rebuild and cultivate the land and they again multiplied greatly, having fifteen years of health and good weather and the last year was the most fruitful of all. At the time of harvest, there came upon the land some contagious fevers which lasted twenty-four hours. After the fever the victim would swell up and burst open, being full of worms, and of this pestilence many people died leaving the fruit ungathered.

After this pestilence there was another sixteen good years in which they renewed their passions and ravagings. In this way one hundred and fifty thousand men died in battle. After this massacre they were more calm and made peace and rested for twenty years. Then came another pestilence. Large pimples formed and they rotted the body and emitted offensive odors in a way that the members fell off by pieces within four or five days. This plague has passed more than fifty years ago, the massacres

---

[1] "The Four Winds" is a Maya expression.

of the wars twenty years before that; the pestilence of the swelling and worms sixteen years before the wars; and the hurricane another sixteen years before that and twenty-two years after the destruction of Mayapan, which, according to this record, makes one hundred twenty-five years since the destruction. Thus by the wars and other punishments which God sent, it is a wonder there are as many people as are now living, although there are not many.

This quaint account by Landa sheds some light upon the condition of the Mayas during the century preceding the Spanish invasion and indicates that the golden age of the race had occurred not many centuries before.

The legendary history of the coming of the Mayas to Chi-chen Itza is alluded to by Landa in several passages. He states:

It is the opinion among the Indians that with the Itzas who populated Chi-chen Itza, there reigned a great man called Kukul Can, and the principal temple of the city is called Kukul Can. They say he entered from the west, that he was very genteel, and that he had neither wife nor children. After he left Chi-chen Itza he was considered in Mexico one of their gods and called Quetzal Coatl and in Yucatan they also had him for a god.

In another place Landa says:

The ancient Indians say that in Chi-chen Itza reigned three brothers. This was told to them by their ancestors. The three brothers came from the west and they reigned for some years in peace and justice. They honored their god very much and thus built many buildings and beautiful, especially one. These men, they say, lived without wives and in great honesty and virtue, and during this time they were much esteemed and obeyed by all. After a time one of them failed, who had to die, although some of the Indians said he went to Bak-halal. The absence of this one, no matter how he went, was felt so much by those who reigned after him that they began to be licentious and formed habits dishonorable and ungovernable, and the people began to hate them in such a way that they killed them, one after the other, and destroyed and abandoned the city.

Virtually the same stories are contained in a document found at Valladolid and dated 1618, which goes on to state that the newer part of Chi-chen Itza was built about 1200 A. D.

The ancient city consists of two parts, the southern, which is ruined to such as extent that it contains almost no standing edifices, and the newer city built to the north, which contains many buildings—some of them almost perfectly preserved. I believe that much of the older city was built at least a thousand years prior to most of the buildings in the newer city, and there is ample evidence to substantiate the belief that the old city was ruthlessly robbed of its carvings and cut stones for use in the construction of the new.

The Nahuatl influence is seen in the newer buildings. It is thought that Chi-chen Itza reached the height of its civil power, though not its artistic supremacy, after it had been conquered by the Aztec warriors from the north, and the native inhabitants were reduced to slavery and driven by their masters to the speedy building of many temples—an undertaking which they would have gone about in much more leisurely fashion had there been no compulsion.

Don Pedro Aguilar, one of the earliest historians of Yucatan, states that six hundred years before the coming of the Spaniards the Mayas were the vassals of the Aztecs and were forced by them to construct remarkable edifices such as those found at Chi-chen Itza and Uxmal.

Herbert Spinden, in his admirable little book "Ancient Civilizations of Mexico," has most happily drawn an analogy between the traits of the Mayas and Aztecs and the similar traits of the old Greeks and Romans. The Mayas were like the Greeks, the creative race, while the Aztecs were primarily warriors, as were the Romans.

Just what was the impulse which led these people to undertake the mighty works they accomplished,—whether it was religious fervor or plain fear,—we do not know. We do know that their age of greatest progress was within the era of verifiable history. We know that they built many large cities; and that there was a large population; Chi-chen Itza was a city of at least two hundred thousand inhabitants, and some archæologists believe that at one time its population numbered no less than a million.

During their supreme period they built great pyramids and marvelous temples. They wrote books and set up intricately carved record-stones. They brought the whole of Yucatan into a federation of government that held the people together in a unity which has few parallels in the history of the human race. They evolved a calendar which is ingenious, complicated, and amazingly correct. They read the heavens and knew the planets and their seasons and changes. They displayed in all they did a genius to invent and an ability to execute which cause us to rate their culture very high; and this culture is all the more wonderful because it was purely original and cut off by an ocean on each side from any contact with the rest of the world.

CHAPTER IV

DON EDUARDO'S FIRST VIEW OF THE CITY OF THE SACRED WELL

DON EDUARDO has described to me his first trip to Chi-chen Itza, and his impressions, which are somewhat as follows if my notes and memory do not err:

"I had traveled all of a hot and dusty day, on horseback, through the jungle and over animal trails. In many places my Indian guide, who went afoot, had to lead my horse over or around the huge stones that blocked our path. After the first few miles I was painfully aware that running blithely from my city into Mérida, for forgotten trifles or even for sorely needed supplies, was another of my pleasant fancies thoroughly punctured.

"Darkness overtook us ere we reached our journey's end, and the ensuing coolness was delightfully refreshing even though the dark slowed our already snail-like progress. Just when I had abandoned all hope of making further headway, the moon sailed majestically into view —a gorgeous full moon in a perfect Yucatan night, lighting every object softly, gently, with a caressing touch so lacking in the masculine directness of Old Sol. A more lovely silver and black-velvet night I have never seen. Truly, the moon magic of Yucatan is no less than divine stage-craft which subtly wafts one completely away from the Land of Things as They Are and into the Realm of

49

Enchantment. I should not have been surprised to meet the March Hare, Lancelot, Gulliver, Scheherezade, or Helen of Troy. In fact, I was prepared to stop and chat with any of them and offer a bite from the one remaining cake of chocolate in my pocket.

"Sometime, and most reluctantly, I suppose I must go the way of all flesh. If so, then by all means let it be in the full glory of a Yucatan moon and the going will not be unpleasant.

"For days I had been traveling, first by train, then by *volan,*—that satanic contrivance which leaves one bruised and bumped from head to foot,—and finally in the saddle, dozing over the head of a somnambulant horse.

"Even the witchery of the moonlight could not long hold alert my fatigued body and mind. On and on we plodded, hour after hour. Midnight passed and how many more hours I do not know, when I heard an exclamation in the vernacular, from my guide. Startled out of a half-conscious dream I came erect in the saddle.

"My Indian was earnestly pointing up and ahead. I raised my eyes and became electrically, tinglingly awake. There, high up, wraith-like in the waning moonlight, loomed what seemed a Grecian temple of colossal proportions, atop a great steep hill. So massive did it seem in the half-light of the approaching morning that I could think of it only as an impregnable fortress high above the sea, on some rocky, wave-dashed promontory. As this mass took clearer shape before me with each succeeding hoof-beat of my weary steed, it grew more and more huge. I felt an actual physical pain, as if my heart skipped a few beats and then raced to make up the loss.

"Thus for the first time I viewed the Great Pyramid of Kukul Can, now called El Castillo—the Castle. And I shall always be glad that I had the good fortune to get my first glimpse of it in this fashion. Times without number I have since passed and repassed this grand old structure, yet never have I walked in its shadow without a quickening of the pulse or without recalling undimmed the vision of that moonlit night. And, as I look back through my years of intimate companionship with my City of the Sacred Well, it seems to me that moonlit nights are linked inextricably with nearly all the important events that have there befallen me—or, at least, with those which are pleasant in retrospect.

"By the time I had dismounted and unsaddled my horse my Indian was already curled up and fast asleep. The poor horse was, I think, in sound slumber the minute his feet came to a halt. But for me, weary as I was, sleep was out of the question. I must see more of this magic city. Reaching the foot of the steep ascent, I crawled painfully up what had obviously once been a tremendous stairway, now overgrown with small trees and shrubs. At the end of a breathless climb I reached a narrow, level stone ledge eighty feet above the ground and faced the north door of the temple—the temple of the great god Kukul Can. This sheer pile of perfectly joined masonry pierced by a forty-foot doorway within whose sides I could dimly discern intricate and fantastically carved bas-reliefs; this time-grayed temple of a forgotten faith, viewed there in the silence and solitude of eerie moonlight—is it to be wondered at if my knees shook just a little and if I glanced apprehensively over my shoulder awaiting the terrible, majestic wrath of the

god whose temple was profaned by the eyes of an un-
believer?

"On my eminence I turned slowly and gazed out over
the dead city. Here and there, some near by and some
at a distance, were a dozen other pyramids surmounted
by buildings. A few seemed well preserved, others
were in picturesque ruins, all ghostly white in the moonlight, except where a doorway or a shadow stood out
in inky blackness. I could see the long shadow of that
old temple we call the 'Nunnery.' The stillness was
broken only by the monotonous hum of hidden cicadas;
or was it the distant beat of phantom *tunkuls,* or
sacred drums, warning that the ancient God of the
Feathered Serpent did but sleep and might at any moment
awake?

"And then my eyes were caught and held by a broad
raised roadway leading straight away from the temple
toward a vast black pool overgrown with trees. Breathless, frozen to the spot, I could only look and look, for
in a blinding flash I realized that I was gazing at the
Sacred Way, and at its end the Sacred Well in whose
murky depths even then might lie the pitiful bones of
many once lovely maidens sacrificed to appease a grim
god. What untold treasures this grisly well might hide!
What tragedies had been enacted at its brink!

"I descended and as I walked along the Sacred Way
I thought of the thousands, millions perhaps, of times
this worn thoroughfare had been trodden in bygone ages
where all was now desolate. Here was I, a grain of dust
moving where kings and nobles of countless centuries
before had trod, and where, for all I know, kings and

nobles may again tread long years after I am still a
grain of dust but moveless.

"At the brink of the well I peered into the blackness
and continued to gaze into its depths, picturing in my
mind's eye the awesome ceremonies it had witnessed.
The chant of death begins, swelling softly over the slow
pulsing of the drums. The solemn procession leaves the
holy temple of Kukul Can and the funeral cortège ad-
vances along the broad raised avenue of the Sacred Way,
toward the Sacred Well, the dwelling-place of Noh-och
Yum Chac, the terrible Rain God who must be placated
by human sacrifice. The corn in the fields is withering,
crying for rain. If the anger of Yum Chac be not
appeased famine will follow and the dread Lord of
Death, Ah Puch—he of the grinning, sightless skull—
will walk abroad in the land.

"Slowly, slowly the cortège draws near. At its head
is the high priest, clad in ceremonial vestments and elaborate feathered head-dress, as befits the pontiff of the
Feathered Serpent. And what is this embroidered bower
borne so reverently by sturdy, sun-browned lesser priests?
Is it a bier, a stately catafalque? Is the pitiful victim
already dead? Ah, no! she moves, beautiful, flawless—
the most lovely maiden to be found in the land. Through
every city and village and country-side, for weeks and
weeks, a thousand priests have sought her, this fairest
flower of Maya maidenhood. Her face is pale. She
knows the supreme honor that is hers—she who is to
become so soon the bride of the Rain God. But there
is terror in those lovely eyes, a benumbing, cold fear
of the Unknown.

"And behind them, filling the whole of the Sacred Way, come the king, the nobles, the great warriors and many priests. Already on the far side of the Sacred Well is gathered a silent, grave-faced multitude, the whole populace of the city and pilgrims from afar.

"The high priest enters the little temple at the brink of the well. The dirge ceases, the drums are stilled. He performs his devotions to the Rain God. He lights the sacred incense-burners and the fragrant blue vapor floats, curling, upward. Again the slowly chanted dirge starts, to the muted beating of the drums. He lights a basket of sweet-smelling copal incense, holds it aloft, and casts it into the well. The chant grows louder, the drums beat faster.

"Two powerful *nacons,* or lesser priests, lift the maiden from her couch, their muscular brown arms forming a sling in which she lies as lightly as a leaf on the bosom of a stream. They advance with her to the edge of the well. The pitiless sun glares down into her upturned fear-stricken eyes and she throws one slender arm over her face. Her gauzy garments reveal the tender flesh and adolescent contours of a girl in her early teens.

"Slowly the *nacons* swing the feather-light body backward and forward to the beat of the drums and the rhythm of the dirge; forward and backward in an ever wider sweep, while the drums and chant swell to a roar. At a sign from the high priest the drums are suddenly stilled; the chant ends in a high-pitched wail. A last forward swing and the bride of Yum Chac hurtles far out over the well. Turning slowly in the air, the lithesome body falls faster and faster till it strikes the dark water seventy feet below.

"An echoing splash and all is still. Only the widening ripples are left. The child bride has found favor in the eyes of her lord, the great god Noh-och Yum Chac.

"Thus I imagined the sacrifice at the Sacred Well—a sacrifice enacted not once but hundreds of times through many centuries. Thus has it been handed down in a dozen Maya legends and I wondered whether this grim old well really held at its far murky bottom the relics of the ancient rites or, after all, the sacrifices were mere myths founded on some trial event, which grew and grew with each telling.

"Granting that such sacrifices had been, every vestige of evidence might well have disintegrated into nothingness a thousand years before my time. Assuming even that at the bottom of this watery pit was all I sought, what a mad venture it was for one lone man with but a little money and no great mechanical skill to attempt to recover these evidences!

"And yet my faith was strong. I felt that my quest was not to be in vain and that somehow I would make the well yield up its treasures. At least I must attempt the feat or continue to be haunted by the idea all the rest of my life.

"My wearied brain could no longer sustain these speculations. My whole tired body knew but one desire— sleep. Yet I did not wish to sleep in this gruesome place. Half a mile farther on I should find the Casa Real, the old manor-house that was to be my home. Wearily I strove toward it in the failing moonlight.

"At last I approached the main arched gateway of the corral, built more than two hundred years ago. It was boldly outlined in the pale moonlight, while here and there were long jet shadows cast by some broken portion of a wall or by some partially burned but upright trunk of a great tree. All was desolation, as in the case of the ancient temples, but a newer desolation, for this manor had been built less than seventy years before. As I pushed my way over broken stones a cloud came over the moon and I stumbled full upon what seemed at first the vertebræ of a huge fish. The cloud passed as I halted and an involuntary shudder gripped me as I looked down on the whitened bones of a human skeleton. A little to one side on a slight elevation lay the severed skull; and just beyond was still another and yet another. Ah, yes! I knew the tragic story, but had not expected to be met with so brutal a reminder of it.

"The former inhabitants of this once beautiful hacienda had all been massacred, many years before, by the Sublevados, the untamed tribes of Maya Indians living some miles to the south. These savages had slain every living creature on the estate and had left the several buildings in smoldering ruins. Even at the present time the Sublevados are still untamed and I have often been warned of the menace of a similar fate.

"I turned and gazed at the old gateway under which I had so recently passed—a gateway, so the records say, built in June, 1721. Under it also had passed long lines of weeping captives, and there are men living who remember the event. These poor captives were laden with the booty taken from the villages of Tunkas and Dzitas as they were urged on by their Sublevado captors in their terrible journey to Chan Santa Cruz, the distant Sublevado stronghold. And only the vigorous men with trades and the young women were spared for the journey, while the other prisoners were ruthlessly murdered. Of the prisoners left alive for the journey those who fell by the wayside were despatched with a stroke of the machete and left where they fell. I later found many of their pitiful skeletons.

"Poor boys and girls! What heart-pangs they must have felt; what scalding tears must have fallen on the stone flags as they passed beneath this old arch! Their pangs were soon stilled and the tears they spilled quickly dried, for they all soon came to that tranquil rest which is for eternity. Their lives were like the meteor that flashes for a moment in the sky and is then forever snuffed out. 'Cigar stubs that the God of Night tosses away' is the native vernacular for meteors. The souls of these wretched youths and maidens seem to have been no less carelessly tossed away by the God of the Night.

"I sank down upon the corridor of my new-old home, too utterly fatigued in mind and body to care what army of horrid phantoms might there abide. Let graveyards yawn and specters dance, let witches ride; loose Beelzebub and all his imps, but let me sleep!

"And so I did until awakened by a torrid sun burning down upon me through what once had been a roof."

CHAPTER V

THE ANCIENT CITY

I AROSE cautiously, expecting to find an ache in every bone and muscle, and was agreeably surprised to discover myself without an ache or a pain, though a little stiff. Apparently the hot sun had baked all pains away. In a shady place near by sat my Indian, not sleeping, apparently not even thinking, but just doing nothing at all, an art in which he was an adept.

"I was conscious of an earnest desire for two things,— a bath and breakfast,—and I wanted a great deal of both. Without much difficulty, in sign language, I made my wishes clear to the native and he conducted me a distance of half a mile or so, not to the Sacred Well but to another well or cenote called Tol-oc, which is about two hundred feet to the left of the road leading to the village of Pisté. How he knew so definitely the location of the well is a mystery to me.

"This great cool, crystal-clear pool was the water-supply of the ancient city. A wide flight of steps, now much broken, leads into its depths and the lower steps are at present actually some distance beneath the surface of the water. On the stone rim of the sides of the pool are deep grooves, worn in olden times by the ceaseless raising and lowering of rope-suspended water-jugs or gourds. And can't you picture the women of old Chi-chen Itza in a constant stream passing from dawn till dusk

along the road to the well of Tol-oc?—the servant glad
to escape for a time the sharp tongue of her mistress;
the wrinkled, toothless crone to whom a trip to the well
means an opportunity to exchange the latest gossip; the
comely young matron anxious to get back to her household tasks; the belle of the neighborhood, on her way to
the well, light-heartedly swinging her empty water-jug
and bantering those who pass.   This is a phase of life
as old as communal existence.   One may see the same
scene enacted to-day almost anywhere south of the Rio
Grande or in Spain, Egypt, or the Orient.

"As I swam about in the pool fresh vigor flowed into
my veins, and I emerged with an increased craving for
breakfast.   When I reached the hacienda I found my
Indian had anticipated this and while the repast he provided might not have appealed to a pampered appetite,
I found it a Lucullian feast; and my guide proved no
mean trencherman, either, although I suspect he had
fortified himself with no less heartening a meal two hours
earlier, when he found me asleep.

"While he performed the housewifely task of doing
the dishes, which consisted of throwing away the big
green leaves we used as plates, I sat in the shade of a
magnificent old *yax-che*—the sacred tree of the Mayas
—and puffed my favorite and most disreputable pipe.
Sitting somewhere in the shade around Chi-chen Itza is
the most pleasant occupation in the universe, for there is
a perpetual breeze and no matter how hot the sun, one is
always cool and comfortable in the shade.   Sitting thus
is the favorite and major occupation of the native, and the
white man can very easily acquire the habit.

"As I sat there, at peace with the world, my experi-

ences of the previous night seemed unreal—the fantas-
magoria of a fevered dream and, much as I enjoyed this
shady spot where I sat, the ancient city called me.

"Taking the Indian with me, I returned to make a
superficial examination of the place. My newly acquired
estate of about thirty-six square miles included the abandoned, dilapidated manor, corrals, and other buildings.
And within its boundaries lie the Sacred Well and all of
the ancient ruins and temples that are still standing, not
to mention many others which are now covered with
debris. It also includes several Indian villages. Chi-chen
Itza is really two cities. The more ancient is overgrown
by a thick forest and its location is indicated only by an
occasional grassy, thicket-covered mound out of which
grow great trees and whose sides are covered with scat-
tered carved stones. The newer city is clearly defined
by the buildings which are still standing. The whole,
including the older and the newer city, covers an area
of about twelve square miles.

"There is no apparent plan in the situation of the various structures, although most of them are arranged in
such a way that their openings avoid the direct rays of
the sun at midday. The city was built in this location
because of the two great wells and the lesser one, which
I am sure are not the work of men, although they may
have been altered or enlarged. In all probability there
were no definite and continuous streets; with the exception
of the Via Sacra or Sacred Way, there is little or no evidence of what might be called a city street.

"I reason that there was little need for streets, because
there were no beasts of burden, nor vehicular traffic.
Loads were transported upon the backs of men, just as

they are largely transported at the present time. The ancient builders did construct very good narrow, ballasted stone roads which led into Chi-chen Itza from various directions, but they were roads for human feet to travel. Surely the architects of these wonderful buildings; these people who knew much of astronomy and who could count into prodigious figures had the intelligence to lay out their cities in blocks and squares if any particular advantage or convenience were to be gained thereby!

"The only evident plan is that the present buildings, which are temples and perhaps palaces for the kings and those of high religious or noble rank, are centrally located. Beyond these for miles about are the remains of small rectangular foundations, evidently the sites of what were once the dwelling-places of the large population of the city.

"In the area which I designate as new Chi-chen Itza are twelve buildings in an almost perfect state of preservation, as though built no more than twenty or thirty years ago. Ten of them are still covered with their original ponderous stone roofs and are entirely habitable. These structures alone might house a considerable population. I have lived for months at a time in one or another of them and have found them to be delightfully comfortable and cool. Indeed, these elevated Maya temples are the most ideal living-quarters, much to be preferred to the usual house built upon level ground. Although they contain no windows, they are well lighted by the reflected sunlight striking through the doorways upon the white limestone floors.

"Passing across what is now a lovely flower garden in the rear of my home,—which is no other than the building in whose broken corridor I spent my first night,—my guide and I came at no great distance upon a rise of ground where are situated two most interesting groups of buildings. The first one, a massive structure on our right, bears the curious name Akab Tzib, 'House of the Writing in the Dark.' It is one of the few buildings which has no sub-base or plinth of artificially heaped earth or stone to give it elevation. It is built upon the natural ground-level, which, however, is somewhat higher at this point than the surrounding terrain. And it stands sheer on the edge of a depression in the ground some four hundred feet across.

"It is possible that this depression represents the site of an ancient quarry from which the stone for the building of the city was taken, or it may be simply a natural hollow caused by the caving in of the soft limestone surface rock. The front of Akab Tzib stretches a distance of one hundred and seventy-six feet and in depth the building is forty-eight feet. The structure is low, the façade rising only to a height of eighteen feet. The walls, however, are capable of withstanding a siege. They are of great thickness and constructed of perfectly joined rectangular stones, the surfaces of which are dressed and polished to smoothness. The expanse of the west wall is broken by a shallow recess in the center which divides the wall into three equal sections, with the middle section recessed or offset by a depth of about three feet.

"This central part is pierced by three square-cut doorways. John L. Stephens, who visited the temple more than eighty years ago, says that in the middle section of the interior was a great stairway that led to the roof.

It has since collapsed and is now but a heap of stones and dust.   Apparently it was about forty-five feet wide. Knowing the Maya custom, which was common, of erecting one structure on top of another, we may surmise that this stairway was probably a sort of flying arch and intended as a means of reaching a second temple to be built on top of the low, massive-walled Akab Tzib.   For some unknown reason the upper temple was never erected. Many interesting theories have been advanced as to why the architects abandoned their original plan.   On each side of what was once the stairway are doors leading into chambers.   Besides these entrances there are seven handsome doorways along the western façade of the building. In all, there are eighteen rooms or apartments.

"The whole massive structure is an unsolved mystery. Over the doorway of a small, dim chamber in the southeastern part of the building is a carved lintel on which is depicted in bas-relief the seated figure of a priest or a god, wearing a feathered head-dress and with a long nose-plug protruding from the nostrils.   The figure is seated on a throne and holds in its hand the ceremonial *caluac* or baton of rank.   In front of the figure, at its feet, is a graceful brazier containing what was probably a burnt offering of some sort—copal or incense.   On each side of this well-carved picture are double rows of hieroglyphs, the meaning of which is unknown.   There are no other carvings, glyphs, or pictures in the entire building. This fact is hard to understand, because these ancient builders usually inscribed every available surface.   In one room is a large depression in the floor, and in the center of the building is what appears to be a solid mass of masonry forty-four by thirty feet and reaching clear to the ceiling. Perhaps it contains hidden and secret chambers; that remains to be found out.

"Of one thing, however, I am reasonably sure: the carved lintel was not inscribed nor originally designed for its present position, but was taken bodily from some earlier structure, probably one of the now leveled temples of the older Chi-chen Itza. It represents the period of the highest Mayan art, which occurred before the domination of the Nahuatls, who swept down from the north some centuries later. I believe this building was not erected until after the abandonment of Chi-chen Itza, the long residence at Chan Kan Putun, the return to Chi-chen Itza, and the enslavement of the Mayas by the Nahuatls. Very likely it is the most recently built of all the present monuments in the city, and the one carved piece in it, the lintel, was taken from an older building without reference to the significance of the glyphs. From this lintel is derived the name of the temple, for Akab Tzib means literally 'House of the Writing in the Dark.'

"Leaving Akab Tzib, we walk for the distance of a city block or so through dense shrubbery and over an old stone fence, built perhaps eighty years ago, and come to a most interesting building called La Casa del Monjas or the Nunnery. It is what might be called rambling, yet is of exquisite architectural harmony and richly ornamented, in utter contrast to the building we have just left. It is one of the most wonderfully carved edifices of this old civilization to be found anywhere in Yucatan. It spreads out for an eye-filling distance of two hundred and twenty-eight feet, the center part of the huge pile rising for nearly ninety feet, in three separate tiers, each

The Nunnery, the only three-storied structure in the Sacred City.

The second story of the Nunnery.

All that remains of the third story of the Nunnery. Several inscribed stones
built hit or miss into the wall were doubtless taken from the older city.

smaller than the one below it. Stretching away on each side of this center portion are one- and two-story annexes.

"How well its name fits this grimly beautiful old building is a matter of conjecture. We know that the Maya priesthood was dominant in all matters and that the lives of the people seem to have been governed by a constant devotion to their pantheon of gods and especially to the all-great Kukul Can. Their ceremonies were numerous and elaborate. Doubtless there were many priests and perhaps priestesses. Long training must have been required in the amazing and intricate rituals. And the ancient historians relate that it was the custom to sequester certain girls or women belonging to religious orders. It is not unlikely that this vast building of many rooms and annexes, which seems more fitted to be a place of residence than a temple, may have been the abode of Mayan monks or nuns, or possibly a training school for novitiates. Some believe it to have been the king's palace.

"Not the least perplexing thing about La Casa del Monjas is the plain evidence that what now meets our eyes as a symmetrical whole is, in fact, the result of several different periods of building. The principal structure has been built in stages—for all the world as a swallow year after year builds one nest on top of the previous one. And the annexes evidently were built at various times, as the need for them arose. The whole base of the building is buried in debris, which detracts from the true and lovely lines of the architecture. I have excavated a trench part-way around, to clear out this rubbish, and the trench reveals the fact that La Casa del Monjas has served as a dwelling-place for many people, or that many lived near by even long after the place had lost its sacred

significance and its very name and purpose were no
longer known.

"Without danger of contradiction, I think we may in
fancy reconstruct this Nunnery, in the order of its building. The first structure was a single, rectangular unit
about one hundred feet in length. A later builder caused
it to be entirely filled with great stones and rubble and
cement, so that it formed a solid base or foundation.
More masonry was then erected to the same height, on
three sides, to enlarge this base area, and upon the whole
was erected a building ninety feet long and one third as
wide, leaving a flat promenade twenty-five feet wide all
around, from which there is a delightful view of the surrounding country. We have dug through the masonry of
the sub-structures and into the old, original building
which was filled in with stone-work to provide a support
for the later and upper buildings, so that our theories are
substantiated that far at least.

"To reach the second structure, whose floor is thirty-
four feet above-ground, a great stone stairway of forty
steps was erected, up which twenty men might march
abreast. If they were men of our day they must surely
come tumbling down again, for the steps are each nine
inches high but with very narrow treads, built for bare-
footed or sandaled folk and not for clodhopper boots or
shoes.

"A third and still smaller structure—now little more
than a jumble of stones, except for a part of one façade
and a doorway—was built atop the second temple and
served by another grand and steep stairway, a continua-
tion of the first. This topmost temple was rich in carved
stones, taken, in all probability, from the oft-ravaged

older city. The various annexes were built on to or
adjacent to the first and largest building. All this the
reader will see from the illustrations opposite page 65
and page 69. The custom of enlarging Maya temples by
such methods as just described was not uncommon. Perhaps it indicated growing power or population. Surely it
indicated long residence.

"The main building, constituting the second story, has
five doorways on the south side and one doorway at each
end, and contains many chambers and intercommunicating
doorways. The end rooms extend clear across the building. The central rooms are long and narrow, each with
three doorways. There are also very many shallow
alcoves, scarcely more than niches, which may have contained idols or scrolls—some say books. The center portion is solid masonry, which originally may have contained apartments later filled with stone to provide support for the third story.

"The entire rambling structure is ornamented with
symbolistic carvings and murals in a profusion of designs,
many of them of matchless beauty in inspiration and
execution. The façade of the main building is twenty-five
feet in height, with two handsome stone cornices extending its whole length. The eastern façade in particular is
crowded with ornamentation. The dominant motif is the
face of the god Kukul Can—symbolic masks with upturned snouts which some observers have called 'elephant
trunks.' The same masks are seen again and again in all
these old ruins, but in many cases the projecting snouts
have been broken off by vandals; indeed, a special zeal
has at some time been devoted to this particular destruction. Linking the masks and carrying the whole in a

carefully planned and balanced decorative series are geometrical designs and figures. Above the broad band of the upper cornice and carved in deep relief are geometrical stone screens not inferior to those of the Moors or of India.

"Over the main doorway are two bands of small, undeciphered hieroglyphs, above which project six bold and gracefully curved ornaments. From them, we may imagine, once hung a costly curtain, heavy with embroidery. And still higher above the doorway, interrupting the geometrical sculptures of the whole façade, is a horseshoe-shaped frame within which may still be seen a badly defaced seated figure with feathered head-dress. The lintels over the classic doorways are of huge perfectly cut and polished stones, each bearing a multiplicity of clear-cut glyphs which, like many things in this City of the Sacred Well, tenaciously hold their secrets.

"The Nunnery stands a monument of grace and beauty whose charm is at once evident to any beholder, and doubly so to him who perceives how closely in every line and dimension, yet how subtly, it accords with our modern ideas and rules of good design. But nowhere else in the world is there anything like it. Unique, distinctive, it is characteristic only of this ancient culture. The cut facing page 65, representing one of the best of my many photographic attempts, tells all that a photograph can, but it cannot begin to convey the beauty of this masterpiece. In the great main hall were once many colorful paintings upon the walls and ceilings, still indicated by bits of color here and there or by an interrupted broad band of black or red. And in the various rooms were paintings, nearly all now obliterated. They seem to have reached quite lately their critical age, for many that were almost perfect as recently as twenty years ago are faded or chipped now. In a few years they will be gone forever, and for this reason I have taken pains to obtain the most faithful possible copies of all of them. These Maya paintings represent several periods of culture. Some are childishly crude. Many are of an excellence of line and balance and color not inferior to the best of modern art. Some even are drawn in a most pleasingly free and sketchy manner which so exquisitely portrays an idea without unnecessary detail that one almost expects to see scrawled in the lower right hand corner the signature of some well-known modern artist.

"The eastern or ground-level portion of the added basic structure contains many rooms entered by way of six wide outer doorways.

"Near the main building are two smaller detached ones, the more interesting being known as the Iglesia or Church. It is small in comparison with the bulk of La Casa del Monjas, being but twenty-six feet long, half as wide, and thirty-two feet high. It has three cornices and the principal decoration consists of two seated human figures over the doorway. Hardly a square inch of its surface is undecorated. Formerly it was stuccoed, or plastered, and painted. Much of the original color still clings to the crevices and interstices of its carved walls and it is evident that new layers of stucco were added from time to time and new paint in appropriate colors. Such layers of stucco and color may be seen where the stone has been chipped, with the colors sometimes varying from those of the early coats.

"The carvings again portray the mask of Kukul Can,

with interlinking geometrical designs. A single doorway gives access to the interior, once rich in murals, and the bright sunshine striking upon the white floor floods the whole room with clear light. Close to the ceiling are traces of a row of medallions which originally contained hieroglyphs.

"Another building of about the same size is similarly finished and decorated with the mask of Kukul Can. It contains several small rooms. The entire wall of one apartment has been removed, by not very ancient builders, for the prosaic purpose of making a stone fence. In passing I might mention also that a good-sized pit has been made near one side of the grand stairway of La Casa del Monjas, it being easier to get cut stone in this way than to quarry it.

"No great amount of labor would be required to put this group of buildings in nearly its pristine condition. Nearly all the stones that have fallen lie where they fell and could easily be replaced. Near the grand stairway lie many sculptured images of serpents, birds, and animals, of massive size and carved in full relief. These formed the balustrade and might be replaced even though some are missing. I have no doubt that when the debris at the base of the buildings is removed new archæological treasures will be revealed.

"As an interesting bit of authentic history, the main building was occupied by the soldiers of Montejo, who were besieged there by the enraged native populace. They escaped by night, through the rear of the buildings, by means of a ruse. The besiegers did not discover until dawn that the enemy had fled many hours before.

"Just when one decides that there is nothing new to

surprise him, in this old city, he comes upon something else to puzzle his brain, spurring his curiosity into vain excursions after the why and wherefore of it all.

"We leave the unexplainable Casa del Monjas and, walking westward less than a hundred yards, stand before the Caracol or Snail-shell, which is entirely unlike any other building in the City of the Sacred Well or in all of Yucatan. This curious structure, we imagine, was either a watch-tower or an astronomical observatory—though it may have served a quite different purpose. It is round and built on a terrace two hundred feet square of cut stone, twenty feet in height. Above this is a second stone terrace, twelve feet high. These terraces have sheer vertical sides, but much fallen stone and debris have gathered about them. From the west a stairway forty-five feet wide leads to the first terrace; it was once bordered with great stone balusters in the form of tremendous entwined serpents, their heads on the ground, their bodies forming the balustrade and ending at the top in rattles. The same sort of device is found again and again in Maya architecture. A second similar stairway leads to the upper terrace and the door of the building. A projecting ornamented cornice caps each terrace.

"At the top of the second stairway was once some large object which Stephens thought was an idol, and here was uncovered a hieroglyphed monument bearing the longest inscription yet found in the city. The round tower is forty feet in diameter and forty feet high, with two concentric walls, each two and a half feet thick. The inner wall incloses a circular chamber at the center of which is a core of small diameter, solid except for a winding stairway at its center, extending from the ground-level to the height of the double walls. There is also a passage, now almost obliterated, piercing the lower terrace and connecting with this winding stairway. The building at the top of the double walls has a deep-jutting five-tiered cornice above which rises another and smaller single-walled tower, surrounded by a promenade or ledge, not unlike the balcony of a lighthouse, at the height of the cornice.

"The space between the outer and the inner wall provides an arched chamber five feet wide and one hundred feet in circumference. The inner chamber also is arched and is eight feet wide. The usual Maya arch construction is employed, the arch beginning at a height of ten feet and being about twenty-four feet at the peak. The upper ruined tower, about twenty feet high, contained a stone-lined passage facing due west which might have been used as a line of sight for astronomical observations.

"The outer walls are pierced by four openings—windows or doorways, whichever they may have been—corresponding to the four points of the compass. Similar openings occur in the inner wall but, curiously, they are exactly forty-five degrees out of line with the openings in the outer wall. One of the most novel features in the construction are the many wooden beams placed horizontally between the inner and outer shells of masonry. As these are set in the masonry, it is evident that they are an original and integral part of the building, probably put there to help support the stone-work during construction. Many have stood the test of time and are still stanch and firm. They are hewn from the famous sapote tree, whose wood of steel-like hardness alone could have endured through the centuries. There is no ornamentation within the building, nor upon its walls, and the construction is pure Maya except that it is round where all else is square.

"The curious edifice is on high ground and its construction leads inevitably to the idea of a watch-tower. Its builders knew in their time quite as much about astronomy as did any contemporary race—if not more. The periods of sun, moon, and planets they knew with great accuracy. For these reasons I like to think that their priests and sages came to this tower, making divinations from the stars and laboriously charting their positions and courses. Possibly they were panic-stricken by an occasional eclipse of moon or sun, which they called *chi-bal-kin,* 'the moon or sun devoured by serpents or other beings.'

"But perhaps this tower was no more than a military precaution, a place where solitary watchers by day and night constantly scanned the horizon. Maybe it was merely the local police station or fire department from which could be seen any undue disturbance or the outbreak of a conflagration. I shall leave it to you to make your own conclusions, which may be quite as near to or as far from the actual fact as my own, over which I have puzzled backward and forward for many years.

"To the north a distance of four hundred feet is the so-called Red House, or Chich-an Chob, the latter name meaning 'strong, clean house.' The name Red House is derived from the fact that the antechamber or vestibule across the front of the building has a broad painted band of red running about its four walls. This is the best-preserved building of all my city; scarcely a stone is missing. Its four walls face exactly the four points of the compass; its main entrance is in the western wall, while the eastern wall in unbroken. It now rises from a lovely grassy terrace, slightly sloping from the vertical and about twelve feet high by sixty feet long, faced with large stone blocks and having rounded corner stones at each of the four sloping edges of the pyramided form. Extending around the top of the terrace is a regular Maya cornice, or projecting coping. Approaching the western entrance is a stone stairway, twenty feet wide, of sixteen high and shallow cut-stone steps—a staircase as distinctly Mayan as the mask of Kukul Can. And this stairway is as perfect to-day as the day it was finished, not a stone out of place or broken. It seems incredible that it could have lain there so many centuries at the mercy of the tropical wilderness and of passing vandals and have suffered not at all.

"Chich-an Chob deceives one at first glance, seeming to rise to a stately height because of its twenty-eight foot façade. The roof, however, is but twenty feet above the floor. The false front is nevertheless very lovely, being made of stone latticework which skilfully weaves with geometrical designs the ever-present elongated masks of the great Kukul Can, with the upturned snouts unbroken. The construction throughout is pure Mayan of the highest period, typical of many buildings seen in the southern part of Yucatan and particularly at Palenque. Three square-cut, high doorways give access to a shallow vestibule running the length of the building. Back of this is a wall with three more doorways, each opening into a separate chamber. A frieze of hieroglyphs cut in the stones somewhat above the doors completely encircles the walls of the vestibule. All of the interior walls are plastered and painted and have been replastered and re-painted many times. The outer walls up to the stone latticework are quite plain, the cornices or moldings are unadorned, and except for the absence of pillars it could pass for a gem of Doric architecture. Its very simplicity is a pleasing contrast to the Nunnery; yet it is no less distinctly Mayan.

"Two hundred feet beyond Chich-an Chob is a level terrace, or pyramid, sixty-four feet square, which supports a small three-chambered temple with an entrance to the south. One end has fallen in, but two of the chambers are in good repair. This temple, so far as I know, is nameless and at present is of no special interest. Clustered near by, to the right, are several smaller pyramids whose buildings are merely heaped ruins. Some of these contain tombs. Probably all were burial-places of great men. The principal pyramid of this group contains the tomb of the high priest and it is the scene of one of my most thrilling adventures."

The story of the exploration of the high priest's tomb, alluded to by Don Eduardo, is very interesting and will be related in another chapter.

In about the center of the City of the Sacred Well is El Castillo, whose imposing bulk is by far the greatest of all of the silent old structures of this ancient metropolis. Don Eduardo has told us that this huge pile struck him speechless when he came upon it suddenly in the moonlight upon his first introduction to Chi-chen Itza. He is not the only one who has been struck dumb by the first sight of the rugged and beautiful temple, high and huge above its surroundings. Coming back from the States one year, I made the acquaintance, on the boat, of a middle-aged American and his charming daughter, who with some others composed a small party bound for Mérida, the capital of Yucatan. As I had been to Chichen Itza many times, I naturally, in my talk with this gentleman, was enthusiastic over the idea of showing him the ruined city, and finally the whole party decided to go there. We arrived at the little town of Dzitas, where the gentlemen on horseback, I on an ambling mule, and the rest in *volans* set out for the City of the Well. All the way the members of the party took turns in joking me about my pet city and my stories concerning it. I was in every sense the tail of the procession, as my mule had decided ideas of its own, as mules have, and would travel no faster than a slow walk; but the rest of the party were not traveling on a bed of roses and there was no unwillingness to stop and wait for me while they composed ironical witticisms.

When we came near to Chi-chen Itza I ranged my mule alongside the gentleman who was leader in the heckling. I did this knowing that we would travel almost to the Great Pyramid of El Castillo and then, at a sharp turn to the right, view it completely and suddenly.

My friend was in the middle of another verbal dig when the sight smote him. His mouth simply remained open. I have not yet heard the last of his apologies for his previous jesting remarks and I find my revenge very sweet.

The pyramid, or terrace, on which El Castillo stands is two hundred feet square and rises to a height of seventy-five or eighty feet. The exact height is rather difficult to measure because of the debris at the bottom. The top of the terrace has a level surface, or platform, sixty feet square, upon which stands the temple. The four sides of the pyramid rise steeply at an angle of fifty degrees and the pyramid is terraced, each terrace being nine feet high, with a narrow horizontal offset. The rises are faced with cut stone beautifully paneled. Each of the four pyramid faces is vertically bisected by a wide stone stairway more gentle in its incline than the angle of the pyramid itself but still very long and steep. The stairs start at the top flush with the ledge upon which the temple stands and draw away farther and farther, as they descend, from the plane of the pyramid face, with an increasing ratio of projection so that at the bottom they project an appreciable distance beyond the pyramid base. Thus the stairways pleasingly break the monotony of line—which is good art and good architecture. Like all Maya stairways, they have narrow treads and high risers.

The cult of Kukul Can, indicated everywhere in the City of the Sacred Well, nowhere attains so overshadowing an importance as here in this vast temple. Each of the four corners of the pyramid is bounded by the huge undulating body of a stone serpent, extending from the ground clear to the top of the pyramid. Each undulation of the serpent's body marks a terrace or gradient and to lift a single stone section of one of these mammoth serpents would be a task for a dozen men. Everywhere on the horizontal levels of the terraces springs up each year a thick growth of grasses as high as a tall man's head.

The principal stairway, facing the north, is guarded at the base by two huge heads of feathered serpents, jaws open, fangs displayed, and forked tongues extended. And each of these heads, excepting only the forked tongue, is

hewn from a single solid block of stone, with every cro-
talic detail perfectly carved. The bodies belonging to
these serpent heads, conventionalized into two broad, flat
bands, extend up the mound, one on each side of the stairway, to the principal entrance of the temple. On the
narrow platform and forming the main doorway of this
holy of holies are two more immense monolithic serpent
heads, now partially destroyed. They are used as pillars
trisecting into three parts the great forty-foot doorway.
The conventionalized and foreshortened head of the serpent forms the base of the column and the foreshortened
tail forms the capital which is, in its own way, no less a
worthy architectural creation than the Greek Corinthian
column, with its capital of acanthus leaves.

The triply vaulted ceiling rests upon great sapote
beams supported by three-foot-thick walls and massive
square-faced, paneled stone pillars. This sapote wood,
called *ya* by the natives, is dark red in color and turns
chocolate brown with age and exposure. It is nearly as
heavy as iron and is very hard. In many ways it resists
the action of the tropical elements better than metal, and
insects seem to produce no effect upon its adamantine surface. These beams are wondrously carved and with few
exceptions have faithfully sustained the tremendous
weight of stone put upon them. Only a few have broken
with age, so that but a part of the façade of the temple
has fallen. For a thousand years, at least, they have
stood and at the time of the Conquest in 1540 they were
in much the same condition in which we now find them.

In front of the main doorway originally stood a great
stone table with an intricately carved surface. It was
supported by curious Atlantean stone figures and some of

these strange male caryatids were bearded. Other figures on piers and columns within the temple also are bearded —with one exception the only bearded figures portrayed in this whole city which was inhabited by a beardless race. Close examination shows, however, that the carved figures wear masks and it is the masks which are bearded. This fact only enhances the mystery, pointing to the possibility of a still more ancient past and of ritualistic traditions so remote in their beginnings that all memory of their original meaning has faded and only the ritual or empty shell remains of what was once living fact. Analogous are some of the archaic Greek rituals and Druidical rites.

Who were the prototypes of these bearded figures? Were they the mysterious, blue-eyed, fair-skinned people clad in armor who were supposed to have once landed at Tamoclan near Tampico? Norsemen? Or were they the old Atlanteans whose country Plato says "sank in one day and one night beneath the waves of the ocean"?

Of the many marvelous carvings and paintings in this temple I shall say more in another chapter.

Doubtless upon the wide level roof of the temple were performed religious rites,—solemn invocations to the sun and the like,—for, throughout, this edifice leaves one with the impression that its character was purely religious. There are no warlike scenes pictured, only solemnity and high reverence for the great gods.

Lying within the shadow of El Castillo are the broken remains of another building, called the Temple of the Tigers. It takes its name from a frieze of bas-reliefs which is one of the outstanding treasures of the lost art of the Mayas. In these wonderful carvings the sculptor has perfectly caught the feline vigor and grace of the American jaguar. No doubt he had a first-hand knowledge of jaguars, which were very plentiful then and still abound in this vicinity if one wishes to go to the trouble of looking for them. To the Mayas the jaguar was the "Protector of the Fields" because he lay in wait for the deer in the open and cultivated spaces. It was the custom of the natives to put some gift or friendly token in the corner of the field for this god-like beast. Probably his very life was sacred as are those of many animals in India.

The Tiger Temple is built on a pyramid base with a stairway up the side approaching a wide doorway which is divided by pillars into three parts. Much of the sustaining pyramid has crumbled away, or been removed, leaving the building perched on a sheer wall of roughly cemented rubble as viewed from one side. The façade is thirty-five feet long and twenty-two feet high and at each side of the entrance is a great serpent's head. Each of these monoliths weighs several tons and is carved with amazing skill; every feature and scale is flawless and they are painted or enameled, the colors being still visible if not vivid. The head of each is green, while eyes and open mouth are red. The scales end with the head, and the remainder of the body, elaborately feathered, rises in a graceful cylindrical column, with the tail now broken but originally projecting upward along the face of the building and terminating in well-defined rattles. A portion of the front roof has fallen, due to the breaking of wooden lintels supporting the mass of stone of which it was composed, but fortunately the serpents' heads and the door columns are unharmed.

All of the interior walls are solidly painted with bat-

tle scenes, scenes of domestic life, and pictures of sacrificial pageants. Many of the colors are as brilliant as
the day they were laid on these smooth walls, although
the wonderful paintings have been much marred by
vandals. The many figures, each in a different posture,
each group differently clothed or armed, and all cleverly
drawn, in good proportion, and elaborately colored, are
capable of holding the most casual observer by the hour
and are a never-ending delight to the enthusiast.

The Tiger Temple is in every way the prize exhibit
among the various edifices of the Sacred City, not for its
size but for the craftsmanship and charm of its every
detail. And yet I must make one small reservation, for
just back and at the base of the Tiger Temple is a small,
almost ruined building, nameless, lacking a roof and a
front, yet containing on its three still standing walls and
what little remains of a ceiling more than eighty sculptured figures. There are warriors in armor of metal,
hide, and wood; priests in ceremonial vestments; kings
and chieftains. The various figures are distinct and different from one another and the features are individual,
doubtless recognizable if we but knew the great men in
whose likeness they were carved. Each figure is identified by its own personal and distinguishing sign, or mark,
usually placed overhead. Vivid paint or enamel was
painstakingly applied to the sculpture and in many places
it is still pronounced.

Some of the work is crude, other parts exquisitely refined, indicating that it is not all the work of one man. I
am told by those well versed in stone-carving and the
making of bas-reliefs that even with modern stone-cutting
tools it would take one man at least twenty years to

accomplish this work. For lack of a better name I always call this wonderful roofless place the Temple of Bas-Reliefs. When first observed, the sculptured walls look merely like a variegated patchwork. In order to see it at its best one should arrive at about ten o'clock in the morning, at which time the shadows cast by the background bring out all the raised parts in strong contrast and the whole procession of priests and warriors marches clearly before one's eyes. The south wall, however, can be seen at its best only for a short time soon after sunrise and it is well worth the discomfort of early rising. Very probably there was an arrangement of smooth-faced, light-reflecting pillars in this building which caused all the walls to stand out in bold relief.

In the middle of the floor and facing the entrance squats a stone jaguar. Perhaps upon his broad, flat back may have been placed holy offerings to the gods.

The fallen front of this temple was once supported by two finely carved and painted square columns, still majestically erect, and remindful of those other ancient temples of Greece and Egypt.

And now we come to what is perhaps the most curious thing in the whole metropolis. The Tiger Temple, the Temple of Bas-Reliefs, and two other buildings surrounded a great inclosure having a flat paved floor four hundred and twenty feet long, bounded on the sides by smooth, perpendicular walls more than twenty feet high and thirty feet thick.

A hundred feet from the northern extremity of this extraordinary court and facing it is a building consisting of a single chamber. Its front wall is lacking, but arising from the rubbish are two ornamented round columns which were evidently the supports for the wall. The whole interior of the building, from floor to peak, is covered with worn and faded bas-reliefs. In the center of the rear wall is the perfect figure of a man, bearded and with decidedly Hebraic features.

At the opposite end of the court and a hundred feet back from it is a building extending nearly the entire width of the court. The roof of this structure has fallen, but the remains of sculptured square columns are visible.

And on the two side walls of the court, on the precise middle line, were mounted two great carved stone rings, like millstones, twenty feet above the floor. Each ring is beautifully carved with the entwined bodies of serpents. The rings are four feet in diameter and a foot thick, and the hole in each is one foot seven inches in diameter. One of these rings is still mounted in the masonry of the wall, while its counterpart once on the adjacent wall has fallen, but, happily, is unbroken.

A very similar court and similar rings have been found at Uxmal, another ancient Maya city of Yucatan.

Obviously this court was intended for some public game and it has therefore been given the name of the Tennis-court or Gymnasium. In an account of the diversions of Montezuma, given by Herrera, who accompanied Cortes, is the following illuminating description:

The Emperor took much delight in seeing the game of ball which the Spaniards have since prohibited due to the mischief which often happens at the game. By the Aztecs this game was called *tlachtli*—being like our tennis. The ball was made from the gum of a tree that grows in hot countries, which, after having holes made in it, distills great white drops that soon harden and being worked and molded together, this material turns as black as pitch.[1] The balls made thereof, although quite hard and heavy to the hand, did bound and fly as well as our footballs and there was no need to blow them, nor did they use staves. They struck the ball with any part of the body as it happened or as they could most conveniently. Sometimes he lost who touched it with any other part but his hips, which was looked upon among them as very dexterous and for the purpose that the ball might rebound better they fastened a piece of stiff leather on to their hips. They might strike the ball every time it rebounded, which it would do several times one after another, in so much that it looked as if it had been alive. They played in parties, so many on each side, for a load of mantles or what the gamesters could afford. They also played for gold and feather work and sometimes they played themselves away. The place where they played was a ground room, long, narrow and high and higher at the sides than at the ends. They kept the walls plastered and smooth, also the floor. On the side walls they fixed certain stones like those used in a mill, with a hole quite through the middle. The hole was just as big as the ball and he who could strike it through thereby won the game, and in token of its being an extraordinary success which rarely happened, he had the right to the cloaks of all the lookers-on.

It was very pleasant to see that as soon as ever the ball was in the hole, those standing by took to their heels, running away with all their might to save their cloaks, laughing and rejoicing, while others scoured after them to secure their cloaks for the winner, who was obliged to offer some sacrifice to the idol of the Court and to the stone whose hole the ball had passed.

Every Court had a temple day where at midnight they performed certain ceremonies and enchantments on the two walls and on the middle of the floor, singing certain songs or ballads, after which a priest of the Great Temple went with some of their religious men to bless it. He uttered some words, threw the ball

---

[1] The Spanish Conquerors, as will be seen from this description, were not previously familiar with rubber.

about the court four times (towards the four points of the compass) and then it was consecrated and might be played in, but not before.

The owner of the Court, who was also a lord, never played without making some offering and performing some ceremony to the Idol of the Game, which shows how superstitious they were even in their diversions.

This account which has come down to us will save much head-scratching on the part of future archæologists as to the purpose of the unique court and its carved mill-stones.

The Gymnasium or Tennis-court and the buildings surrounding it were not pure Mayan, but were unquestionably introduced under the Nahuatl or Aztec régime.

Nearly all of the remaining buildings are in too bad a condition to yield much of further interest until careful digging and replacing of fallen parts can restore them to some semblance of their original form. One such fallen temple on a great pyramid is now marked only by four nine-foot pillars whose square sides are chiseled with queer bearded figures, some of whom carry what I can only call a "rabbit-stick"—evidently some sort of ceremonial staff or wand. These pillars were unquestionably the front of an immense temple whose wooden lintels have given way, letting fall the whole edifice. In front of this ruin were several stone tables, and apparently they stretched at one time, end to end, clear across the base of the pyramid. The tables were of various heights and consisted of stone slabs six inches thick and about three feet wide. They were supported by grotesque dwarfish Atlantean figures with upraised hands, the palms held flat and on a level with their heads. While grotesque, these figures have much dignity and sureness of line. Originally they were brightly painted.

The tables have been so disarranged that it is impossible to tell what was their original position or even to guess at their purpose. The temple faced west, as indicated by the broken stairway leading up to it. In the midst of the debris lies a fractured serpent column nearly five feet in length, with a stone tongue projecting two feet from its fanged lips. The column rising from the serpent's head is two feet in diameter and its capital was the creature's tail. The broken outlines of a rear chamber reached through a vestibule just behind the serpent column measure thirty-six by fifteen feet. The doorway of the chamber has square-cut, sculptured jambs.

A few hundred feet to the north is the ruined Temple of the Cones. Strewn all about are large cone-shaped stones like big projectiles, but cut and carved. It is thought that they formed some sort of ornamental frieze. Some are handsomely sculptured. There are also in this vicinity figures of the Chac Mool type—an animal body, usually a jaguar, with the head of a man.

Some distance to the right of El Castillo are the ruins of what must have been a very important temple. They occupy a great irregular mound some six hundred feet long and are bordered by several pyramids and other ruins of varied character. The largest of the pyramids is fifty feet high and stands in the northwest corner of the group of ruins. All that remains of it are columns, but there are almost a forest of them, some round, some square. We have called this ruin the Temple of Columns. It seems as though here must have been an elaborate plaza of temples, colonnades, and sunken courts.

Even now archæologists from the Carnegie Foundation of Washington, D. C., are at work in reclaiming this portion of the Sacred City from the jungle, clearing the debris and working out the jig-saw puzzle of replacing each fallen stone in its rightful position.

Everywhere for miles one comes upon huddled debris-covered mounds and carved stones. In the very heart of the jungle is the overgrown ruin of a tremendous pyramid and temple, while here and there unexpected columns rise amid the trees. More than thirty such ruins have been counted, choked by rank jungle growth—palaces, no doubt, of high priests and mighty chieftains. And I think sadly as I view them that the study of archæology is long and time is fleeting.

CHAPTER VI

AN IDLE DAY IN THE JUNGLE

SEVERAL thousands of years before that sturdy Scotch engineer John MacAdam gave to the world the broken-rock road surface known as "macadam," which has done so much to make communication easier, roads were built in Yucatan that embodied all of his sound principles of road-making. And MacAdam lived and died without ever having heard of them. In fact, he had been sleeping beneath the green sod of his native kirk for at least a decade before Europe or North America knew that these old roads of Yucatan existed. The thoroughness and good engineering of their construction rival the famous roads of the Roman Empire or of present-day highways.

In ancient times Chi-chen Itza and all the great and lesser cities of the Yucatan peninsula were linked by a network of smooth, hard-surfaced highways. The Mayas of to-day call these old roads *zac-be-ob*, or white ways. The name is of ancient origin, used, perhaps, by the very builders themselves and no doubt these roads were like ribbons stretching mile after mile through field and forest and deserving quite as much the appellation of "White Way" as any of our blazing night-lighted thoroughfares.

But alas! they are no longer white, no longer even distinguishable as roads for any great distance, but are buried beneath matted roots and brown earth. And this land which once had the best roads on earth became a place where until recently good roads were unknown, where every cow-path was called *camino real* or royal road but was decidedly unregal.

Don Eduardo has painstakingly studied the old highways and for the rest of this chapter I will merely repeat what he has so often told me:

"The old roads, each and every one, went down to bedrock, and upon that solid foundation was built up a ballast of broken limestone, with the larger stones at the bottom. As the surface of the road was reached, smaller stones were used and the crevices were filled in. And the whole face of the road was given a smooth, hard coating of a mortar cement of lime and finely sifted white earth, known then and to-day as *zac-cab*. The hard-pan of Yucatan is limestone ledge rock and as a rule it is not very far beneath the surface soil. Often in the building of roads the first layer or ballast consisted of large boulders, not merely tumbled in haphazard, but carefully placed and with the interstices filled in with smaller stones, painstakingly fitted and hammered into place. Thus a firm anchorage was provided that has held through the centuries. The second and third courses, each of smaller boulders and stones, were quite as carefully placed. The final course was constructed of stones the size of a bushel basket and smaller, wedged together with rock fragments. Within a foot or so of the desired road-level, rock fragments from the size of an egg to that of a small walnut were leveled in, a grouting made, and the whole pounded until a hard, level surface was obtained. Mortar or cement was then applied in a thin coating and when this had hardened sufficiently gangs of stout-muscled laborers armed with smooth, fine-grained polishing-stones rubbed the plastic surface until it became compacted into a polished flatness almost as smooth-coated as tile and nearly as hard.

"The majority of the stones used were not quarried but were isolated boulders rounded by erosion and stained with iron from the 'red earth' in which they are usually found. Seldom was any rock used which could easily be cut and used for the construction of buildings or temples.

"These old highways—what a tremendous labor they must have been! What miles and miles of carrying the stones to build them! And nothing but man-power to move the huge boulders. Centuries, perhaps, were spent in the building, and millions of sweating men.

"Their traffic problems did not concern vehicles, not even horses nor other beasts of burden. The roads were built for travelers afoot and the burden-carriers were men, traveling in single file as human carriers do the world over. And yet there must have been much traffic, for some of these roads are twenty-five feet in width, so that four files of men with their loads could easily pass, two lines going one way and two in the opposite direction.

"The largest and longest of these ancient roadways connects Chi-chen Itza with the once important cities of Uxmal and Tiho. It is twenty-five feet wide. The long road from Chi-chen Itza to ancient Zac-ci (now Valladolid) and the unnamed but important towns between Zacci and Lake Co-ba, is bifurcated again and again into more and more narrow highways, resembling creeks flowing together to form eventually a mighty river.

"What a picture these forgotten roads must have been in the golden age of the Mayas!—pulsing with life, crowded with water-carriers, venders, idlers, pious pilgrims, nobles with their retinues, farmers bringing their produce to the city, itinerant craftsmen, rich men, beggarmen, thieves; a cheerful jostling of motley and purple; a riot of color and of all the things men buy and sell.

"Came a squad of soldiers, crystal-tipped lances glinting in the sunlight; or a solemn procession of priests and devotees with sacred whistles shrilling or the boom of the *tunkul,* while the laughing crowd parted and made silent obeisance to the holy ones.

"Along the sides of the road every now and then are low raised platforms, or elevations, which have lost all semblance of their pristine contours, so that one can only guess at their purpose. It has been suggested that they were originally hollowed out and were *holtunes,* hollow stones, or water-reservoirs, where the traveler might quench his thirst. My own examination of them convinces me that they were, for the major part at least, nothing more than resting-places where the carrier might deposit his load, letting slip the band from about his forehead which held the burden on his shoulders. And well he might rest, this ancestor of the present sturdy Maya, for he bore just as incredibly heavy burdens for as incredibly long distances.

"There is a striking similarity in the practical engineering of the Maya roadways and the construction of the stone terraces upon which the temples were built. One day, bent upon the study of such construction and to verify certain conclusions I had reached, I had recourse to a deep excavation made in the base mound or pyramid of an important fallen structure which is located some distance north of the Great Pyramid of El Castillo.

This excavation, so some of the natives told me, had been made by a 'stranger' (white man), short of body but thick-set and very powerful. He was, they said, 'a very positive man, with a long gray beard, and this was so long ago that few are now alive who remember.' No one who has ever seen and known the late Doctor Le Plongeon, intrepid investigator and discoverer of the famous monumental 'Chac Mool' figure, could fail to recognize the faithfulness of this native description. And from all his years of labor Doctor Le Plongeon evolved a Mayan theology which is either inspired or the result of a mentality unhinged by too great labor. Certainly it seems to be imagination run wild, with little of fact to bear it out. It is no less than tragic, for never did archæologist drive himself to more herculean effort than did Le Plongeon.

"To resume my story, this excavation was like a deep chasm, bisecting the crowning platform and going clear down to bed-rock, and thus it fitted perfectly my purpose. Nearly forty years had passed since Le Plongeon made the excavation, and Nature had done her best with wind and rain and vegetation to heal the wound. Loosened material from the sides of the cut had fallen in, providing an excellent bed for climbing vines, saplings, and big-leafed plants. The roots of big trees, no longer supported by the stones, had given way and the trees had fallen, bridging with their trunks the crevice. Vines, saplings, and flowering plants grew up and twined about and embraced the bridging tree trunks, so that one would scarcely know without close scrutiny that an excavation had been made. The two tree trunks which lay side by side, bridging the space overhead, were both of hardwood. One was a *yax-nic,* light-colored and with bark of silver gray, while the other was a *chac-ti,* dark red and with loose-held bark, in decay separating from the trunk in long, curling ribbons.

"Near me were many big spiders, flat, crab-like and motionless, yet with bright pin-point eyes that seemed fiercely awake, waiting and watching for whatever prey might come to their nipper-like jaws. Their long legs and still longer caliper-pointed antennæ lay sprawled flat against the tree trunks so close that on casual inspection the creatures might pass for bits of tree fungus. Small lizard-like reptiles, with beautiful diamond-like eyes and heads as ugly as sin, sprinted up and down the tree trunks and under and over the branches, skilfully avoiding the spiders and other dangers. Both spiders and tiny lizards on the *yax-nic* trunk were gray in color, blending perfectly with the bark surface, while those on the *chac-ti* trunk were dull red to match the bark—an example of natural camouflage or protective coloring as striking as any I have ever seen.

"Out came the powerful pocket magnifying-glass which I always carry. While looking at a gorgeous little insect decked in gold and green, I became aware of a commotion in the *yax-nic* tree and turned the lens in that direction. What I saw was a fearsome-looking head and a body that was no less than an walking horror. The head seemed to be all jaws and glittering eyes—deep, powerful grinding mandibles that worked like steel-cutting shears; eyes lidless, unblinking, bulging, and coldly cruel. And the whole body and pointed legs were incased in gray armor of metallic luster. It was with a sigh of relief that I laid down the lens and realized that I had been gazing only at a spider and not some antediluvian monster. Except for the comforting fact of relativity of size between man and these creatures, I doubt if there ever existed three more terrifying animals than the crab-like spider, *chin-tun,* the tiny crested lizard, *hu,* and the giant-armored ant, *choch,* whose sting is worse than that of the scorpion, often producing fever and sometimes death.

"Directly overhead, between the fallen trees, I could see growing at the top of the mound the thorny *katzin,* one long branch of which swayed over the brink of the man-made chasm. And almost at the very tip of this branch hung the pensile nest of an oriole, with the brilliant feathered male singing his lungs out beside it. The gold-and-black plumage against the green leaves and the glossy jet-black Spanish moss of which the nest was made produced a picture that Gauguin would surely have longed to put on canvas. Suddenly his song ended in a high-pitched scream, as a brown hawk swooped from the sky and clutched not the bird but the nest. With one scaly talon the pirate gripped the neck of the nest, while with the other he tore at its woven bottom. He worked like a flash, but my revolver flashed yet more quickly and effectively. The mother bird and the eggs, I think, were saved, but the nest was sadly in need of the work of an expert in oriole nest-repairing and I imagine it was some time before the master of the house recovered sufficiently from his fright to resume his liquid melody. At least I heard no more from him that day, although every other bird in the neighborhood immediately dropped what he was doing and came over to view the damage and condole with or congratulate the victims of the assault, so that it was a full ten minutes before the jungle resumed its habitual quiet and the averted tragedy was sufficiently forgotten for the near-by *dzaypkin,* or tree cicada, to resume his not unmusical note that sounds like a muted automobile siren.

"I had outlined my work for the morrow, selected the place where the shovel should follow out the prodigious work of Le Plongeon, gone these many years. I had even snapped the rubber band back on my note-book and was turning my thoughts luncheonward when almost between my feet I heard a frightened squeak and saw a small brown rabbit dart from the opening under the stone ledge on which I was sitting and scurry into the adjoining underbrush at a speed incredible even for a much frightened bunny.

"This looked promising and I concluded to sit a while longer and wait developments. Only a few seconds elapsed before there emerged from the same hole the blunt ophidian head of an enormous boa-constrictor. The unpleasant creature came out uncertainly and the ugly head wavered about nearly on a level with my knees and much too close for comfort. Boas, I think, have not a very keen power of scent. This one, at least, seemed to take up the trail of the rabbit with some difficulty. Yet I can believe, too, that that particular rabbit got over the ground so quickly that he left no scent whatever. Or it is possible that the near presence of an unseen human being bewildered the scent faculties of the huge snake.

"You may be sure that I had kept very, very still, trying to believe what has so often been told me—that few jungle creatures recognize man by his form alone as long as he remains silent and motionless. At any rate, the big reptile finally started in the general direction taken by the rabbit, which no doubt was several hundred miles away by that time if he had maintained his initial rate of travel. Apparently the same idea came to the boa, for he soon reappeared and, still heedless of my presence, passed almost between my legs and reëntered what appeared to be his permanent home, on the ground floor of the pyramid, in the interstices between the big stones which formed its base.

"After making sure that he had entirely gone in and, figuratively speaking, closed the door after him, I took his measurements from observations on certain stone projections he had passed. He was not less than sixteen and a half feet long. Deciding that I had had quite enough adventure for one morning, I bade the spot adieu and went home to lunch."

CHAPTER VII

THE SACRED WELL

YUCATAN has a peculiar geological structure. The soil is usually very thin, and beneath it is porous limestone rock. Owing to the thinness of the soil, vegetation, prolific as it is, does not grow high and the few large trees grow only where the bed-rock has in some way been broken, thus providing depth of soil for the roots.

The limestone foundation is of minute sea-shells, for it was all once sea-bottom; and this porous rock is very subject to erosion, so that the whole peninsula is honeycombed with subterranean streams and channels and caves, while every here and there are natural wells, or cenotes. Some, like the two greater wells at Chi-chen Itza, are very wide and deep; others are tiny. Nowhere is the elevation above sea-level great, and many of these natural wells extend down to sea-level and are fed by seepage from the sea. Others, of course, are partly fed by surface drainage and nearly all provide an inexhaustible supply of water. Indeed, I believe that it would be practically impossible to provide any pumping equipment which would drain the huge Sacred Well.

In the case of nearly all these wells, except those very close to the sea-coast, the water does not contain salt or minerals evident to the taste, as the limestone rock is a perfect filter. The water, however, as might be expected in this tropical setting, is fairly alive with animalcula. One soon becomes accustomed to such fleshy nourishment in his beverage and ceases to find it unpleasant.

In the dry season the cenotes provide virtually the only water-supply, because there are almost no lakes or surface streams. Owing to the porosity of the rock, moisture sinks into the earth very rapidly and in only a little while after a heavy rain the ground is again quite dry. To-day, as in ancient times, life is dependent upon the natural wells and it is easy to see why the city of Chi-chen Itza was located as it is. On every hacienda, the manor is built adjacent to a cenote. So, too, are the villages. While cenotes are not rare, still they are not common enough to provide a convenient water-supply for the majority of the populace.

In Mérida the wealthy inhabitants have cenotes upon their grounds, providing delightful places to bathe. And around them many pretty grottos or underground chambers have been hollowed out from the rock by artificial means, where it is always cool and where the families resort in the heat of the day. Cenotes are often found in the jungle and sometimes are ideal places for hunting. Where the well has sloping walls or a reasonably good path down to the water, it is sure to be patronized by wild animals of all kinds. Many cenotes contain fish, especially catfish.

One device employed in olden times and still used to augment the water-supply is a shallow reservoir, or cistern, called a chultun (stone calabash), which fills with water in the rainy season and tides over, to a certain extent, the arid months. But it is usually a dry hole before the dry season is far advanced. These rain-cisterns are of all sizes and shapes. There are a few ruined cities, like Uxmal, which had no cenotes or other natural water-supply and which must have depended solely upon the impounded water of many chultuns.

The inexhaustible natural wells were early utilized by the Spanish plantation-owners, who in the irrigation of their fields employed the noria, that ancient, rather clumsy big wheel with water-buckets or dippers fastened to its periphery. It is in operation to-day in Yucatan just as it is in Spain and the Levant.

At Chi-chen Itza are three main cenotes and some lesser ones. The Sacred Well was called "Chen Ku" (*Chen* means "well") and was never called *dzonot,* or cenote, which gives the impression that the great well may have been made by human effort or at least was thus enlarged. Perhaps, however, this idea that human agency was employed in its construction may have arisen mostly from the fact of its circular form and perpendicular sides, which may quite logically have been the work of Nature alone, or Nature aided by man. De Sander speaks of this well as having been formed in part by man, and I think his theory is not improbable. But surely the great well is, for the most part, a work of Nature.

Tol-oc, the next largest well in the Sacred City, was the main source of potable water. In ancient times a stone stairway led down into its waters. To-day the upper steps are gone, but one can see a clearly defined line of chiseled steps some three feet or more beneath the surface and adjacent to these is distinguishable another line of steps. Don Eduardo thinks the stairway origi-nally consisted of a broad flight leading from the top of the well down to the water-level and that at its base was a narrow stone platform. It is impossible to determine now how wide the stairway was, or whether or not his surmise is correct that there was a platform at the bottom.

His conclusions were made several years ago, when the water in the well was unusually low. The fact that the rise and fall of the water-level in this cenote bears little if any relation to local rain-fall leads to the belief that its principal source is far distant and comes down through some permeable rock strata, until by reason of a rock fault it gushes up into the well of Tol-oc. Overhanging the wall are large trees, orchid-covered, whose delicate perfume floats down to meet the water. There are orchids here that would quickly make a fortune for a New York florist.

At first sight the water seems dust-covered and turgid, but the dust on the surface is only pollen from the orchids and the big lilies that cluster against the cliff-like walls. It is therefore good, clean, and deeply poetic dust, and beneath the surface the water is crystal clear and cold as any bubbling New England spring. To bathe in Tol-oc is an unalloyed joy.

The large cenote of X-Katum also is on the outskirts of the city and is famous among the natives to-day for the purity and softness of its water. It has no recorded history nor traditions, but the worn grooves in the solid stone of its brink, where ropes have raised and lowered countless jars for countless centuries, is testimony more eloquent than words.

The many other cenotes in and around the city all contain very pure water and are apparently inexhaustible. Around them are the remains in stone and mortar of what

were surely important structures. Near the cenote of
Yula, which is almost six miles from the center of the
ancient city, Don Eduardo was fortunate enough to
uncover a large stone tablet, one side of which is entirely
filled with clear, minutely carved hieroglyphs.

The Via Sacra—the causeway, once so straight and
smooth, leading to the Sacred Well—is now in bad condition, its outline dulled by time. Great trees border it
and their branches arch overhead, while their roots have
raised and broken the smooth avenue until it no longer
resembles a road. Smaller trees are rooted in the roadway itself.

The Sacred Well is a great pit, with sheer stone sides
which are slightly irregular. Its form is elliptical, almost
circular. At the side nearest the Great Pyramid is a
small ruined sanctuary where the last rites were performed before a maiden was thrown into the well to
become the bride of the Rain God. The ground for
some distance about this sanctuary was paved with stones.
The Sacred Well, at whose bottom dwelt Yum Chac,
the Rain God, is more than one hundred and sixty feet
wide and as one gazes down its vertical sides, the drop
to the water seems tremendous; indeed it is fully seventy
feet.

The sheer wall of the well is laminated, split horizontally into two thousand bands or strata of limestone, of
various widths. Some of these bands appear hardly
thicker than a sheet of paper, others as wide as a house is
high, and every lamination is separated from its neighbor
by a sandwich filling of thin lime-powder. The striated
appearance is very striking, because the laminations are
dead black except where vines, trees, and orchids or other

parasitic plants or fungi cling to and lend color to the surface. The layers of lime-dust between the strata of rock are either pure white or cream-colored. The powder has a hard-packed coherency, but the elements—sun, wind, and rain together—loosen enough of it so that the

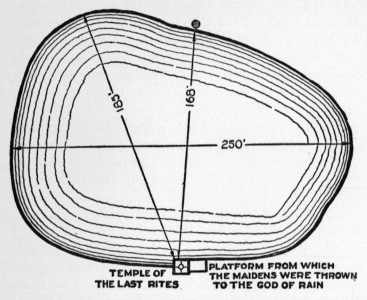

TEMPLE OF
THE LAST RITES

PLATFORM FROM WHICH
THE MAIDENS WERE THROWN
TO THE GOD OF RAIN

THIS PLAN INDICATES THE GENERAL SHAPE AND SIZE OF THE SACRED WELL AND
THE LOCATION OF THE SHRINE OF THE LAST RITES

plants and the surface of the water are always covered with a thin film of dust. All about the edge of the well is a fringe of trees, and a surprising amount of vegetation has found a root-hold between the rock laminations of the perpendicular walls.

The placid water of the pool is jade-green, due partly to the great depth, and partly, I believe, to traces of certain salts or solubles in the water, although I cannot speak with certainty on this point, as I have never subjected it to chemical analysis. I have tried many, many times to get a really good photograph of the Sacred Well and have come to the conclusion that only the motion camera, or an airplane view can ever succeed in reproducing the sight. The "still" photograph, taken from the brink, shows either an expanse of wall and little water or much water and little wall. For this reason the illustration opposite page 116 fails to show the whole well and does not begin to do justice to this most interesting, historic spot.

As Don Eduardo and I sat on the crumbling walls of the shrine, at the very brink of the Sacred Well, he told me of his famous undertaking, now so successfully carried out—the removal of the ancient treasures from the very bottom of the Sacred Well.

"For many years," he said, "the thought of exploring the bottom of the Sacred Well had filled my mind. I thought about it by day and dreamed about it by night. It became a mania which would not let me rest and earned for me the reputation of being a little queer in the head. A thousand times I had gone over in my mind the practical ways and means that might be employed. Draining, dredging, or diving—it must be one of these three. I early became convinced that probably the well could not be drained, and certainly not with the slender finances at my command. I concluded at last that it could be dredged, and with comparatively simple equipment consisting of a stiff-legged derrick with a hand windlass, a long boom which might be swung out over the well, and a steel orange-peel buck-scoop, or bucket.

"Simple as the undertaking sounds, it was beset at every turn with difficulties. The equipment, especially contrived and designed, was easily ordered in the United States and put aboard ship. Getting it ashore at Progreso, where it had to be unloaded five miles out and lightered to shore, was the first hard job. Loading it on flat-cars and finally unloading it at Dzitas, sixteen miles from my city, was no less difficult. With only native assistance, without trucks or anything adequate on wheels, and over the poorest excuse for a road, the equipment was moved piecemeal, until, after months of the hardest work I have ever done, it was all piled beside the Sacred Well.

"Assembling the machinery was a task of shorter duration but no less strenuous. I would at that time have given gladly some years of my life for the services, for a few hours, of one or two brawny, profane, and competent Yankee 'riggers.' Time and again, before the cumbersome outfit was completely in place, I expected it to topple into the well or fall upon me and my Indians.

"At last all was ready. My Indians, about thirty in number, each had his appointed task. The most trusted were to man the windlass and the turning of the boom from whose projecting end hung the cable-suspended dredging-scoop. The boom was swung out until it extended far over the well. I gave the signal and the steel bucket descended, disappeared under the green water, and at last came to rest on the bottom. Slowly the boom was swung back toward the brink of the pit and stopped. Eager hands manned the windlass to raise the bucket. Seemingly endless feet of wet cable were

wound about the drum before the filled bucket broke
the surface of the water. Up and up it rose, until it was
on a level with our heads; then it was swung in by the
boom and lowered to the spot which I had selected, where
every precious scoopful should be minutely and painstakingly examined on the sorting-tables I had erected.
No treasure must slip through our hands; nothing must
be damaged by careless handling. Anything perishable
must be immediately treated with the preservatives which
were ready and waiting. My hands trembled, in spite
of my effort to control them, as I emptied the contents
of the scoop upon the sorting-tables, for soon I must
be either 'that clever chap who recovered the treasures
from the Sacred Well in Yucatan' or else the prize idiot
of the whole Western Hemisphere.

"I went over the muck, spreading it out, examining
every bit of it, and found nothing; not a trace of anything
interesting. It might just as well have come from any
cesspool.

"Again the winch revolved, its ratchets clinking against
the brake. The big scoop, with its hungry steel lips wide
open, plunged into the still water. The Sacred Well
seemed sullen in the reflection of a black cloud overhead,
as though determined to the very last to withhold its
secrets.

"And so it was, day after day. The winch rolled and
unrolled its cable of steel and its manila ropes. The
triple-pointed steel jaws dived into the soft, yielding muck
many feet below the surface of the well, and came dripping up to deposit their burden. And day after day I
found nothing but ill-smelling rotted leaves and a few
stones, prevented from sinking into the mud by rotting

tree branches which had fallen into the well and which, when not too decayed to stand the bite of the steel jaws, were brought up by the dredge. Sometimes whole trees were brought up and their weight made our steel cable sing like the string of a bass viol as the sodden mass was swung underneath the surface to free as much of it as possible and so reduce the weight before raising it clear of the water and dropping it again in another part of the pool where it sank with a splash and swirl of water.

"At times the dredge, working between two entangled trees, was caught as in a trap and we experienced very real difficulties and dangers in freeing it. When the whole mass could be raised to the surface, agile natives with axes and machetes always managed to get down to it and, clinging precariously to cable and bucket, free it from its rotting incubus. For hours at a time we labored with such delaying obstacles, but always in the end the winch again rolled out its cable and then coiled it up with nothing but a mouthful of the mucky bed of the pool.

"Several times we brought up the skeletons of deer or of wild hogs and once the tangled skeletons of a jaguar and a cow, mute evidence of a long-past forest tragedy——the cow feeding quietly, probably at night; the spring of the hungry forest cat and the agonized, purposeless flight of the bleeding quarry with the clawing jungle beast clinging to it; the last frantic leap into the well where both were doubtless stunned or killed by the seventy-foot drop to the surface of the water.

"Then, for a long while, finds even as interesting as these ceased. Absolutely nothing was brought up but mud and leaves, leaves and mud, with an occasional stone

thrown in for good measure. My high hopes dwindled
to nothing and became less than nothing. The work was
interminable, nauseating. Doggedly I kept at it, however, determined not to stop until the absolute rock
bottom of the well was reached. I tried not to let my
Indians see that I was discouraged, but they did see it
nevertheless and I think wondered every day how much
longer the crazy stranger would persist in his foolish-
ness and pay them high wages for bringing up mud, useless even as fertilizer, from the bottom of an abandoned
well.

"But Fate was even then preparing a pleasant surprise,
for one day when things seemed darkest—a gloomy,
rainy day when everything was soggy and sodden with
moisture—the dredge brought up what first appeared to
be two ostrich eggs, cream-colored and oval against the
black mud in which they rested. These proved to be balls
of copal incense and they revived at once my waning
hopes. We had several times previously brought up
fragments of earthenware which seemed to be of ancient
origin and probably were, but I could not permit myself
any illusions about them. Similar ancient potsherds
are not uncommon on the surface of the ancient city. A
boy . . . some boy . . . this year . . . ten years ago
. . . a hundred years or ten centuries ago . . . might
have taken up a potsherd and skittered it into the well.
Boy nature has not changed through the centuries and
certainly no boy with a nice, flat chip of a water-jug at
hand could have resisted the urge to see it skip far down
and across the water of this big pool. And so the potsherds we brought up might well be ancient without having
been long buried in the well.

"But the balls of copal, or aromatic resin, left no doubt. Surely they were thrown into the Sacred Well as an offering to the Rain God in those long-past centuries when Chi-chen Itza was a great and holy city, the Mecca of the Mayas! With the evidence that this day brought forth came the conviction that the long siege was at an end and that it was merely a question of time before other and more important treasures would be brought to light. They proved to my satisfaction that the well did really have a religious significance in the olden days and therefore the legends concerning it were doubtless true in the main.

"From that time on, nearly every shovelful contained some trove—balls of copal incense or baskets that had been filled with plastic copal. The basket-work had nearly all rotted away, but the deep impress of its weaving still remained on the masses of hardened copal. There were tripod vessels often filled with copal and rubber incense; wooden fragments of various forms and of unknown use but indicating the skill of some ancient craftsman. And among these wooden things were several pieces of wood made in the form of an old fashioned English bill-hook or of a pruning-knife. My natives looked at them as they came up from the sacred pool and called them machetes of wood, but my heart sang with joy as I viewed them. No sword of damask steel, no Toledo blade could compare in historical value to these simple wooden implements, for they were, in the most primitive form, those strange weapons of the ancient Mayas and kindred races which the eye of the twentieth century had never previously beheld except in pictured form. These wooden weapons were dart-throwers—

the *hul-che* of the Mayas; the *atlatl* of the Nahuatls. They are pictured many times upon the walls of the old temples. Warriors are shown in every attitude of throwing the dart from the *hul-che*.

"The *hul-che,* or throwing-stick, of the Mayas is in its most primitive form more elemental than the bow and arrow, more elemental even than the *yun-tun,* or sling, for throwing stones. The first ones we brought up from the well were so near the birth-type that the hook was actually formed by the natural twist of the wood where the branch had been cut from the parent stem. In ages past, some jungle man, lacking a club and needing a weapon, pulled up a sapling that had attached at its root a secondary branch. As he gave the sapling a downward whirl, the secondary branch flew off at a tangent and straight as an arrow. Thus, probably, came the idea of the *hul-che*.

"It is a singular and interesting fact that the *hul-che,* so universally used by the Mayas and their contiguous neighbors, is almost exactly duplicated by the bone or ivory throwing-stick of the Eskimos, while there are absolutely no traces of its use by the Aztecs or other northern Mexican peoples. In those dim ages when the human race was young—those ages as vague to us in outline and substance as the clouds that float across the sky—the *hul-che* and not the bow was the common weapon of battle and the chase. Then we must suppose some great gelid cataclysm blotted out all humans throughout a whole region, leaving an ethnic break between the two extremes. Gradually the break was filled in by intrusive fragmentary races having no knowledge of the arts and weapons that had been before, leaving only the extremes, the arctic and the tropic, with their descent of man and his arts unbroken.

"Later on I was to have the keen pleasure of finding several votive and ceremonial examples of the *hul-che* representing the highest artistic development. Possibly they are the very ones which served as models for the carvings showing such weapons in the hands of stately priests and other figures portrayed upon the walls and square stone columns of my Sacred City.

"While the Mayas seem never to have used the bow and arrow, their neighbors to the north did. Possibly the Mayas actually preferred the more primitive and possibly more powerful weapon in whose use they were very expert, holding it in the hand with the hooked portion down and resting the feathered end of the dart upon it. The shaft of the dart lay between the fingers grasping the *hul-che,* with the pointed arrow-head even with the wrist. A powerful overhand motion of the arm or a side swing and release of the dart sent it hurtling through the air, and legend says that the dart thus thrown by a strong man might be driven clear through the body of a deer.

"When these weapons of wood were brought up from the Sacred Well they seemed to be in as good condition as on the day, centuries before, when they were cast into the water; but almost immediately upon being exposed to the air they began to decompose and it was only by treating them immediately with preservatives that I was able to save them.

"With the copal balls and baskets and the wooden objects, we also brought up great quantities of rubber incense and rubber objects. The early legendary people

who are supposed to have settled Yucatan were called
Hulmecas, which means literally 'rubber people,' and the
name was derived from the extensive use of rubber in
their religious and public rites; just as the Sapotecas, or
'sapote people,' are so called to this day because of their
extensive use of the sapote tree and its fruits and deriva-
tives. So says the gifted historian Torquemade, following much the same line of reasoning as other writers,
who say that the name of the tribe called Olmecas was
derived from their general term or name for their chief
or overlord.

"Whatever the answers to these mooted questions of
etymology may be, it has become evident, from the finds
brought up from the Sacred Well, that the Mayas were
users of rubber in various ingenious ways. Many of the
masses of copal which I raised from the well bore, im-
bedded at or near the surface, nodules or small cylinders
of rubber, and in some cases wooden splinters still pro-
truded from the rubber insets. Obviously both the
splinters and the rubber portions were intended as lighters
for the copal, and this evidence substantiates Torquemade's statement: 'They light the fires in their vessels
containing the copal used in their sacrificial ceremonies
with rubber.'

"Upon several of the balls or masses of copal, as found
either in their original baskets or vases or without their
containers, small figures of rubber, built around the
wooden splinters, were placed in a standing position.
At times the legs of these little rubber grotesques were
half buried in the copal. Evidently they were merely
more elaborate forms of lighters or fuses.

"One day when the dredge came up with its customary

load of decayed leaves and silt and one of my natives had, as usual, pushed his arms, clear to the elbows, into the oozy mass, he leaped back with a cry of terror. We all clustered about him to see what was amiss. Silently he pointed to the head of a small dark-colored serpent with a white-ringed neck, which stood up menacingly from amidst the muck. It was precisely of the shape, size, and appearance of a small and extremely poisonous viper which is native to Yucatan. Some seconds elapsed before we became convinced that it was, after all, made of rubber. Although made by hands dead, possibly, ere Christ was born, it turned sinuously in our fingers as we drew it from the mud. It has retained the elasticity of vulcanized rubber, a substance reinvented by Goodyear in modern times. After its centuries of immersion it would surely have shriveled and crumpled to bits if it had been long exposed to the air. I took no chances, but at once put it in a rubber-preserving fluid.

"A number of dolls were found, made of wood and adorned with plastic copal and rubber. They are perfectly formed and artistically colored and decorated. Several have movable arms and legs, with joints made of rubber.

"There was evidence that human nature has not changed—that there were cheats and dishonest sharpers then as now. Some of the copal balls, instead of being clear, heavy, and pure throughout, as were the majority, had a perfect exterior appearance but within were a conglomeration of leaves, sticks, and rubbish— evidently the skimming or residue from the melting-pot. Doubtless some ancient and not too honest profiteer grew wealthy through their fabrication.

El Castillo, the Temple of Kukul Can, on its great pyramid, is the center of the Sacred City and the largest edifice.

Looking down into the Sacred Well. Because of the size of the well and the fringe of trees about it, the whole scene cannot be readily photographed.

"Weight for weight, I imagine we accumulated ten times as many potsherds as all other specimen material combined. At times a large portion of the silt in the dredge seemed to consist of terra-cotta grains—an indication of the enormous number of earthenware vessels which must have been hurled into the well. Probably for centuries the custom was observed of casting into the pool these containers filled with burning incense or copal. Very likely some, heated by the flaming incense, disintegrated almost at once when they struck the cold water, while others lasted for a time and finally crumbled into dust. But to furnish all this red-gray mud and burnt earth-silt an almost incalculable number of vases and jars and basins must have been required. Luckily, by no means all of them were destroyed or even broken beyond repair. Scores were saved entirely whole and among them are many strange and interesting ones.

"The range in pattern and workmanship of potsherds is wide. The larger vessels or fragments of them—cinerary urns and incense-holders—were generally of a coarse, granular biscuit mass, well turned but unevenly burned. They are capable, however, of withstanding a considerable degree of heat. Between this class and a hard slate-gray ware almost as thin and fine as porcelain, are many grades and numerous interesting forms, such as well-made models of human heads, manikins, animals, reptiles,—especially crocodiles,—grotesque Atlantean figures, and tripodal temple vessels used in the sacrificial ceremonies, to hold votive offerings or viands.

"Not always did we have such good fortune in our dredging. At times the soft upper layers of mud caved into the pits we had excavated and we spent many days and weeks in hauling up this mud before we again reached the treasure-level.

"And then, one day, the dredge brought up a perfect skull, bleached and polished to whiteness. Examination showed it to be that of a young girl. Later came other skulls and human bones, scores of them. Most of the skeletons were those of youthful maids, but every now and then one was raised which had the breadth of shoulders, the thick skull, and the heavy frame of a powerful man—no doubt some mighty warrior sacrificed in the flower of his vigor, sent to grace the court of the Rain God.

"I remember as if it were but yesterday finding in the mud raised by the dredge a pair of dainty little sandals, evidently feminine, once worn by some graceful, high-born maid. These more than the bleached skulls and bones, more than any other of the finds, brought home to me the pathos and tragedy of those ancient, well-intentioned, and cruelly useless sacrifices. Frequently bits of cotton fabric were brought up, perfectly preserved but carbonized. My own theory was, and still is, that the copal incense, falling upon the robe of the victim, together with the substance with which the body was painted ere it was sacrificed, exuded an oil which penetrated the fabric and gradually carbonized it, thus preserving it. These specimens of cloth, many of which are lovely in design and texture, are, I believe, the only relics of ancient Maya fabrics in the world to-day.

"Detached skeletons were raised until we had upward of ninety, and at sight of the whitened bones my heart was wrung with pity for the young creatures whose lives had been snuffed out just when living was sweetest. Our finds proved conclusively that the statements made to Landa in 1565 by the natives were true—that both maids and warriors had been frequently sacrificed to the god of the well.

"The female skeletons were those of girls ranging in age from fourteen to twenty. The first one we raised and completely assembled had a small, thin-walled skull, with the sutures almost separate. The skull was delicate, shapely, with small, regular, perfect teeth. The sympathetic imagination without effort clothed the naked bones with flesh and substance, so that one saw instantly the graceful, lovely, high-bred maiden and the last solemn act that had stilled the poor girlish body, clad in all its finery and left to sink into the ooze at the bottom of this terrible pit.

"By comparing the female skulls with those of modern Mayas, obtained from the cemeteries of several villages, I came to the conclusion that there was no appreciable variation or difference. These century-old skulls might pass as typical crania of pure-blooded young Maya women of to-day.

"The male skulls are a contrast to the female ones. Some are relatively large, thick-walled, with protuberant surfaces, receding foreheads, and prognathic jaws. Evidently their possessors were ferocious, primitive, almost gorilla-like—not of the same race which bred the girl-brides of the Rain God. Again this tallies with the tradition that the warriors sacrificed were captives— fighting-men of high renown, who, after being made drunk with *bal-che* (the sacred mead of the Mayas), were hurled into the well as fit offerings to the deity.

"Some years before the time of which I am speaking

I had the good fortune to discover in a sealed stone-walled grave the now famous Sabua skull. I had to work on it for three days, with atomizer and glue water, because the skull, which was perfect in shape, was no more than lime-dust which would crumble at the least touch. By this treatment I saved it and it is to-day a priceless museum piece kept under glass. In view of this experience it seemed strange, almost uncanny, to see these perfect skulls and bones come from the well, so wonderfully preserved that they required no other treatment than cleansing and rubbing with a weak solution of formalin to render them ready for packing and shipment. In the Sacred Well, big and gruesome as it is, are no large reptiles, no saurians, no fish which would or could tear apart a human body or gnaw or crush the bones. I know this to be true, in spite of the local traditions which speak of huge serpents and strange animals to be seen about the well and to be unpleasantly encountered should one be so foolish as to roam about in its vicinity at midnight. I have been that foolish many times and have never met anything of the sort. On the contrary, in the glorious moonlight of Yucatan the big pool has for me an even greater lure than it has in the sunlight.

"As the excavations in the well became deeper and deeper we passed from mud to powdered limestone, which became more and more compact until we reached a marl-like bed into which the steel-lipped bucket bit with difficulty, finally making almost no impression at all. It became obvious that, although we had by no means dredged the whole well, we had literally reached the end of our rope as far as dredging was concerned. I was convinced that further work of the sort would bring us many more finds, but I was quite as certain that they would not differ greatly in character or variety from those already accumulated.

"I could not quarrel with our good fortune thus far. I felt well repaid, even if we should discover nothing else, for all my effort and expense. My highly speculative venture had amply justified itself. I had proved conclusively the history of the Sacred Well. But our dredging operations, together with soundings made from time to time, indicated clearly that the bottom of the well was very uneven—a series of hummocks; almost a miniature mountain range. And in the pockets between those hummocks, where our dredge could not reach, might there not be other treasures?—objects heavier and smaller in size than anything we had yet found; things which, because of their weight, would sink through the mud to the very bottom of the well.

"Never could I leave the spot until, by some means or other, this last and final ghost was laid."

CHAPTER VIII

WE had reached the stage where it was very slow work for the dredge to get even a mouthful of the stiff, almost shale-like bottom of the well, but, while we brought up fewer treasures than previously, I was not ready to discard the derrick and dredge as long as the bucket brought up any finds whatever.

"To facilitate the work at this stage, a plan which I had long considered was put into effect. We built a big flat-bottomed scow, crude but serviceable, and capable of holding ten scoopfuls of muck from the dredge. The scow was constructed, right on the brink of the well, of logs and such other materials as we had at hand. Then we lowered it, by means of the derrick, until it floated easily seventy feet below, on the still surface of the water.

"I fancy if the grim old Rain God, Noh-och Yum Chac, the Indra of the Mayas, was enraged when the dredge first began to rob him of his long-held treasures, the presence of this clumsy craft, as it tipped and yawed on its slow seventy-foot descent to the water, must surely have excited him to frenzy. Yet inexorably we continued our quest, undaunted by the thought of the god's wrath and determined to strip him of every secret. We moored the craft, by a long rope, to a projecting stone knob on the sheer wall of the well, so that it was directly over the area where the dredge had been working. Our system was to lower the bucket, raise it, and pour its dripping contents upon the scow, and this we continued to do until we had heaped upon the boat ten buckets of bottom mud. Loaded to its capacity, the scow was drawn to a narrow sandy shelf or beach which had formed at one side of the well. Then we transferred and examined the load, handling ten buckets from the dredge in about the same length of time it had taken us previously to dispose of one. And thus, for a while, the dredge was made to work profitably even under the increasing scarcity of 'pay dirt.'

"During this phase of our labor we accumulated a great quantity of potsherds, copal, and rubber nodules. Each time the filled scow came to the little beach, the big toads retreated into their rocky cavities amidst the roots and the myriad eyes that usually shone in these twilight depths became invisible. Only the iguanas and the lizards in the branches of the cork-trees that shadowed the tiny beach remained sleepily undisturbed, while the little painted tortoises on the half-submerged logs or branches floating near by became so accustomed to the sight of the scow that they stayed brazenly in their places and eyed the proceedings without fear.

"As the work went on, the tailing or discard from our dredge began to spread out and extend our little beach until it became a solid peninsula jutting out into the well and making our labors easier by providing much-needed footing and elbow-room.

"Long hours I spent gazing over the side of the scow, waiting for the dredge to come up with its load, and while I waited I glimpsed fascinating high lights of a hitherto unknown world—a world with its tragedies, grotesqueries, and surprises; a world in which humans took no part; one unseen until then by human eyes. Drifting past on the turgid waters were curious jelly-like formless creatures and tiny water-insects, some moving slowly as with effort, others like an arrow in shape and speed. Here was a plethora of twisting, darting, gyrating forms of life, all intent on the one object of preserving life— that bitter jest of Nature who instils in us each, great or small, the belief that our own particular and individual existence is of amazing import when she herself values it so lightly.

"Floating on the water were many small red worms no larger round than a pin and perhaps a quarter of an inch long. As one floated lazily by, a small red ant, blown or fallen from the land above, struck the water and instantly was attacked by the worm. The struggle was titanic but brief and the worm, which was more slender than its victim, simply swallowed the ant—body, struggling legs, and all. As the swallowing continued the body of the worm became almost transparent and I could easily follow the journey of his dinner inside, until diner and dinner drifted out of sight.

"Close by the cliff-like wall of the pool was a school of tiny jet-black catfish—pouts, we used to call them in New England when I was a lad. They were but a few days beyond the egg state and were carefully herded by a portly, motherly old catfish. Her inclination evidently was toward dignified, unhurried movement, well tempered with complete repose, but the erratic and swift excursions of her hundred or more infants kept her on the qui vive to head off their ceaseless turnings and dashes, for they seemed possessed to venture into the outer and unknown world, even as other infants since time began. To add to her trials, the whole school was more or less surrounded by tadpoles just as black and even more lively than the baby fishes. They seemed not to have nor to require any motherly care and, like impudent street gamins, they delighted in teasing and leading astray the more tenderly nurtured youngsters. Slyly they tried to swallow the little fishes, tail first, in their sucker-like mouths, and were dissuaded only by the wrathful dash of Mother Catfish.

"It was during this time, which I call the intermediate stage of the work, that many of our specimens of lighter weight were obtained. Among them are pieces of gourds, copal fragments, parts of wooden objects, and bones, all wonderfully preserved in this colossal silo—for the Sacred Well is in many respects like a silo. Some of the potsherds and wooden objects, and even a few of the gourds, had been covered with a thick white paint, almost as hard as enamel, and upon the surface of this the artists of old had worked and drawn figures and hieroglyphs similar to those found in the Codices. Some of the finest pieces of ancient fabrics were recovered at this time. The gradual caving in of the mud about the cavity we had scooped out permitted these fabrics to slip gently into the hole and to be brought up unharmed by the steel lips of our dredge. They are all carefully preserved and are the only authentic specimens of their kind known to archæological science. I deem them among the most important of my treasures from the well.

"There came up ropes and cords, both of bark and fiber, and curiously knotted masses of copal; images carved from light wood and covered with rubber and copal; and always bones and more bones, of maidens and warriors.

"At last the dredge bit only on rock and boulders, against which the steel jaws made no headway. Again and again the bucket came up empty and with its jaws twisted and bent.

"If the first stage—the beginning of the work, when the steel bucket first plunged into the still water of the pit—was exciting, I found myself now laboring under a still greater emotion, for the time had come which I had long foreseen, when the dredge unaided by human hands could accomplish nothing more. There must be hands at the bottom of the well—not the dead hands of pitiful maidens, but live hands of sturdy men to explore every inch of the uneven rocky bottom. From dredging with windlass and bucket, we must pass to a season of deep-sea diving with all the paraphernalia of diving-suits and hose and air-pumps.

"What could be more interesting, more romantic than to go down under sixty feet of water to the very bottom of this grim pit?—to tread the corridors of the most sacred and abysmal abode of the Rain God? I might possibly remain at the bottom, myself, a modern sacrifice to the ancient deity, but I was willing to take that chance; for nothing could now keep from the world the treasures already recovered from the well and if I perished in the attempt at further discoveries, my effort would be, as a whole, not in vain. It was almost like trying to push aside the veil that separates living man from the nether world. Who might say but that the ancient people spoke the truth when they said that the entrance to the habitation of the Rain God was guarded by huge serpents and that none might pass but those expressly summoned by the god, to carry out his mandates? Or might there not live in that deep ooze slimy-bodied monsters of the ante-diluvian era, to which the passing of the centuries was but as the passing of hours? This was no time for specu-lation. I did not crave to serve as a brontosaurian break-fast, yet I must know the bottom of this well.

"Long hours and many days must be spent down on the bed-rock, under high water-pressure, in total darkness and in a temperature but little above freezing. My hands must explore the cracks and crevices and corners and pits where the dredge could not enter, and each find must be carried to the bucket and placed carefully within it, to be raised later.

"I went over every detail of the plan with great care, for not only my own life but the lives of others depended upon its practicability. A hitch, an unforeseen obstacle, a piece of bungling, and one or more of us would never return alive to the sunlight. I was prepared for this part of the business, having become an experienced deep-sea diver back in the United States. But diving under bright skies in open water spaces bathed to some depth by clear sunlight reflected from the sandy sea-bottom is not at all the same as descending into turgid, green, almost opaque water confined by high-cliffed walls overgrown with mighty trees and festooned with huge vines twist-ing and turning like giant serpents. I knew it to be very different from and far more dangerous than clearing off the barnacles and seaweed from the clean-lined bodies of United States cruisers and lighthouse tenders.

"Early one bright morning my crew who worked the windlass and managed the bucket stood grouped about the derrick. The winch which had so long rattled and clanged as the steel jaws of the dredge opened and plunged down to their task, was silent and motionless; but its silence, like that of the men grouped about, seemed to be a sort of watchful waiting rather than the lazy inertia that comes with a holiday hiatus. The cogged wheels were hooked introspectively, as it were, but the jaws of the bucket hung loosely open like those of a school-boy, agape with interest and wonder. On the refuse-built level space between the derrick and the examination platforms were strewn strange-looking suits of armor, canvas-lined and metal-covered, piles of rope and rubber hose, canvas-covered rope ladders, a small but powerful air-pump, and divers other things. Yes, even the divers themselves, for he who was to be my aide in this undertaking had come under contract from the sponge-banks of Florida with his striker, or pump attendant, and all the necessary equipment. Both men were Greeks, young, lithe, handsome as Apollo himself. All that day we spent assembling, testing, and getting everything ready for actual diving operations early the next morning. As fast as the apparatus was put in order we placed it on the scow, which had been scoured and cleaned and was now transformed into an ideal diver's craft. Before nightfall the air-pump was securely fixed on the scow, the air-tubes and life-lines were in place, and the rope ladder dangled over the side and disappeared into the green water. From its bottom rung I should, on the morrow, step off into the unknown.

"The morning of the next day was heavy with clouds that soon broke in a deluge—a three-day norther that kept us all under cover except for a diurnal excursion

when the Greeks and I and my native striker went to the
edge of the well and from there carefully scanned the scow
to make sure our equipment was weathering the storm.
Luckily, the entire apparatus, pump and all, was almost
amphibious by nature and habit, and so far as the eye
could see the wetting was doing no damage.

"Dawn of the fourth day was clear and bright and the
leaves and grass, even the sky, seemed to have been
washed clean by the long rain. After a hasty break-
fast we hurried to the well and descended via the air
route, in the dredge bucket, to the rain-soaked, water-
covered deck of the scow. We bailed out the water and
sponged off the deck, on which we then laid out with
minute care the two rubber-lined canvas diving-suits, making sure that there were no holes through which the com-
pressed air could issue in lines of silver bubbles into the
surrounding water. Our wrists were carefully soaped
and we stepped into the clumsy uniforms, forcing our
hands through the tight-fitting rubber wristlets. The
neck-bands were adjusted and the copper helmets, cloth-
lined and with glassed goggle eyes, were put over our
heads and securely fastened. Then came a necklace of
lead plates and finally heavy metal-soled boots.

"A trial puff of air from the pump, a touch of the
valves in the helmets, and we were ready to call on
Noh-och Yum Chac at the bottom of the Sacred Well.
With a final hand-clasp all around and with my Indians
looking very awed and solemn, I waddled to the edge of
the craft and clambered down the rope ladder about
as gracefully as a turtle falling off a log.

"I must confess that as I loosed my hold of the last
rung and went swirling down into the watery darkness

my heart beat far faster than could be reasonably accounted for by the increasing water-pressure; and my mind, like that of a drowning person, reviewed at lightning speed all the errors of commission and omission of my whole life. But almost automatically I took the precautions of every experienced diver, making sure that the air-line and life-line were free and clear of obstacles. Almost at once the weak, greenish light faded into utter blackness. Once or twice during the descent my lines brushed against some sunken tree roots or branches and I was instantly alert, for in such encounters there is always an element of real danger. These woody projections were, however, quite rotten and with no more strength than soaked punk, and fortunately always broke off at the mere touch of the stout rope.

"Meanwhile, as I went down and down, at a distance of every ten feet or so I felt acute pains in my ears, as though sharp objects were being thrust into them. By adjusting the valves in the helmet and opening wide my mouth, I succeeded in equalizing the air-pressure on the ears, causing a sound like the exhaust of a motorcycle on the ear-drums but relieving the pain. Once I was at the bottom, the helmet valves alone required attention; for only by opening them frequently is fresh air forced down from the pump and the vitiated air expelled.

"I had reached the bottom but a moment before I sensed that the Greek diver had also descended and was close beside me. He had waited only long enough, before joining me, to make sure my native pump attendant was handling my air-supply properly. The darkness was complete, a perfect blindfold, but I reached out and

touched the Greek so that we might be sure of our
relative locations and not get our lines entangled.

"Standing upon the uneven, rocky bottom of the well,
I was thrilled with the knowledge that I stood where no
living man had stood since time began. I think I felt
much the same high elation that must have filled Peary
and Shackleton at the end of their respective dashes to
the polar caps.

"I had foreseen the need of light and had provided
myself with the very latest and best submarine electric
light obtainable. What any illuminant could do, this
light would do. But what light can force its beams
through a lake of chocolate-colored porridge? Our
lights were of not the slightest use in this grim old water-
pit and we had to depend entirely upon the sense of
touch. And this sense served us well, for under constant
use our finger-tips grew highly sensitive. The palpi in
the skin whorls and curves became so responsive that we
were frequently able to distinguish the form and texture
of the objects we touched and even got so far as to guess
at colors, although we made many wrong hazards.

"Another modern invention which we carried at the
bottom of the well was the submarine telephone. It
operated satisfactorily, but we found little use for it, as
it was less bothersome merely to give the required number
of tugs on the signal rope when we wanted to communicate with those above. The Greek and I found also that
by touching the metal fronts of our helmets we could con-
verse easily with each other. The voice tones were
muffled, but with a little practice we had no trouble in
understanding each other. I even recollect hearing the

chattering of the strong white teeth of my Hellenic companion. The water was very cold and every time we came to the surface after our daily two hours of immersion our lips were blue and our bodies covered with goose-flesh and trembling with chill. Coffee, very hot and very strong, was our first requisite.

"The water-pressure at a depth of sixty feet is considerable, and both the air-tubes and life-lines were buoyed in several places by tightly corked quart bottles. When drawn up after the day's work, the lower ones were always half full of water, in spite of the fact that the empty bottles had been corked as tightly as possible before being lowered into the water. This will give some idea of the tremendous pressure.

"This pressure, offset by a corresponding pressure of air in the diving-suit, affects in a peculiar manner the movements of the diver. In spite of my necklace of leaden plates and my two-inch lead soles, I seemed to weigh nothing at all. A slight stamp of my foot upon the bottom would take me soaring upward perhaps ten feet in the water, and I would then come slowly down to rest two yards from my original position. It took good judgment to land in any precise spot, because it was so very easy to overshoot the mark. It seemed as though one real leap would carry me clear to the surface of the well and perhaps entirely up the cliff-like sides.

"On one occasion I became so interested in the finds on the bottom of the well that I quite forgot to let out the accumulated air by means of the helmet valves. I had been working diligently, feeling along the silt-filled cracks of the rocky bottom; then, satisfied with my examination, I gave a stamp of my foot and started

upward. But my diving-suit was so filled with com-
pressed air that I turned in the water topsyturvy and
finally hit the bottom of the scow feet up, with a resounding thump of my metal soles which almost caused
a panic among the natives on the deck of the craft.
Meanwhile I swung around turtle-wise from under the
boat, found the rope ladder, and started to climb over
the side. My henchmen, pallid with fear, were pumping
for dear life, while I, at the side of the boat but below
their line of vision, opened wide the helmet valves to
prevent them from blowing me up like a toy balloon.
When I appeared over the side they all crowded around
me and Juan Mis, my faithful old servant, took my
helmet-encased head in both his hands and peered eagerly
through the thick glass insets. 'God be praised, he is
laughing!' shouted Juan, and they all chuckled with
happy relief, while I sat on the gunwale and was divested
of my cumbersome habiliments.

"Our first task was to discover the nature of the stone
objects that had so often cramped the jaws of our dredge
and strained its chains, costing us hours of hard work
in repairs. The fact that the dredge had never secured
a sufficient purchase on any of these stones to bring them
to the surface led me to surmise that the majority
were smooth-faced and probably hieroglyphed. Mere
rocks or boulders rarely were so smooth that the steel
bucket could not grip them and bring them up after a
trial or two.

"By feeling over the bottom of the well with my hands,
I located the stones one after another and found my
surmise correct. We managed to fasten chains about
them and by means of the derrick raised them from

their watery bed. One by one the heavy, wondrously carved stones were hauled up through sixty feet of water and up another seventy feet until they rested upon the brink of the well. One great stone was a perfectly sculptured statue of a seated god or priest which reminded me of 'The Thinker,' by Rodin.

"The next day we again descended into the well, this time not in search of large objects such as carved stones, but rather in quest of small things lying in the silt between the humps and in the crevices at the bottom.

"I remember distinctly my sensations as my fingers touched upon curious small objects like coins, small nuts, and rings. I could hardly contain my curiosity as I tucked them into my pouch, and my eagerness to get up to light and air to examine them was almost irresistible. When I had collected perhaps twenty or thirty I gave the signal and started upward. Before my diving-dress had been more than half removed I plunged my chilled fingers into the dripping pouch and drew out beautiful embossed rings, small bells of copper, and several bells of pure gold. There were bells and ornaments and medallions of gold repoussé and gold filagree, of exquisite design and craftmanship. There were lovely carved jade beads and other objects of jade. Just as truly as any mining prospector, I had struck gold, but gold tremendously more valuable than his raw nuggets; for, whatever might be the mere intrinsic value of my golden finds, each bit was in reality beyond price.

"This was but the beginning. We now had at our command two means of bringing up the treasure. The big carved stones having been removed from the well, the dredge could again be used, or we could don the diving-suits. In many instances the Greek and I directed from the bottom the work of the dredge. The golden objects brought up, if simply thrown into the goldsmith's melting-pot, would net several hundreds of thousands of dollars in bullion—dividend enough, if one were sufficiently sordid of mind, to justify all my investment of time, effort, and money in the undertaking.

"One particularly wet and dreary day the dredge had worked all morning long, in a monotonous round in which nothing of value was brought up. Toward lunch-time I had about decided to send the men to their quarters for the rest of the day, to let them recover from their half-drowned state. Just then the men at the receiving-platform gave a shout that brought me running. For several blissful minutes we were busy picking lovely little copper bells from the black ooze. The rain was forgotten. Bearers were sent to bring our lunch, and eagerly we sent the steel bucket down again. And again it came up with a pudding of mud plentifully plummed with copper bells. All afternoon we plied the dredge, and nearly every load contained more copper bells, of all sizes and shapes, none larger than our old-fashioned sleigh-bells and many much smaller. In fact, they so resembled sleigh-bells that I could not rid my mind of the idea that they were modern bells used for barter and exchange, like the hawks' bells of Spain. At the end of the day we had piled up over two hundred of these curious specimens of Maya workmanship, and even the most cursory examination showed them to be of genuine ancient origin.

"We carried the bells to the plantation house, where all the servants looked with awe and wonder at *los cascabeles de los antiquas,* the bells of the ancient people. From that time on hardly a day passed that we did not add a handful of copper bells to our growing collection. The bells are mainly capsule-shaped or spherical. Some still have a carbon core within, showing clearly the method by which they were molded. Very rarely did the bells contain clappers or rattles, and this fact supports the tradition that the ancient people believed that all things had life and souls. By removal of the clappers the bells were 'killed,' made mute forever, and their souls, thus released, entered the realm of Ah Puch, the God of Death. Incidentally, the portraits of Ah Puch show him with anklets of bells.

"Certain of the larger copper bells have rope-like designs embossed on them, while others are fashioned like animals and birds and the grinning heads of Cheshire cats. Some represent the heads of foxes or of the ant-eater, showing unmistakably the long, tapering snout.

"Intermingled with the bells were copper circlets like finger rings, and curious flat copper ferrules, from a fourth to three quarters of an inch thick and about an inch long.

"One day we brought up a handful of small masks, about an inch long and half an inch wide, made of thin, well-worked copper. By a strange coincidence they came to us on the very day of a modern native carnival when every one wears a mask. My Indians commented upon the fact and seriously debated whether Yum Chac had not sent them up to us in remembrance of the day. And it is a fact that no other masks of the kind were found previously, nor have any been found since.

"Specimens of well-modeled hard copper chisels were

recovered at various times. Some are small, others of
the customary size and shape of modern chisels, but with
the heads burred, showing much use. All of the copper
chisels, rings, and masks have the reddish color of pure
copper, but many of the bells, particularly the smaller
ones of round sleigh-bell shape, are of a color indicating
copper alloyed with silver or tin. Some of the other bells
contain a considerable percentage of gold, which may be
either a natural admixture from the ore itself or an
alloy added by the ancient artisans.

"One of the most prized treasures was brought up
one day while visitors were present—Mr. and Mrs.
James of Mérida and Dr. Marston Tozzer, now pro-
fessor of American archæology at Harvard University,
who knows the Mayas intimately and has lived among
them and shared their huts and hammocks. We were
all standing at the edge of the Great Well when the
dredge bucket heaved itself from the roiling swells of
green water. As it came up toward the level of our eyes
we saw dangling precariously from one of its fangs a
gray, nondescript article which some one in the party
facetiously remarked must be a cast-off overshoe of the
Rain God. We all laughed at the witticism and then
stopped short as the bucket swung around, bringing the
object into plainer view, and we discovered it be a large
copper disk covered with figures in repoussé and representing the Sun God. My heart was in my mouth for
fear it would drop off and sink back into the well before
my eager hands could reach it, but grasp it I did after
what seemed an age of waiting. It is so beautifully and
intricately worked, so fine in artistry that I deem it one

of the most priceless of all these antiques. What it loses by not being pure gold is more than compensated for by its mass of exquisite ornamentation.

"From copper to gold, so John Hays Hammond once told me, is but a short step and one likely to be bridged at any unexpected moment, and this I found to be the case in the Sacred Well.

"One fine day I discovered, among the several copper bells brought up by the dredge, one small round bell of pure gold, shining as bright and clear as if newly molded. After that every day was literally a golden day with finds of yellow gold—golden bells of all shapes and sizes, some as small as a pea, others large and heavy. And these gold bells were all more or less flattened, as though they had been struck with a hammer or even mauled with a sledge. Some were so flattened that the shape of the clapper within was outlined on the outer side of the bell. The clappers were, like the bells themselves, made of pure gold, but most of the smaller bells, like our previous finds of copper ones, had been 'killed' by having the clapper removed.

"Many disks of gold were brought up, which are covered with finely worked figures in repoussé, while around the outer edges are characters and symbols and sometimes hieroglyphs. Some of these disks were originally flat and others have curving surfaces like breastplates. A few are plain or nearly so, but the majority are completely covered with incised work. One disk, a mask, is two thirds the actual size of a human face and represents a face with the eyes closed. Upon the closed eyelid is engraved a symbol of unknown meaning. Another disk of solid gold is eleven inches in diameter and weighs nearly a pound. It contains no carving or design and I judge it to have been some sort of temple basin or standard.

"Among the golden objects are two very handsome tiaras representing entwined feathered serpents, worked partly in repoussé and partly in filagree. There are also a number of emblematic figures, dancing frogs and monkeys, and several queer objects like brooches. They are from one to three inches high and very thick. There are objects like sandals and objects similar to candlesticks. Some of the latter are of copper, gold-plated. I found, too, a considerable amount of gold-leaf nearly as fine and pure as that of to-day.

"Also among the golden treasures are several specimens that look like the heads of canes. These I believe to have been the tops of the official wands or emblems of authority—the *caluac* pictured many times upon the walls of the temples.

"I found virtually no silver and no metals other than those mentioned, except iron pyrites. This substance, backed with hard-baked clay or stone, was used for mirrors, and I found large fragments of several such mirrors with the mirror surface of iron pyrites still bright and shiny. One metal object about three inches in diameter is white like silver, absolutely uncorroded, and seemingly as hard and refractory as tin alloy or hard steel. I do not know yet what the metal is, but shall know as soon as it can be examined by metallurgists. Can it be that rare, indestructible metal, platinum?

"And with all the precious objects I have taken by force from the Rain God I am very sure that I have wrested from him not a tenth of his jealously held treasure. There are many, many more golden ornaments hid away in the recesses of the uneven floor of the pit, and many, many things even more priceless than gold to the antiquarian.

"All this I leave to the engineer of a future day—and I say engineer advisedly, for it is going to be an engineering task to strip the old well of all it holds. It will first have to be dredged over its whole area, not with the crude hand-operated device which I have used, but with more powerful and modern, mechanically operated equipment. Then a huge, specially designed diving-bell will be required, so that men may work under it quite protected from the water and with ample illumination.

"Among the treasures we found are three sacrificial knives. One is perfect, while the flint blades of the other two are broken close to the hilt. I am inclined to think that the two broken ones were purposely broken or 'killed' before being thrown into the well and that the perfect one was not cast into the pit but fell in by accident. These knives have intricately worked and fluted handles of gold. The one which is unbroken is especially lovely—a bit of perfect artistry worthy of a Cellini.

"One golden bowl is nine inches in diameter, and we obtained several smaller ones about three inches in diameter. These, I think, were temple dishes used by the high priests. The several gold disks of the Sun God vary from seven to eleven inches in diameter. And we recovered forty flat gold washers about an inch and a fourth in diameter, each with a hole in the center. Regarding the use to which they were put I have no clue and can only surmise that they were fastened to the garments of priests or of sacrificial victims.

"The several brooches, as indicated by the designs upon them, were used for personal adornment. The finger rings are peculiar in that they have an enlarged face like a signet-ring, but the enlarged portion is designed to fit at the side of the finger, rather than on top, and this enlarged part always contains a pictured face.

"There are many golden figures of animals and insects, the most interesting being frogs with exaggerated flat feet, such as are found in the graves of Puerto Rico. Among the great quantity of other articles, too numerous to describe here, are twelve plain disks of gold which I imagine are blanks, originally intended by the goldsmith for some craftsman to ornament with designs, but for some reason or other thrown into the Sacred Well in their uncompleted state.

"Many of the larger golden objects, apparently, were not 'killed' before being offered to the Rain God, but nearly all the smaller articles of gold were crushed. Most of these have since been painstakingly straightened into their original shapes.

"Of the pottery vessels, very few were recovered unbroken. Some, as I have said, were containers for copal and rubber incense. Others, I am led to believe, contained the ancient libation of *bal-che* or sacred mead which was thrown into the pool together with the captive warrior victims. This fermented drink made of rainwater, wild honey, and the bark of the *yax* tree, according to tradition, was for men only. Women were never permitted to taste it nor to be present at the ceremonies where it was used as a libation to the gods. The narrow-necked vessel in which it was contained was called a *pool* and had a flat clay stopper fastened to the neck with cords of bark. We brought up several of the necks of such containers with the stoppers still held in the orifices by the bark binding.

"Several of the open vessels with tripod legs are glazed with red inside and out; others have a blue lining, and many were red on the outer surface but left the natural clay color upon the inside. The legs were either rounded and hollow, containing rattle pellets, or thin and solid. They are often fashioned as the heads of alligators or as human grotesques. Many large flat vessels and shallow circular dishes, some nine inches in diameter, were found, of the same design and finish as those I have unearthed in ancient graves in Labna and other old Maya cities.

"The ancient devotees seem to have been especially partial to a certain cylindrical vessel about six inches in diameter and nine inches high. These were often of thin structure and covered with designs and hieroglyphs or bearing the outlined figures of some deity surrounded with the conventional symbols of his attributes.

"A large circular earthenware pan, seven inches in diameter and with a long, thick handle which frequently ended in a carved head, was in common use as an incenseburner. It was rarely made of well-kilned ware and was evidently intended only for brief service. We found many broken utensils of this sort, but only one perfect specimen, which is exceptional in that it is of betterkilned material and of most artistic workmanship. Its pleasing outline is ornamented with openwork spaces intended to give needed draft to the burning copal in its basin. Nearly all the incense-burners of this type have hollow legs containing burned clay pellets evidently designed to produce a rattling sound at religious dances and rituals.

"The mortuary urns are large vessels ornamented with the likeness of a human figure surrounded with a conventional design. The figure usually bears upon its back a vase-like receptacle doubtless designed to receive and preserve the ashes of the dead. I do not know whether these urns were empty when thrown into the well or actually contained human ashes. I hope this point may be settled by laboratory examination.

"The finding of copal and the intimate association of the copal masses with the potsherds and unbroken earthenware vessels, leaves no doubt as to the use and purpose of both. The employment of copal resin as a medicament and as a sacred offering seems to have occurred almost simultaneously with the appearance of man upon the peninsula of Yucatan. In the primitive rock sculptures in the famous cave of Loltum is shown the burning of copal as a religious rite, while the earthen vessels found in the cave contain the blackened residue of burnt copal—a residue that, despite its antiquity and long inhumation, gives forth, when burned, the characteristic odor of copal resin, a fragrance not to be mistaken for any other. The copal tree, anciently known as *psom*, still grows sparsely in nearly every part of Yucatan and in ancient times it was carefully cultivated, while the gathering of the resin partook of the nature of a religious ceremony. One of the early Spanish chroniclers says:

Psom is the name of a tree from which the natives take out a certain kind of resin-like incense which they burn before their idols and in their houses. We Spaniards took advantage of this resin to cure many diseases and we called it copal, which is a Mexican word.

"The first piece of copal we found was nearly round and about the size of a baseball. The resin when fresh is light in weight and almost transparent, but time and the pressure of water at the bottom of the well have given our copal specimens the general lack-luster appearance of the bog-butter found in the lacustrine deposits of Switzerland. Several hundreds of these copal masses were brought up in round or oval form and many with the marks on them of wicker containers or baskets. One of the largest of these copal specimens, weighing several pounds, was thus incased, some portions of the basket fabric still clinging to the copal. Evidently the copal was still plastic when placed in the baskets. A number of the copal nodules had been wrapped in leaves, the veined imprint of which upon the copal surface is so clear that I doubt not that any good botanist would be able to identify the tree or vine from which they were plucked.

"Quantities of bark were brought up which have upon the inner surface pellets of copal arranged in the conventional symbol or prayer for rain. Several of the copal masses are molded in the semblance of human figures or faces, many of them fantastic or grotesque. Many are in the form of frogs and some of these frogs hold a small ball of rubber in their mouths.

"Gourds of all kinds we brought up—small tree gourds which broke even under the most careful handling and which were preserved with the utmost difficulty; *leks* or big gourds, some measuring a foot across and with a two-gallon capacity; gourds cracked and mended with bark lacing, just as they are still mended and used by the Mayas of to-day; gourds coated with the same whitish enamel used on terra-cotta vessels and painted or hiero-glyphed. The gourds were undoubtedly used not only as containers for liquids but for other things such as corn and beans, as they are used by the modern Mayas. None of these gourds was found with a top or stopper in it, but we brought up separately many of the top sections which had been removed to permit the hollowing out of the gourd. Some still had an inch or two of stem left on them purposely to provide a handle and were undoubt-edly used as covers or stoppers. Possibly some of these gourds with their contents of food or drink were origi-nally sealed before being cast into the well.

"Among the wooden objects, the *hul-che,* which I have previously described, is the most interesting, and our finds in the well represent the whole history of the de-velopment of this weapon, from its most primitive bill-hook appearance to its most finished and ornamented ceremonial form.

"The highest stage in the development of the *hul-che* is represented by two specimens from the well. One represents an entwined serpent, its fangs at the hook; in its now hollow eye-sockets probably were once glit-tering eyeballs of jade. The shaft of the second speci-men is formed of human figures and is fronted with a fine mosaic or mask of burnished gold. The whole weapon is as elaborately and minutely carved and inlaid as the finest example of Japanese wood-carving. And we found the stone-headed darts which were used with the *hul-che*. They are pictured clearly on the walls of the temples, but an actual dart or any part of one had never been found before we raised our specimens from the well. Any one may now view them in the Peabody Museum at Harvard University—some without the stone heads but showing the cleft in the wooden shaft into which the head was fitted. There are also several of the sharp stone dart-heads, made of common chert and flint. A few are beautifully formed and fashioned of translucent chalcedony, jasper, and even jade. These specimens represent the highest known development of ancient stone point-work of the American continents and probably of the whole world.

"Portions of lance-poles were found, and stone lance-points. Some of these, like the beautiful dart-points, still carry traces of the hard black bitumen—possibly hardened copal—that once fastened the stone point to its wooden shaft.

"Wooden objects shaped like the incisors of a jaguar and bearing fragments of handsome mosaics encrusted on them are probably parts of what were once jaguar head-masks. Other similar objects are plated with gold—portions of golden jaguar-masks. Parts of large trough-shaped wooden objects are doubtless the remnants of shields. The wood is Yucatan cedar, light and easily worked, yet resistant to the destroying effect of weather and insects. All of the wooden objects required quick and skilful application of preservatives, for, while they had about the consistency of wet punk when they came from the water, even a few moments' exposure to the air would have been sufficient to crumble them into dust.

Happily, I was fully prepared for this contingency, and not a single important wooden find was lost or injured for lack of proper treatment.

"Next to the *hul-che,* the most important of the wooden treasures is the *caluac,* the wand, scepter, or symbolic badge of high priesthood or nobility. Many times upon the temple walls are pictured dignitaries holding this device, as a king might hold a scepter or a bishop his crook. The general form is that of a forked rabbit-stick. It may be significant that the figure portrayed carrying the *caluac* is never depicted as carrying also the *hul-che,* and perhaps the *caluac* may be a ceremonial weapon, symbolic substitute for the *hul-che.* Whatever its purpose, we have several specimens. Some are nearly perfect and there are several sizes. The most common of these finds is about half an inch thick by three inches wide and twenty-four inches long.

"In addition to the wooden dolls and figures I have previously mentioned, I obtained a curious ritual rattle inlaid with mosaics, and several spatulas somewhat like Japanese praying-sticks. The spatulas are thin and about three inches wide by seven in length. Both faces show traces of the same hard white enamel found on several of the gourds and potsherds. The faint characters on these spatulate wooden objects are so precisely like those in the Dresden Codex that one might readily believe them the work of the same artist.

"That phallic rites were practised in some, if not all, sections of the peninsula is indicated by a phallus, well carved from hardwood, which we brought up from the well. It was recovered from the deeper layers of the well-bottom, and this fact precludes any chance that it

is a later intrusive artifact. Some distance to the south
of El Castillo lies a straggling line of large stone phalli,
evidently taken from some portion of the ruined city by
early Spanish settlers and then abandoned by the roadside. The House of the Phalli in old Chi-chen Itza further emphasizes the fact that the cult here existed and
there are unmistakable evidences in the ancient ruins of
Uxmal.

"The several wooden labrets, or lip- or cheek-plugs,
are of some dark, hard wood, possibly *circicote* or ebony.
The frontal surface is a sunken panel on which is usually
carved in relief the figure of a plumed warrior. The
carving in many cases is as fine as that on the best cameos
and is brought out by red pigment. Slight traces of
green are indicated, also, following the same general
scheme as the large carvings on the temple walls, where
green and yellow pigments are used to indicate respectively jade and golden objects or ornaments. That these
colors have withstood centuries of immersion is truly
remarkable; I doubt much if any of our modern color-
ings would have the same lasting qualities.

"Now I come to the last and perhaps most important
of our finds—various objects of jade. We brought up
from the very lowest part of the well seven jade plaques
or tablets, broken but later fitted together with almost
no parts missing. They measure, approximately, three
by four inches, and are well carved with cameo-like designs of Maya deities. Of similar design and length, but
only two inches wide, are nine additional plaques.

"Of jade personal ornaments we recovered a hundred
and sixty large, handsome carved beads and pendants
of varying sizes. These are nearly all perfect. There

are seventy carved jade ear, nose, and labret ornaments, from two inches in diameter down to half an inch. They are all well cut and polished. Among the loveliest specimens are fourteen jade globes or balls, an inch and a half in diameter. These are beautifully polished and several of them are finely carved with human figures and other designs.

"The most prized of all the jade objects is a figurine four inches wide and of like height. It represents a seated figure of the Palenquin type, with an elaborate head-dress, and is probably the finest figurine of the Maya era which has ever been found. It is of flawless jade, perfectly carved and polished, and absolutely unharmed by its centuries at the bottom of the well. It alone is worth, a thousand times over, the hard years of my life spent in solving the mysteries of the great green water-pit whence it came.

"I have purposely left the mention of the jade finds to the very last, for they are the culmination of our discoveries, treasures which, instead of enlightening our ignorance, only add another unanswerable riddle, another intriguing enigma.

"These plaques and ornaments, green, gray, or black; this wonderful figurine—all are of genuine jade, and jade is simply not indigenous in America. Despite all seeking and all investigation, not one single outcropping vein of jade has been found on the American continents, not even an elementary nodule or crystal. Nephrite, or near-jade, and soft serpentine are common to both North and South America, but the jade of the ancient Maya cities is real jade, as easily distinguishable from nephrite as a real diamond from ordinary glass. Furthermore, I have never found, nor have I seen, any similar objects taken from the ancient Maya cities which are of nephrite, though the present-day Indians, particularly in northern Mexico, file out objects of soft serpentine and sell them to the gullible tourist as *chal-chuitl*. The Nahuatl word *chalchuitl* originally meant nephrite or American jade—near-jade—but even before the coming of the Spaniards the word had become prostituted to mean almost any greenish stone.

"To the ancient Mayas jade was very precious—immeasurably more valuable than gold (sun metal), of which they had great store—even as in China to-day one may pay thousands of dollars for a string of perfect jade beads. The following authentic tale concerning Cortes and Montezuma illustrates the point. The story was recorded by one of Montezuma's followers and has the ring of truth:

"Although Montezuma was, toward the last, virtually the prisoner of Cortes, he was for a long time treated not as a prisoner but as an honored guest. Cortes and Montezuma were accustomed to play each day a native game which in many ways resembles chess, and both became much interested. It was their further custom at the close of each day's game to present each other with some gift.

"At the close of one day's game the Aztec monarch presented Cortes with several large disks of gold and silver handsomely worked. Cortes was greatly pleased and so expressed himself. Montezuma smiled and said: 'The gift of to-morrow shall be such that to-day's gift will seem in value and preciousness, when compared with it, as no more than a single stone tile of the roadway.'

"As may be supposed, the mighty Cortes spent a sleepless night in anticipation of the priceless gift he was to receive. At length the morrow came and the game was played to a long-drawn finish. The gift of Cortes to Montezuma does not matter, but the royal treasurer of Montezuma brought in on a golden salver the royal gift, four small carved jade beads. The bitter disappointment of Cortes was so great that he could scarcely conceal it, but Montezuma had acted in good faith, for jade had throughout the Aztec ages possessed an intrinsic value far above that of gold and silver.

"So far as I can learn, the ancient Mayas considered silver of slight value, and they esteemed gold or sun metal more for its adaptability and malleability and its supposedly sacred origin than for its monetary value. It was an object of barter simply because of its utility in adornment and as a temple metal. Possibly copper may have had nearly as great a value in the eyes of these ancient people.

"Of all the jade objects we recovered, not more than a fifth are unbroken, and the broken jade ornaments were broken not by chance or accident but deliberately and by a practised hand. The fractures are not the result of a casual crushing blow, but of the splitting or cleaving impact from a sharp-edged instrument guided by a deft hand, so that the jade was broken but not pulverized or marred. Like so many of the relics from the well, they had been killed, just as the bottoms of terra-cotta vessels were punctured and weapons were broken so that the departing soul of him who died might be accompanied by the souls of the material objects he had most loved or used during his earthly life. And when the departed souls completed the long journey and at last stood before the almighty Hunal Ku, the supreme god in the heavens, each would wear the souls of his earthly jewels and have at hand the souls of his earthly implements.

"Although virtually all of the ancient rites and beliefs are unknown to the modern Mayas, this one belief has persisted in an esoteric fashion. Many years ago I attended the funeral of a young Maya woman whose husband had been devoted to her. Her burial attire was of the richest the family could possibly afford, the *huipile* and *pic* wonderfully embroidered of *xoc bui chui* (embroidery of the counted threads). Her slippers of pink silk also were elaborately embroidered. Long slits had been cut in both *pic* and *huipile* where they would not be noticed, and the soles of the slippers each had three longitudinal slits cut in them. When I asked the old grandfather why this had been done, he professed ignorance and would only reply that it was the custom among his people. But when I told the old *H'men* of Ebtun what I had seen, and of my conviction regarding it, he admitted that I was right and that the ancient belief and custom have been handed down through the generations, although the subject is never discussed with the Catholic clergy.

"Always since that time and the finding of the jade in the great well I have thought of these lovely stones as 'soul jewels,' although, according to the Maya belief, their souls are departed.

"Unfortunately, some of the finds from the well were stolen. How many I do not know—not a great many, I think. But these things are priceless and it is cause for grief that even the least of them should fail to reach a safe place of exhibition. One of my natives abstracted some gold from the finds and had it melted up and made into a chain before we detected him. Later I found, also, that one of my straw bosses had been bribed by another archæologist to secrete and hand over for a price whatever of the finds he could. While I shall never know just what the sum of these losses was, it could not have been great, because no finds were brought up except in my presence, and every find that came under my eye was catalogued and accounted for."

CHAPTER IX

TWO LEGENDS

ON one of Don Eduardo's trips into the country of the Sublevados he chanced across an old Indian, the troubadour of his tribe. This man had a wonderful store of ancient traditions and legends and was an excellent spinner of tales. As nothing pleased him more than to sit by the hour and tell his stories to Don Eduardo—a most interested audience—they spent many pleasant days together. The following legend, especially, remains fresh in Don Eduardo's memory and seems to me worthy of being recorded ere it dies for lack of appreciative ears.

IX-LOL-NICTE

My grandfather told me this, as his grandfather related it to him, and so on back through many grandfathers; and before that —who knows? There was in the north of this great land a city, and this city existed a thousand years before the coming of the white man. The dwellers in the land were called the children of Kukul Can. Afterward the Itzas, who were a mighty people, discovered this city and dwelt about the edge of its Sacred Well for many *katuns*.[1] But before the time of the Itzas, the first dwellers had come to this land in big canoes, from the land of the mountains of fire. They were led by a great and wise man who aided them to build the city. The name of this man is written in stone in the ruins of the city.

[1] A *katun* is a little less than twenty years.

In the city was a high-born maiden, a princess named for a flower, for on the very night she was born, when the goddess Ixchel caressed her beautiful mother and placed in her loving arms a tiny girl child, the *zac nicte* tree growing on the terraced platform of the big house on the hill burst into bloom for the first time and the tiny princess was named for its flowers, Ix-Lol-Nicte—She the Flower of Sweet Perfume. Each year thereafter the *zac nicte* tree, the Mayflower tree of the Mayas, flourished and brought forth its fragrant snowy blossoms. Each year the princess grew in comeliness until she became the most graceful, lovely maid that eyes ever rested upon. Sixteen Mays had the *zac nicte* tree been crowned with blossoms and sixteen Mays had passed since the girl-child was born to the beautiful mother in the great house on the hill.

As the summer passed, the trunk and branches of the *zac nicte* turned to ashy gray, but its leaves remained green and its blossoms lingered in masses of white fragrance. So beautiful had the maid become that it seemed the greatest honor in all the land must be hers. She must become the bride of Noh-och Yum Chac, the Rain God, whose palace is at the bottom of the Sacred Well. Surely the god would be pleased with her, for never had he had a bride half so fair. The time was at hand for the wedding of the water-god and a mortal maid. The god, who controlled the vase of waters, the dew, and the rain, and at whose will the corn grew luxuriously or withered and died, must be mollified. Each year, if it became evident the Rain God was angry with his people, the most beautiful maiden in the land was chosen to be thrown into the well, to sink quickly to his watery home and become his favorite handmaiden and win his forgiveness for her people.

Ix-Lol-Nicte grew in loveliness, and yet no man had seen her, nor had she looked upon the face of any man, save only those of the trusted household retainers. The home of the princess, with its carved stone walls, thick and massive, loomed majestically above the palm-thatched homes of the common people. In the spacious garden was a riot of tropic flowers, exotic shrubs, and twisting vines, giving forth wave upon wave of sweet perfume. Among the trees of grateful shade was the *yax-nic,* whose bark is used to make the drink of the gods and whose clusters of lilac blooms formed a perfect background for the vivid flame of the *copte* tree.

Care-free, with no thought of the future to darken her innocent pleasures, the princess drifted happily about the garden, with only the companionship of the wild creatures that peopled the inclosure. And they sensed with unerring intuition the gentleness of her presence and bared not against her claw, fang, nor sting. In the sunny garden the little wild honey-bees, shining black like bits of jet, clung to her glossy tresses, loath to leave her fragrant presence. The big, lazy black-and-yellow butterflies lit fearlessly upon her shoulders, fanning her lovingly with their slowly opening and closing wings. The *bec-etch-ok,* the bird of a hundred songs, seemed to save for her his choicest selections as she wandered along the garden paths.

Her first knowledge of sadness came with the death of her pet fawn which had fed upon a poisonous vine that grew in the garden undetected by the servants and gardeners. All day she sat in the shade of a big sapote tree, thinking of her little dead pet. Suddenly she heard a sound in the forest depths beyond the garden and she looked up to see a youth chasing a wild fawn which bounded over the undergrowth and into the garden, coming close to her as though beseeching her protection, and she stood up and kept the youth from further pursuit. Not knowing her to be a princess, he was very angry with her for spoiling the chase and called down upon her the curses of Cacunam, god of the hunters.

But the princess was not at all alarmed, because, not knowing the ways of men, she did not realize that the wrath of a man is a very dreadful thing to a woman.

"Beautiful boy," she said, "why do you chase the baby deer? Go find Ek Balam, the black jaguar, or Noh-och Ceh, the giant grandfather deer who lives in the deep forest! No brave man would hunt such a defenseless little creature as a fawn."

The lad, who was of her own age, hung his head and was ashamed. Abashed by her imperious manner, he felt that one far superior addressed him, yet his pride was stung. Flinging back his head, he gazed at her with flashing eyes and said:

"I come of a line of great warriors and I will show you I can fight even the wild *tzimin* or the *chacmool* [tiger]." So saying, he rushed off through the forest and was gone.

A jungle pheasant gave its staccato whistle in the forest depths and all was still. For the first time in her life the princess felt loneliness creep over her, for she had not wished the youth to rush away.

"Thus do the gods of our people upset the plans of man," said the story-teller, as he paused to roll and light a corn-husk cigarette. Looking up with a quizzical smile, he said, "Is it not so with the gods of the white people?" I assured him heartily and from personal experience that the plans of mice and men, white or otherwise, do have a peculiar faculty for going awry.

With his fag burning freely, he continued the legend:

The memory of this meeting kept coming before the eyes of the youth and a strange restlessness possessed him, so that even the excitement of the chase no longer gave him pleasure. He himself knew not what had bewitched him and he fancied that he suffered from some fever. But ever the beautiful form and flower-like face of the maid floated before his eyes. Asleep or awake, it was the same; he could not banish the lovely vision. He did not know her to be a princess, but he knew the big house on the hill and that nobility dwelt there.

At length he went to his uncle, the great *ah-kin-mai,* the high priest, and said:

"Tell me: am I not also of noble birth, like those who live on the hill in the big house?"

His uncle regarded him curiously, for he was a wise as well as a very learned man and well he knew that when a youth asks about those of a house, he is not interested in any of the inmates but the maid who dwells there.

"Be still, my son," said he. "Forget that you have asked this question. The people on the hill are of the royal house, while you are but the son of a chief. Does the bird in the high tree-top know who is on the ground below? So it is with men."

The youth turned silently away and from then on held his own counsel, for he knew that the high priest, his uncle, held no thought of love or romance in his breast. But the next day he warily scaled the hill beyond the city walls, vowing in his heart that he would at least gaze once more upon the maid who had woven about him so potent a spell. As he reached the hilltop there was nothing to see but the tall, rough tree trunks and the heavy branches. The tree under whose shade the lovely maid had sat but yesterday was there, but its branches sheltered only a gay-plumaged motmot perched on the lowest branch, jeering at him with its raucous voice. A weight lay heavy on his heart.

"Hateful bird! Pitiless sun! Unfriendly forest!" thought he. Was it possible the gods might be angry because he dared to invade the privacy of the big house on the hill? He turned sadly to depart, but determined to come again even though the gods be wroth. He had taken but a few steps when a sweet voice directly behind him asked mockingly:

"Do you hunt the baby deer to-day? Or, perchance, the blue-bird, that sings so sweetly in the tree-tops?" The boy turned at the first word and his courage returned, for the evil bird had flown, the sun was never more glorious, and the forest suddenly seemed friendly.

"I hunt a rare flower that grows high up in the dwellings of men," he replied, "and there is joy in my heart now, for at last I have found it."

The maid did not answer, for she was unused to the ways of men and of flatteries, but she sat down under the tree where she had sat before and said:

"Tell me, handsome youth, are the people who dwell in the city below as good to look upon as you?"

The youth did not know what to say or answer, for he realized at once how far above him the maiden must be to dare ask such a question, and how closely guarded she must be to know so little of the dwellers of the city. But this only increased his determination to come again and again, until the heart of the girl should respond to the beating of his own.

In a short time a path was worn up the hillside and through the forest, and often the birds looked down upon the lovers as they spoke of the plans of the girl's family that she become the bride of the Rain God. The princess had been taught that to be called to serve in the subterranean palace of the god was the greatest honor and happiness that could come to any maiden, whether high-born or of lowly birth. Until now, until the coming of this youth, she had accepted eagerly the possibility of becoming the bride of the Rain God. But of late her heart had grown strangely chilled whenever she thought of this honor that might be hers.

Meanwhile, the youth, who came from a family noted for its energy and decision, bided his time and kept his own counsel. His plan was formed. The princess must not be sacrificed to the grim keeper of the Sacred Well, whether god or devil. He would steal her away and bear her off to some distant province before ever she could be chosen for the Rain God. He dared not tell the princess of his plan, for he knew her awe and fear of the gods. But to himself he said:

"Surely if I take her away before the day of the choosing, that will not be opposing the will of the gods, for they will not yet have spoken their decree."

Now Ix-Ek [Brunette], daughter of the great war chief Ek-Chac [Dark Red One], was as beautiful to the eye and in outward semblance as gentle as Ix-Lol-Nicte. It had been rumored that the high honor of serving the Rain God in his deep home might be hers. Those who knew her best, who knew the workings of her artful mind and cruel heart, shook their heads and said in secret:

"Surely the gods who can read the minds and what is in the hearts of men, even as *H'men* the high priest, does with the ills of the body by means of his magic crystal—surely they will never choose Ix-Ek!"

But Ix-Ek knew nothing and cared less about the secret whisperings. The desire to be the chosen of the gods became stronger and stronger in her heart as she perceived that Ix-Lol-Nicte was a rival for that coveted honor. And the hour for the final choice drew nearer and nearer.

It was by the merest chance that the handsome youth passed within the sight of Ix-Ek. At once it came to her like a bolt from the blue that she did not in the least want to serve the Rain God in his damp abode, and that the only happiness in the world for her was to bask in the tempestuous adoration of this unknown youth. Artfully she found a way to know him and to make it seem that he had sought her of his own volition. To him, unused to the wiles that an artful woman ever has at her command, she seemed so tender and compassionate that he, knowing nothing of her passion,—for who can see the moon when the sun is shining? —impulsively confided to her his love for Ix-Lol-Nicte. And Ix-Ek, concealing the jealousy that seethed in her heart, that she might better work out her terrible design, sweetly promised to aid him in securing his heart's desire.

As silently as the poisonous yellow spider of the jungle spins and spins its web, so did Ix-Ek spin her web of deceit and false-

hood to bring the choice of the gods upon Ix-Lol-Nicte and thus
separate her by death from the youth upon whom Ix-Ek had
set her own evil heart. The jealous rage of an unscrupulous woman
knows no bounds, obeys no laws, sacred or otherwise, and stops
at nothing. So Ix-Ek schemed in secret and acted upon her plan.

Just as the plans of the youth were perfected, even to the litter
that was to bear Ix-Lol-Nicte away with him, and stout bearers,
men of his own service, the high priest announced that the day of
the choosing had arrived and that all who were to participate in
the ceremony were to be in instant readiness. The young man
knew that as one of the *hul-che* bearers and especially appointed
guard to the king he must be present at the ceremony. Failure
on his part to be on hand, by an ancient, unchangeable law meant
degradation for his entire family beyond all pardon and for
himself enslavement.

On the great square before the Pyramid of Sacrifice stood the
platform of Noh-och Can, the Great Serpent, where would be
enacted the ceremony of choosing the betrothed of the Rain God.
At the very center of the platform was a massive seat, or throne
of carved stone, used in this ceremony since the earliest days of
the Sacred City. Over the seat was a gorgeous gold-embroidered
canopy with a circular opening in the top, so that the rays of the
sun might shine directly upon the person seated there.

This was in the month of the New Sun. The early summer
rains had passed, though every now and then a fleecy cloud swam
through the azure and obscured the direct brightness of Ich-Kin
[the Eye of Day]. Earth was at its best, covered everywhere
with a tender verdure accustomed to plentiful moisture and now
suffering the first pangs of thirst which might wither and parch
it should the Rain God not relent.

At a given point in the solemn rites, the high priest would call
one beautiful maid after another to occupy the sacred seat and
the one upon whom the unclouded sun shone longest was the
choice of the gods for betrothal to the Rain God. Thus Ich-Kin,

the greatest of the gods, would choose the virgin bride for his brother, the Rain God.

A vast crowd from the city and from far regions had gathered to witness the majestic ceremony. An oppressive stillness was over all, and in the silence was the solemn feeling of the nearness, the very presence of the gods as they awaited the choosing of their lovely mortal handmaiden.

Shattering the stillness came the shrill, weird notes of the flute and the keening of the sacred whistle, mingled with the rolling boom of the drum as the multitude joined in the slow chant of the ritual music, rolling out in a mighty sea of sound.

At length the high priest raised his hand and the music ceased. Taking a vase of fragrant smoldering incense, he approached with measured pace to each of the four corners of the platform, symbolizing the four corners of the earth, and as he came to each corner he wafted the smoke of the incense toward each of the symboled *Bacabes* who support the four corners of the earth upon their faithful shoulders and asked, by invocation, their blessing upon this ancient ceremony.

Four times he did this and then announced that the gods were favorable. The priestly blower of the sacred trumpet blew two long blasts from his great conch-shell, and as the echo died away, Ix-Lol-Nicte descended from her curtained palanquin and, trembling from head to foot, walked toward the throne. She was attired in a long pure-white robe, adorned only at the throat and hem with the exquisite embroidery of the counted threads, worked by the temple nuns. Clusters of *chan-cala,* black and shining as jet beads,—the color worn in honor of the West God,—lay against her fluttering breast. Before her went attendants, scattering large white and yellow blossoms, flowers of the gods of North and South.

Slowly, with graceful dignity, unfaltering yet fearful, she approached the great stone chair. In her heart she prayed desperately that the choice of the gods might not fall upon her, for how could her adoration turn even to an immortal god when before her eyes was the beloved image of the mortal youth of the hillside?

Upon her the throng gazed with wondering eyes. Beauty had been expected, but not this vision of virginal loveliness—a maid upon whom even the gods must gaze with rapturous and humble admiration! As she seated herself upon the throne it seemed to the onlookers as if the gods had already endowed her with sacred attributes, and an involuntary sigh came from each bosom in the dense throng.

Again the high priest raised his hand, and now the drum alone beat in pulsing cadence to the movement of the *caluac* or scepter which he held. Seated before the maiden was the *Uinic-xoco,* or counter, who recorded the beats of the drum. At length the *caluac* in the hands of the high priest came to rest, the drum ceased to beat, and Ix-Lol-Nicte with her attendants left the platform.

Then came Ix-Ek, and she too was beautiful; as vivid as the scarlet berries that shone upon her breast. A murmur of admiration came from the onlookers and Ix-Ek turned and gazed at them disdainfully, for to her these people were as the dust underfoot. She bore herself with haughty pride, and if she felt any fear her bearing did not show it. A short time before, she had craved the honor of becoming the bride of the Rain God, but now she was passionately enamoured of a mortal youth and she was pulsating with the love that filled her heart. Whatever the honor, she no longer wished that sleep in which the eye of life is forever closed.

Once more the high priest raised his hand, the drum-beats ceased, and the people silently returned to their homes. The solemn ceremony of the choosing was over, but the choice of the gods, by ancient custom, might not be made known until ten days had passed.

With heavy heart the young man returned to his father's

house, for he had seen not even the tiniest cloud pass over the face of the sun while his adored Ix-Lol-Nicte sat in the great stone chair. It seemed inevitable that she would be the choice of the gods and the thought was as a knife in his breast. As he lay upon his couch, stricken with anguish, there came to him a messenger from Ix-Ek, saying:

"Come to me. I will help you and yet not anger the gods, for I know that Ix-Lol-Nicte was chosen."

Swiftly he went to the house of Ix-Ek and shook the string of hollow shells before the curtained entrance. At the first sound Ix-Ek stood beside him, brilliantly beautiful in her rich garb, her cheeks flushed and eyes bright with excitement. Even the love-blinded and despairing lover of Ix-Lol-Nicte gazed at her, spellbound for a moment with admiration, before his poignant grief once more engulfed him and he listened in hopeless silence while she spoke.

"You must tell Ix-Lol-Nicte that if she is really chosen she must hold her body straight and like an arrow, so that it will enter the water as the jade-tipped dart from the *hul-che*," she said. "I know the under priests who are to hold her at the brink of the well and fling her in. I will tell them that the gods have whispered to the high priest that the Rain God desires no new bride this year and that they are to fling her carefully so that her body shall not turn in the air but shall cleave the water like an arrow. Thus she shall come again to the surface, unharmed. Be you ready to rescue her and it will seem merely as though the Rain God had refused the sacrifice. Fear not. I know the priests and they will do as I say. Is not my father their chief, with power of life and death over them? Have no fear; they will obey me without question."

Hope returned to the heart of the youth and he called down the blessing of heaven upon Ix-Ek, his ears dulled to the serpent hiss of her voice, his sight unheeding the crafty, cruel glitter of her eyes. And that night he haunted the forest close by the royal

abode of Ix-Lol-Nicte, while the Ox-ppel-Ek, the stars of the
Three Marys, like white sentinels, gazed down upon him in pity
as he gave the familiar signal, the cry of the night-bird. Soon the
white-robed, weeping Ix-Lol-Nicte was locked in his arms. And
when she could speak she whispered between her sobs:

"Let this be our last farewell. It is the will of the gods and
I must go quickly, for since the choosing I am watched con-
tinually."

Kneeling at her feet, the youth told her of the plan of Ix-Ek
and she was convinced by his eager young eloquence. Her stifled
sobs ceased and the flame of hope warmed her and calmed her
fears, for her faith in her lover was as great as her love for him.

Alone once more and without the reassuring nearness and vital
strength of the boy, her fears returned and she distrusted Ix-Ek,
because the intuition of a woman often reaches where the reasoning
of a man fails to penetrate, and in her heart the maid knew that
Ix-Ek sought only to destroy her. But she resolved to say nothing to her lover to dim his hope, and to trust only that the gods,
knowing all that was in her breast and that she could never serve
the Rain God with a whole heart, would in their all-seeing
beneficence refuse her pitiful sacrifice.

When ten days had passed, the high priest announced that Ix-
Lol-Nicte was in truth the choice of the gods, and soon came the
fateful day. Ix-Ek, aided by the nether gods and guided by Hun-
Ahau, the arch-fiend himself, carried out her evil plan. She
had seen and instructed the two brawny *nacons* who were to cast
Ix-Lol-Nicte into the Sacred Well, but instead of directing them
as she had promised the youthful lover of Ix-Lol-Nicte, she told
them that the high priest had had a vision and unless Ix-Lol-Nicte
were accepted by the Rain God, priests and all would die before
sunset; and she urged them to fling the maid with all their strength
so that she should turn again and again in the air and strike the
water with fatal impact.

The sturdy, slow-witted under priests, befuddled by the words of Ix-Ek, did not, as was the custom, fling the slight form of the victim far out toward the center of the well, but let fall the tender body of Ix-Lol-Nicte so that it struck the terrible rocky side of the pit. A mutilated, bloody corpse at last sank beneath the green waters.

Her lover, standing at the brink of the well beside the covered bower of the king and poised to dive into the water to aid Ix-Lol-Nicte the moment her lovely head should reappear above the surface, saw her body strike the rocks. Turning like a flash, he rushed to Ix-Ek and threw her far out into the well as one would throw a small stone. Then he leaped upon the two dazed under priests and dragged them over the brink so that all three fell like plummets into the watery pit.

Horror overwhelmed the high priest and all others who stood there. They knew that a portentous thing had happened and that the wrath of the gods would swiftly be upon them. Enormous clouds, as black as the berries upon the dead breast of Ix-Lol-Nicte, came rushing from the four corners of the horizon and surged high up in the heavens, meeting as one. A single bolt of lurid lightning split the firmament and entered the Sacred Well, and the thunder made the rock walls shudder and the whole earth to tremble. The Rain God, angered that his people had turned the sacred sacrifice into a day of evil, caused the heavens to pour down upon them such a deluge that hundreds were swept into the well and battered to death on its jagged, rocky sides or drowned in its depths.

Others fled, to escape the wrath of the gods, but few reached the shelter of their homes.

When the terrible storm was at last over, only a few houses were left and a decimated population. The big *zac nicte* tree, which had blossomed for the first time when Ix-Lol-Nicte was born, now lay upon the ground, its gray trunk split and torn and its lovely fragrant blossoms bruised and crushed. But if one had looked closely he might have seen that the heart of the tree had been eaten out by a big, dark worm with stripes of brilliant red, red and vivid as the carmine berries on the breast of Ix-Ek.

The old man—soothsayer, story-teller, wizard of Zactun—also told the legend of Xkan-xoc, the forest bird, choosing his words carefully, with long waits between puffs of his husk-wrapped cigarette; and the measured cadence of his voice, together with the white magic of midnight moonlight, made his stories live and clothed his legendary characters with flesh and blood for the enchanted eyes of the listener.

XKAN-XOC, THE FOREST BIRD

There was a time when the wrath of the Rain God was over the land. He had sent the dry wind to work his will and all the country of the Mayas lay parching and dying. The leaves of vines and shrubs and trees first twisted and contorted in their agony of thirst and then crumbled away. The black earth turned to dust, blown about by the winds, and the red earth was baked as hard as the tiles in the roadway. The old men, wise with the knowledge of years and many famines, and whose ears knew the inner meaning of small sounds which most people think insignificant, said that the deep earth cried out and groaned in its hot anguish.

The *ah-kin,* priest of the Rain God, who lived at the verge of the Sacred Well, told his people that the mighty God of Rain was displeased because more copal incense had not been burned at his shrine, and that he must be appeased at once or no corn, no beans, no peppers would grow in the whole land.

A new maid must be sent to him, one so beautiful that he would wish to keep her as his bride and his gratitude would be shown by gentle and frequent rains that would revive the dying maize. The mortal messenger must be the loveliest virgin in all the country, without a flaw, absolutely without the slightest blemish on any part of her body. Her voice must be as sweet as that of *Xkoke,* the wood-thrush, so that the sound of it as she spoke to the god in behalf of her people might be as music to his ears.

The great and wise men met in council,—the king, the lords, the priests, the mighty warriors,—and picked men, hundreds of them, were sent to comb the country-side and the cities and the depths of the forest to find a fitting bride for the god. There was not a maid in Yucatan or even in lands far to the south upon whose face one or another of these ambassadors would not look. And only a few maidens, those of surpassing beauty, would be sent to the sacred city for the ceremony of the choosing.

From the humble house of her father in the depths of the Tiger Forest came Xkan-xoc, carried swiftly on a flower-decked litter, borne by strong young men, the sons of nobles. Garlands of flowers and sweet-scented herbs shaded her from the heat of the sun. Her thirst was quenched with the milk of new corn and wild honey. Her food was especially prepared by the vestal virgins of the temple.

And upon the day of the choosing her *pic* and *huipile* were made of shining, soft tree-cotton, lustrous as the wings of a sea-bird, that clung to her slender gracefulness. Glinting green stones hung pendent from her ears, while about the lovely slender column of her neck were entwined many small fretted chains of gleaming sun metal. Her eyes were big and dark like those of a fawn; her voice as soft and sweet as the dawn breeze swaying the fronds of the *cocoyal* palm or ruffling the petals of the hibiscus flower. Tiny sandals of softest doeskin covered her feet as she was led to the temple to be prepared for the sacrifice.

The high priest donned his vestments, the lesser priests brought rich votive offerings and baskets of incense, both copal and rubber. The king and his guard of noble *hul-che* bearers took their stations and all the people of the city gathered at the edge of the Well.

The first dulcet tones of the sacred flute were heard from the temple of Kukul Can at the far end of the Sacred Way and the shrilling of the sacred whistles joined with the flutes and the reverberating boom of the *tunkul,* the sacred drum. A sudden silence, a strange ominous stillness—then was heard from the depths of the temple the wailing of all the white-robed virgins. And swiftly the news traveled. Xkan-xoc cannot be sent as the messenger to the Rain God, for, in preparing her for the ceremony, the vestal virgins have discovered a tiny mole or birthmark upon her breast, which had been overlooked previously.

The ceremony stopped and the people dispersed with heavy hearts, for Xkan-xoc might not be sent to the Rain God, and beside her all other beautiful maidens seemed unlovely. Another maid must be selected for the sacrifice and how might the Rain God be moved by a bride, however lovely, after seeing the divinely fair Xkan-xoc?

CHAPTER X

THE CONQUEST

IN "The Fair God" General Lew Wallace has given a somewhat fanciful but in the main faithful description of the conquest of Montezuma and the Aztecs by Cortes and his Spanish knights and men-at-arms.

The conquest of the Mayas is a similar story of blood and plunder in which the Mayas, although far outnumbering the Spaniards, were no match for the superior knowledge and weapons of the white men. And, as always, where the flag of Spain went the church followed close behind and consolidated and held the conquered as arms alone never could have done.

Bishop Landa says that Gerónimo de Aguilar with some companions was the first to try his luck in Yucatan. He and his men took part in the destruction of the city of Darien in 1511. He accompanied another leader, Valdivia, in a caravel from Santo Domingo. They ran aground at a place called Viboras, on the coast of Jamaica, and the ship was lost with all but twenty men. Aguilar and Valdivia with the few survivors set out in a small boat without sails and without food and were thirteen days at sea, before, by chance, they reached Yucatan. In that time half of the little band died of starvation.

Upon reaching land they fell into the hands of a bad Maya chief; he immediately sacrificed Valdivia and four others to the native gods, and the people feasted upon their bodies. Aguilar, his chief lieutenant, Guerrero, and four or five others were left to fatten for a subsequent sacrifice, but they escaped and reached another tribe which was at war with the bad chief. Here they were kept as slaves, and though they were mercifully treated, nearly all of them died of disease except Aguilar and Guerrero. The former was a good Christian, according to Bishop Landa's account, and kept his prayer-book, and in 1517 he returned to Spain with Hernan Cortes. Guerrero, however, appears to have been less pious; he allied himself with a native chief and together they conquered many native tribes. Guerrero taught the natives how to fight and how to build fortifications. He conducted himself like an Indian, painting his body, letting his hair grow long, and wearing ear-rings, and married the daughter of a chief. It is thought he became an idolator.

In 1517 Francisco Hernandez de Córdoba set sail from Santiago de Cuba with three ships, for the purpose, some say, of obtaining new slaves for the mines. Others say he went to discover new land. He arrived at length at the island of Mujeres (women), which name he gave it because of the native goddesses of the island—Aixchel, Ixche-beliax, Ixhunie, and Ixhunieta. The Spaniards were surprised to find the women fully clothed and to see buildings of stone and articles of gold. The latter they took with them. Sailing into the bay of Campeche, they landed upon the coast of Yucatan on the Sunday of Lazarus and called the place of their arrival Lazarus. They were well received by the natives, who were struck with awe and wonderingly touched the beards and persons of the strangers.

Near the sea the Spaniards beheld a square stone monument with steps leading up to it on all four sides. On the summit was a stone idol, with the figures of two wild animals gnawing at his flanks, and a huge stone serpent in the act of swallowing a leopard. All were smeared with blood from frequent sacrifices. A little way inland was the city of Champoton, which the chief would not permit the Spaniards to enter, bringing forth his warriors against them. This saddened Francisco Hernandez, but he put his forces in order and caused the artillery of his ships to be fired.

The natives, however, did not cease their attack, although the noise and smoke and fire of cannon must have been terrifying to them who had never seen nor heard such things before. The bloodshed was terrible, for the natives died in hundreds, but still they pressed on, driving the Spaniards back to their ships. Of the Spaniards, twenty were killed, fifty wounded, and two taken alive who were later sacrificed. Hernandez himself received thirty-three wounds.

Returning to Cuba, he told Diego Velasquez, the governor, of the richness of the land and of the abundance of gold, and Velasquez despatched his nephew, Juan de Grijalva, with four ships and two hundred men, on May 1, 1518, to undertake the conquest of Yucatan. One of the ships was commanded by Francisco de Montejo. They cruised along the whole coast and finally attempted to besiege the city of Champoton again, but with no better fortune than their predecessors. One Spaniard was killed and fifty wounded, among them Grijalva.

When the Spaniards returned to Cuba Hernan Cortes
became greatly excited upon hearing the news of so much
land and such riches and determined to conquer the
country in the name of God and his king. He outfitted
eleven ships, the largest being of one hundred tons.
Among their captains was Francisco de Montejo. There
were five hundred men in the expedition, horses, war-
gear, and goods for trading or ransom.

On the voyage one ship was thought to be lost, and
with the ten remaining vessels an attack was made on the
city of Cotoch, which was captured and plundered.
Later the ship that was thought to be lost rejoined the
rest. Cruising down the coast from northern Yucatan,
the fleet came to the inhabited island of Cuzmil.

The natives, seeing so many ships and so many soldiers,
abandoned the place and fled inland. After despoiling
the city, the Spaniards made a foray into the hinterland
and came upon the wife of the chief and her children.
They conversed with her by the aid of a native interpreter
and treated her kindly. Many gifts were bestowed upon
her and her children and she was induced to send word
to the chief and bring him before them. When he came,
he too was well treated and presented with gifts.

The chief ordered all the dwellers to return to their
homes and all of the loot that the Spaniards had taken
was restored to its owners and confidence and friendship
were established. The natives became converted to
Christianity and the image of the Virgin was set up to
replace the old stone idols. From the Indians Cortes
learned that some white men were near by, in the power
of a barbarous native chief. The friendly Indians were

afraid to venture into the domain of the chief, but Cortes finally induced them to deliver the following letter by stealth to the white men:

NOBLE SIRS:

I left Cuba with eleven armed ships and five hundred Spaniards and arrived here at Cuzmil, from where I write you this letter. Those of this island have assured me that there are on this land five or six cruel men and in all very similar to us. I do not know how to give or say other descriptions, but by these I guess and am sure you are Spaniards. I and these nobles who came with me to discover and populate these lands, request you that within six days after receiving this you come to us without other delay or excuse. If you come we shall all know one another and we shall reward the good work that from you this fleet receives. I send a brig in which to come and two ships for security.

This letter was carried by the natives, concealed in their hair, and it reached Aguilar, of whom I have previously spoken. He was not able, however, to make connection with the ships Cortes had sent and after six days the brig and its convoy ships returned to Cuzmil and Cortes immediately set sail with his whole fleet. Soon after embarking, one of the ships was damaged and the whole fleet returned to Cuzmil while repairs were made. The following day Aguilar arrived, having crossed the sea between Cuzmil and the mainland in a canoe. He cried for joy at finding his countrymen and knelt down and thanked God. He was taken, naked as he came, to Cortes, who clothed him and received him kindly. He told of his privations and of Guerrero, but it was not possible to reach the latter, who was then eighty leagues inland.

With Aguilar, who was an excellent interpreter, Cortes

again preached the worship of the Cross and made a great impression upon the inhabitants of Cuzmil. The fleet upon its return voyage touched at Campeche and at Tabasco, where the inhabitants gave to Cortes an Indian woman who was afterward called Marina. She came from Jalisco, was the daughter of noble parents, and had been stolen when small and sold as a slave in Tabasco and later in other cities. Thus she knew the language and much of the condition of the country.

After his arrival in Cuba, Cortes and the governor determined to send Montejo to the Spanish court, to carry to the king his fifth of the treasure resulting from the expedition and to secure a grant for the conquest and settlement of Yucatan. When Montejo reached Spain, Bishop Juan Rodriguez de Fonseca was prime minister, with full power over New Spain. The reports rendered to the minister by Diego Velasquez, governor of Cuba, were by no means in praise of Cortes, and as a result Montejo, his emissary, found himself in a most unfavorable position. It was only after seven years of what must have been heartbreaking delay that he persuaded the president of the council and Pope Adrian to approve the mission. The king had been long absent in Flanders, but now an audience with his Majesty was granted and Montejo succeeded in clearing Cortes and in getting the king's grant for the conquest of Yucatan, and with it the title for himself of governor of the new province.

As soon as possible he outfitted three ships and sailed with five hundred men. His destination was the island of Cuzmil, which was safely reached and where he was well received by the Christianized natives. After a brief time he went to the mainland, where his first act was to plant the flag of Spain with the words, "In the name of God, I take possession of this land for God and the King of Castile." He then sailed down the coast to the city of Conil. The natives were greatly alarmed and sent word throughout the country of the advent of the Spanish. All of the chiefs for some distance about were persuaded to visit Montejo, who received them with honor and respect. But one chief of great strength was accompanied by a negro servant, who carried, concealed, a cutlass, and at a favorable moment the chief seized the weapon and tried to assassinate Montejo, who defended himself while his men disarmed the native.

This event was disquieting; Montejo realized that in spite of his conference with the natives, they were unfriendly and that it would be unwise to risk his little army against their combined strength. And so he weighed anchor and proceeded farther down the coast, seeking the largest sea-coast city, which proved to be Tecoh. Here, either by friendly overtures or by threats, he gained permission to establish a city which he intended to make the capital of his new dominion. Traveling about the country, he came upon Chi-chen Itza, which seemed to him an ideal location, probably because of its stone buildings and its plentiful water-supply. He at once set about the task of making it habitable. Houses of wood with thatched roofs were put up and with the assistance of friendly natives he began the task of subduing surrounding tribes, placing some one or another of his men in charge of the villages as they were conquered, until he had two or three thousand natives in his power.

By this time the natives awoke to the fact that they were fast becoming slaves to the Spaniards, and rebellion set in everywhere. For a time Montejo with his men was able, by cruel and bloody treatment, to keep the people in subjection; but at last they forced him to draw in all his forces to Chi-chen Itza, where they besieged him. Each day the armed and mailed Spaniards took heavy toll of their besiegers; and each day the Indians were reinforced, while the Spaniards counted every victory a defeat which lost them even a few in killed or wounded. And the food-supply was nearly exhausted.

Finally Montejo perceived that he and his men must escape and return to the island of Cuzmil or they would all be slain. Through the day they wearied the native besiegers with skirmish and sortie and that night they tied a famished dog to a rope attached to a bell and just out of reach placed some food. All night the dog tried in vain to reach the food and all night the natives heard the sound of the bell and thought the Spaniards were preparing a night attack. But the wily Montejo and his followers had escaped from the rear of the ancient "Nunnery" and it was several hours before the besiegers discovered what had happened.

Not knowing which road the fleeing enemy had taken, the Indians set out at once by all the roads to the seacoast. Some of them actually caught up with the retreating forces, but were too few in number to attack successfully. The Spaniards reached safely the town of Zilan and the Christianized tribe of the Cheles (Bluebirds) and from there they easily made their way to Ticoh, where they were secure for some months.

Montejo saw that conquest to the southward was

blocked, and, with the aid of the friendly Cheles and taking the chief of the town of Zilan and two young nobles, the sons of a still greater chief, he traveled with his force up the coast, the young natives of his escort obtaining safe conduct for him through the various tribes. Thus he reached Mexico, which was held by the iron hand of Cortes.

Montejo was next sent to Honduras as viceroy, but the project of subduing Yucatan seems always to have been his dream. Some years later he went to the city of Chiapa and from there despatched his son, at the head of an expedition, to Yucatan, in a further effort to conquer it. The younger Montejo had in the meantime traveled through Mexico and even into lower California and had been made viceroy of Tabasco.

In the years since the attempt of the elder Montejo to subdue the Mayas, Yucatan had suffered greatly, first from internecine strife and then from a famine, so that the younger Montejo found almost no organized resistance. The city of Champoton, where the Spaniards had twice suffered defeat under Hernandez de Córdoba and under Grijalva, and where the first Montejo had not dared to risk a conflict, now offered no battle at all. From there the younger Montejo went to Campeche and established friendly relations, so that with the aid of Champoton and Campeche, gained by promises of rich rewards, he reached the city of Tiho, meeting with almost no resistance.

Here he established his capital, renaming the city Mérida, and so it has remained to the present time as the seat of government of Yucatan. The army of a few hundred men was quartered in Mérida and the subjugation of the country was carried on from there. Captains were sent to different towns as local governors. The young Montejo sent his cousin of the same name to Valladolid, to govern that important city and subdue the surrounding territory. When things had pretty well settled down, the elder Montejo came from Chiapa, first taking up residence in Campeche, which he renamed San Francisco in honor of himself. A little later he moved on to Mérida and became governor in fact, as well as in name, of the land of Yucatan.

The rule of the Spaniards was exceedingly brutal for some years, but it is believed that most of their cruelties were committed without the knowledge of Montejo and certainly not at his command. There is the well-worn excuse that the conquerors were few in number and the conquered numerous, and that diabolical treatment was sometimes necessary, to hold the masses in check. Rebels were burned alive and hanged in great numbers. The important people in the town of Yobain were gathered together in a large house and locked in stocks, then the house was set on fire, so that all perished horribly.

Diego de Landa himself saw a tree upon which were hanging many Indian women from whose feet their little children had been hanged. In another city two Indian women, one a maid, the other newly married, were hanged for no other reason than that they were beautiful and the Spanish captain feared that his men might seek their favor and thereby stir up trouble with the natives.

Perhaps the greatest cruelty of all was the deportation of the natives of the thickly populated provinces of Cochua and Chectemal. Hands and arms and legs were lopped off. Women had their breasts severed and, with gourds tied to their feet, were thrown into the lagoons. Children were stabbed because they could not walk as fast as their captors, and men, women, and children were slain without excuse.

Because of this treatment the native population decreased very rapidly and the towns and cities were abandoned. A serious outbreak occurred in Valladolid, where the natives slew seventeen Spaniards and four hundred natives who were servants of the Spanish. Hands and feet of the slain were sent through the country as a signal for a general uprising, but none took place.

Evidently the priesthood complained to the king regarding the atrocities that were being committed and of the making of servants or virtually slaves of many of the natives. An edict from the king deprived all governors of native servants. Montejo was impeached and sent to Mexico for a hearing, and from there to the royal council at Madrid. And there he died, as Landa says, "full of days and work."

The younger Montejo left the imposing gubernatorial mansion which his father had built in Mérida and resided for some time in the city merely as a private citizen, much respected by all. After a time he went to Guatemala and then returned to Spain, where he eventually died after a prolonged illness.

As has been said, the church followed close upon the heels of the conquerors and there seems to have been little love lost between the priests and the soldiery, both jealous of power and wealth. With the forces of the elder Montejo was only one cleric, Francisco Hernandez, chaplain of the expedition, who later attributed the failure of the venture to the lack of priests. Before the real conquest by Montejo the younger, it became necessary for Antonio de Mendoza, who was viceroy of all New Spain, to carry out the orders he had long before received from Queen Juana to the effect that priests should be sent to Yucatan—one of the conditions upon which the province had been granted to Montejo.

Mendoza had no choice but to send priests from other Spanish possessions under his command, as there were none in Yucatan. For this duty Fray Jacobo de Testera, who held a high clerical office in Mexico, volunteered. In 1531 he and three other priests arrived at Champoton and, having asked leave of the Indians to enter the country, made an auspicious beginning. But they soon lost the good-will of the natives because they insisted on burning the idols, and, on finding they were making no progress, became disgruntled and returned to Mexico. In 1536 another band of friars essayed the task of Christianizing Yucatan, but after proselyting for two years they returned to more settled Spanish dominions.

The conquest actually effected, after the founding of Valladolid in 1541 and Mérida in 1542, a church was built in the latter city and in 1544 Bishop Bartolomé de las Casas and his Dominican friars came to Yucatan and gradually spread the creed of the Cross throughout the land. But while we speak of the conquest as becoming an accomplished fact with the founding of the two principal cities of Valladolid and Mérida, it was not until more than eighty years later that the whole country was pacified, and during this time the Itzas in the southern part of the country remained unconquered and unChristianized. These eighty years constitute a long period of guerilla warfare and sporadic attempts on the part of the Spaniards to conquer the stubborn Itzas and efforts of the priests to convert them, and, throughout, showed a lack of concord between the military and the church. At one time two native Christians set up claims as pope and bishop respectively and gained a considerable following.

As has been mentioned earlier in this work, some of the Maya tribes never were conquered; they do not, to this day, pay taxes to or otherwise concern themselves with the Government of Mexico. Catholicism, generously mixed with the old paganism, has, however, permeated their villages.

Whatever we may think now of the means and methods followed by the old padres in bringing the heathen to the Christian faith, we can but admire and reverence their motives, for no earthly reward could possibly compensate for the incredible hardships despite which these zealots persevered. Only a stanch, all-abiding faith, supreme over mundane things, could have carried on.

CHAPTER XI

THE FINDING OF THE DATE-STONE

ALWAYS in my earlier days in my City of the Sacred Well," says Don Eduardo, "the question was in my mind as to the age of the city. Every carved stone I found, I scanned eagerly for some clue and I should say, perhaps, right here, that while we can often gain only an inkling of the meaning of the Maya hieroglyphs and in some cases no understanding at all, the date-glyphs are plain sailing. We can read them, I think, as readily as we would read dates written in English. With but a little training any one may do this.

"But though I looked on engraved stones by the hundreds, there were no dates. Again and again I questioned the natives: 'When do you think these buildings were erected and who built them?' Invariably came the patient answer, *'Quien sabe?'*—'Who knows?'

"Among these Indians was an old fellow whose face hauntingly reminds me of an ancient picture of a Hebrew patriarch that I have seen in some forgotten place. One day we were clearing the brush from a gentle terrace to make ready for the planting of corn. I called the attention of my overseer to several mounds upon a large near-by terrace, telling him that we must surely dig into them as soon as we could find time, to see if they contained any relics. Suddenly my grizzled patriarch straightened up and gazed at the mounds and then came over to me, saying as he pointed to the tallest of the mounds, 'That one has in it a stone book written by my fathers.' Here at last was something, of no value, possibly, but better far than the eternal *'Quien sabe?'* Eagerly I asked him how he came by this idea and he said that in the days of his great, great grandfather this temple mound was known as Mul-huun-tunich, the Hill of the Stone Book. He said that he had been told this by his father and his grandsire had told his father and a high priest had so told his grandfather. I could get no more out of him, but he stuck doggedly to this brief tale.

"I had passed the mound several times and now I gazed at it with fresh interest. It was covered with a tangled growth of vines and thicket and well-grown trees, reminding me of what some philosopher has so truly said—that the most perfect works of men are soon covered by forests which grow an inch a day. If this mound had ever been a stately edifice, all semblance had long since passed. The bat or serpent might find a cavity in its ruined space, but if any carving of god or hero were to be found, it was well hidden from my prying eyes.

"At once I began the task of clearing away the young growth and the stumps of what had been sizable trees and beneath these were other decaying tree stumps. In this ruined area, which is perhaps three thousand feet to the south of the Great Pyramid of El Castillo, is a terrace, rising about twenty feet above the general level. On this terrace, which once had smooth, sloping sides, are ruined buildings with a bit here and there still standing, surrounded with shapeless heaps of fallen stone.

The hill of the stone book, as it was called by my old Indian, was on the northeastern edge of this terrace, pyramidal in form and sharply defined.

"My better judgment told me I was wasting time in heeding the vaporings of the old Indian while more important tasks waited, but my interest and curiosity were touched and I urged my men to strenuous effort, resisting with difficulty the temptation to dig at once into the center of the mound. We cleared the undergrowth in patches and burned it, so that the valuable timber would not be injured by the heat, nor the stones in the mound calcined. While most of the men were thus engaged I selected a few picked workers and we began the excavation of the pyramidal mound. We found not only trees growing above buried stumps, but charred stumps even below these. My old Indian examined carefully the cuts upon these deep-buried stumps and logs and said that these marks had not been made by ax, hatchet, machete, or any modern implement that he had ever seen. In all probability this earliest felling was done before the coming of the white man with his cutting edges of metal.

"I wondered who could have cut down the big trees around the pyramid. How could trees have been permitted to grow here or have been burned so close to buildings inhabited or in use? Evidently the burning and cutting, ancient as it might have been, had yet been done many, many years after the structure was abandoned.

"At last we had a space cleared all around the base of the mound and we sorted over the loose stones, looking for inscriptions, but came across nothing of unusual interest. We found the mound to be four-sided and truncated, with broad steps leading up all four sides and with the principal stairway facing the west. The pyramid was in ruins and the upper outline obliterated. Close to the base of the main stairway we uncovered a semi-recumbent stone figure, part man and part animal, of the so-called Chac Mool type. It was still firmly cemented in place and, like the stairway, faced the west. Just in front of this stone figure we unearthed a small elaborately carved stone urn of pineapple pattern, and a similar urn was dug up just to the rear of the Chac Mool figure. The Chac Mool and the incense urns were much marred and pitted by erosion, and the finding of charcoal in fragments and granules all about indicated that a deliberate effort had been made to destroy these priceless things.

"Gradually we cleared the earth and fallen stones and mortar from the main staircase. Many nests of lovely mauve-colored wood-doves were destroyed as we felled the trees. We saved as many as we could, but for several hours the mournful cries of the bereaved feathered creatures sounded from the neighboring forest like the wails of the departed spirits of those who had lived and died beside this old, old temple.

"On the southern slope a huge *chaib,* a species of boa-constrictor, beautifully marked with splashes of green and brown, was awakened from its slumbers deep in some rocky cavity of the pyramid and came surging down the mound with watchful head held high and graceful body bending the bushes in its path as it disappeared into the thicket below.

"The bees of Yucatan are kindly and have no sting,

but the wasps more than make up for the impotence of the bees. The most venomous wasps, the *x-hi-chac,* build flat nests that cling as closely and unobtrusively to the tree trunks as porous plasters. One of the trees we felled contained such a nest. Lightning is slow compared with the speed of these insects, and I, personally, would just about as willingly be struck by lightning as to encounter the sting of the *x-hi-chac.* I think lightning would be less painful. Several of the men were badly stung and while I gave them first aid by applying ammonia to their hurts, and provided drinks of a refreshing nature, the victims spent a sleepless, feverish night. They were weak and in low spirits in the morning, but we resumed our task nevertheless.

"Clearing the way a step at a time, we finally reached a level, well-built platform at a height of thirty feet. At the rear of the platform was the jagged outlined wall of what had been a small temple and directly before it were two large Atlantean figures of unusual type. I had seen many squat stone figures in and about the city but never before such large ones or figures carved with such fierce grandeur of expression. They were intricately carved and highly conventionalized. Each was garbed in an embossed head-dress, breast pendants, loincloth, and sandals. Every detail was clearly worked, even to the carved strands of rope holding the sandals—sandals bearing a striking resemblance to those worn by the prehistoric or archaic Gauchos of the Canary Islands, which again suggests the plausibility of Plato's Lost Atlantis.

"And as we cleared the debris away it became evident that these massive figures, so stiff and majestic, had originally sustained the front or façade of the temple. My curiosity and excitement had now reached a point where every slight delay was nerve-racking and the two grim guardians seemed to me like silent keepers of age-old secrets, ready to come to life and destroy the prying humans who dared invade their sacred domain.

"Little by little we removed the earth and rubbish. Slowly we progressed between the colossal figures, excavating with great difficulty the compacted mortar and stone which had fallen and become almost as a single stone. About three feet back of the statues was a huge stone covered with inscriptions. Was it the stone book? I cast aside all philosophic calmness and dropped to my knees, clawing away with my bare hands at the debris which obscured the inscriptions, until my nails were broken and my fingers bleeding.

"Here indeed was the Huun-tunich, the Stone Book, the Rosetta Stone of my ancient, lovely, and forgotten City of the Sacred Well! I am not ashamed of the fever of excitement which possessed me and communicated itself to my wondering Indians, who had not the slightest idea why the mad white man should become so wrought up over the finding of merely another stone with queer writings on it. But, then, what matter! White men are always a little insane, anyway, and one never knows what folly they will attempt next.

"With sharpened twigs I cleaned out all the incised lines, until the inscription on the exposed face stood forth clearly. Not till then did I attempt to read it. And there, among the glyphs I could not at once decipher, my eye caught a date-sign fairly jumping out to meet me. Cycle Ten, Katun Two, Tun Nine, Uinal One—in other words, 600 A. D.!

"It had been my secret hope that somewhere, somehow, I should be able to find an authentic date in Chichen Itza, some inscription which had eluded the eyes of other searchers. The Chronicles mention various dates in connection with the ancient city, but this added proof was needed to carry us over the threshold from probability into the realm of incontrovertible fact, just as the finds in the Sacred Well proved for us the veracity of the legends.

"This date-stone does not by any means indicate that the city was founded in 600 A. D., but that this particular temple, whatever its purpose may have been, was built or dedicated at that time. Imagine some terrible catastrophe befalling the United States, wiping out all our people and leaving our cities to fall in ruins and become covered with forests with the passing of hundreds of years. Then imagine an archæologist, even one as mad as myself, digging into these ruins and coming upon that block of granite which now stands over the entrance to the New York Corn Exchange and tells us in unmistakable terms when the building was erected. His find would be of tremendous historical value—a definite date standing out clearly from the misty past. But still he would not know nor have any clear idea of the date of the founding of New Amsterdam and no clue to the interesting history of those sturdy Dutch patroons who first built a village at the mouth of the Hudson.

"And so it is with my Sacred City. There is not in all the world a metropolis living or dead more mysterious, more dowered with romance. Its age, its origin, even the racial identity of its builders, are each and all sunk in mystery so profound that I doubt if we shall ever fathom them.

"I was so elated over my discovery that I at once promised double pay to each man for the month and declared that we would have a fiesta that all would remember for miles around and describe in later years to their sons. I tried to tell them how important was our find, but the double pay and the fiesta were much more eloquent to them than any words I could utter. I singled out the old Indian whose great, great grandfather had passed down the tale of the stone book. His face was as impassive as the faces of the stone gods about us, as befitted his dignity, but I could see it cost him a tremendous effort not to shout with glee and dance about like a small boy, and he gloried in the fact that he had not led me astray. Drawing his bent frame erect, he said, 'Did I not say so and did my great grandfather ever lie?'

"Careful measurements showed that the stone had been the lintel of the doorway. Each end had rested upon and was securely cemented to the heads and supporting upraised arms of the huge Atlantean figures, thus forming an integral portion of the main temple entrance. This is not an unusual Mayan arrangement and, as previously mentioned, there is in the Akzab Tzib, or House of the Writing in the Dark, a similar lintel but without a date.

"A very long time must have elapsed since the abandonment of this temple. A seed of the *chac-te* tree was carried by the winds or the birds and dropped in the entrance, a little to one side of the center. This tree is of extremely hard wood and it grows slowly. It grew to a sapling and at last into a big tree whose roots by their upward thrust toppled over the central portion of the façade. The lintel fell to the ground, but its fall was softened by the pile of powdered mortar and stone which had already sifted down, and fortunately the priceless relic was unbroken. Time passed; the big tree died and decayed. All this we know by the casts of the gnarled roots left in the grouting beneath the temple platform. Once again fertile Nature planted a seed under the tablet, carried to its earthy bed down under the fallen stones by some rodent or fruit-eating bat. And this was the seed of the *yax-nic*—a tree as hard as iron and as long-lived as its predecessor. It too grew to great size and its roots tilted the stone tablet to one side and, finally dying, left its epitaph written in root-casts or molds. Again ever-vigilant Mother Nature planted a seed, this time of a tree of soft, quick-growing wood, and the roots encircled the tablet as in a mighty hand; and thus we found it when we cut down the tree. Fortunately, the previous trees, which exude an acidic sap, had done the tablet no harm and the last tree had by its clasp rather protected the tablet than harmed it. And how easily Nature might have contrived, with her cycles of life, for the destruction of this treasure!

"The day passed and darkness came, but I could not leave the spot. I dismissed my Indians and took the photographic cloth from my camera and covered the tablet and then piled over it some pliant boughs of trees. But, like the youth who lingers over his adieus to his sweetheart, I uncovered the stone again and sat beside it until the moon was bright overhead. My vagrant fancy carried me back over the centuries and I saw smooth highways crossing and recrossing, and along these highways populous cities with the towering outlines of massive temples and the carved edifices of kings and nobles. I could hear the soft, silvery laughter of women bearing water-jugs, as they met in groups along the tree-shaded avenues, and there were merchants and bearers of burdens traveling to and fro from the market-places, and resplendent warriors and haughty peers and solemn priests. And there was the scent of incense smoke and a high, clear voice was chanting the invocation to Kukul Can. . . .

"I was aroused by the voice of one of my Indians, a quaint fellow who always addressed me as Ah Kin (High Priest)—why I do not know. 'Ah Kin,' said he, 'Master, the voices of the birds are stilled; your food is cold and untasted; I beseech you to come and eat.' I arose and went with him, but I could not eat; and all night, as I tossed in my hammock, I saw the tablet and its every inscription as clearly as though it were actually before my eyes, and early in the morning I was back at its resting-place. That day we carefully raised it and replaced it firmly upon the heads and uplifted arms of the impassive stone guardians—serene, majestic figures that have witnessed a mighty civilization and its passing into the dust of oblivion. Once again their arms hold the graven tablet as of old, but their mute lips which might tell so much are silent and in their changeless gaze is the haunting, immutable introspection of the Sphinx."

CHAPTER XII

THE CONSTRUCTION OF MAYA BUILDINGS

WHOEVER views the pyramids along the Nile is inevitably intrigued as to how they were built— how the massive stones were transported and placed in their elevated positions. And likewise at Chi-chen Itza one is bound to speculate as to how the heavy stonework was transported from its quarries, how it was so intricately carved, and by what predetermined plans it was erected into buildings which have stood for centuries, defying tropical nature.

I have found the Sacred City an absorbing topic upon which to ponder, fitting together the known facts and drawing upon imagination to piece in the gaps, until the mental picture of the building of its ancient temples is an unbroken fabric. My own visualization of the process of building a Maya temple is no doubt faulty in many respects, and I have no wish to precipitate an archæological controversy by claiming it to be hole-proof; I offer it merely for the sake of the reader who has not the opportunity to create his own vision of the subject from a first-hand view of these ancient edifices.

Imagine an army of workers—a hundred, yes, a thousand times as many as would be employed in the erection of a great modern building,—short, squat, powerful, sun-browned men, sweating at their task of quarrying and moving huge stone blocks.

In the quarries the blocks for the monolithic serpent heads, the column sections, and all the larger pieces used in the building are being channeled from the solid ledge rock, or from isolated boulders, by the *pa-tunich,* or quarry master, and his many assistants. The ring of blows struck with stone or wooden mallets upon chisels tipped with flint or calcite attests their industry. Some workers do not use the mallet and chisel, but score the soft limestone ledge with flint-bladed hatchets, while others ply long wooden poles as wedges and levers. On the quarry floor the master stone-cutters are squaring and smoothing the rough blocks and laying against them, from time to time, their wooden gauges, satisfied only when the stones are smooth and square and of the right dimensions. Under the finished stones are inserted wooden rollers and about them are knotted cables made of fiber or of tough vines, and long lines of men grasp the cables and bend their backs to the task of hauling the big blocks from the quarry to the building site.

Lines of men like toiling ants carry on their shoulders baskets of earth and stones. Slowly the terrace or sub-structure is built up to the first level, its sides faced with smooth stones, and each side bisected with a broad stair-way. And up to this level is built an inclined roadway for the workers and their burdens. And slowly, up and up, grows terrace after terrace, each smaller than the preceding one, and the pyramid takes shape, leaving a flat stone platform at the top upon which the temple will be erected. Here the *pol-tunich,* the master stone-mason, and his artisans are busy in the finishing of the stones and in their intricate carving. Flint-edged hammers are used to work the grosser outlines, but the finer details are worked out with more delicate implements—gouging-tools of flint and calcite and keen-edged chisels of polished nephrite. Such a chisel Don Eduardo dug up near the base of one of the temples.

The finished stones, one by one, are dragged up the long inclined roadway, to the floor-level of the temple, and put into their places under the direction of the master builder. Stone upon stone, the walls take shape and the column sections are set in place. Then come the workers in mortar. Every crevice is filled and the column sections firmed into place with small stone wedges and thick lime mortar. With a cement-like plaster of sifted lime and white earth mixed with water and the juices of the *chi-chibe* plant, the workmen fill each crack in the walls and columns and burnish it to stony hardness and exceeding smoothness.

Next come the sculptors—men of renown, artists famed for their skill, who spend months and years with knives of obsidian, nephrite and flint chisels, and tiny cutting-tools of copper and calcite. At last the stone-and-mortar surfaces are covered with deep-carved masks and portraits and battle scenes and hieroglyphs and friezes, until scarcely a square inch of plain surface remains. With pencils of red *chac-ti* wood and with soft-plumed brushes dipped in brilliant pigments the carvings are further adorned—various shades of brown, the blue-green of the sacred quetzal bird, the emerald of the forest, the azure of the cloudless sky, the ultramarine of the deep sea, the gold of the noonday sun, the velvet blackness of a cloudy night, twilight purples in the long shadows of trees reflected in the pool of the Sacred Well, the gray of aged stone that has battled for countless

years with the elements; vermilion of the turkey-head
blossom, the rusty hue of red-earth dust. From triple-
vaulted roof to temple floor the colors are applied with
consummate artistry.

Speaking of the tools used by the sculptors, the finds
of Don Eduardo throw a new light upon this previously
puzzling subject. Many cutting-edges and rejects of
flint and calcite have been found. Some archæologists
have stated that chisels of metal were not used, and
probably these were but little employed, yet from the
Sacred Well were raised several small hard copper
chisels. There can be no doubt, to judge from the shape
and the marks upon them, that they are chisels. One
of Don Eduardo's most precious finds is a nephrite chisel
discovered at the base of the Great Pyramid. Concerning it he says:

"While working one day around the base of the Great
Pyramid of El Castillo, taking measurements and digging
below the surface accumulations to get at the base line of
the structure, I came upon a curiously shaped fragment
of worked stone—heavy, close-grained, and dark green in
color. Closer inspection showed it to be the edged
portion of a cutting-tool.

"The unbroken tool must have been of the typical
celt type, about six inches long and three inches wide at
the cutting edge, tapering to a rounded head. The part
found was rather less than a half of the whole, but
nevertheless the more interesting and important part
because it contained the polished cutting-edge. It was
an unusual find, indeed. Stone points and cutting-edges
of local material, like flint and calcite, are not uncommonly encountered in favored places after heavy rains

that wash away the earth covering and expose them to view, but tools fashioned from costly, imported material like nephrite were rarely used and were not carelessly cast aside when broken, for even the fragments had their value and could be worked over into smaller implements or into ornaments.

"The location in which this broken nephrite chisel was found, no less than the chisel itself, has an antiquarian bearing. Here was not only an authentic museum piece, but testimony as to its use, for clearly the chisel was used in making the sculptures of El Castillo and was lost there in the course of the work.

"Nephrite, or kidney-stone, was used in prehistoric, ancient, mediæval, and later times as a remedy for kidney diseases. It was taken, of course, in pulverized form. In prehistoric times nephrite was as needful to the skilled artisan as tempered tool steel is to the modern craftsman. Nephrite was found in lands far distant from the Mayas; and pieces of unworked nephrite were bartered and sold, as was nephrite dust. This dust packed on a rawhide surface became an effective abrasive for shaping and polishing the nephrite tool. Nephrite carried by ancient ways of commerce, by barter and trade and conquest and plunder, reached the Mayas to a limited extent. I have no doubt its value to these ancients was greater than that of gold."

Century after century has passed and the work of these amazing craftsmen still stands, even to the hair lines of the lintel carvings and the faint traces of pigment still clinging to the smooth walls. The epitaph is imperishable, even though the names of the artists, like their very bones, have vanished.

Those who directed the work of temple-building not only built well, but had an eye to efficiency, also. No stone was wasted; rejects, fragments too small for carving or fashioning into building blocks—all were utilized as filling or ballast for the terraces. The stone chips from the mason's hammer and chisel were used as grouting. Even the stone-dust was collected and sifted and mixed, in the ratio of three to one, with powdered lime, plant juice, and water, to make mortar. When the temple was completed to the point where the sculptors and painters took up their task, the inclined roadway was removed.

Then when the massive temple, smooth-walled and roof-crowned, stood complete on its serrated pyramid of receding terraces; when the broad stairways were finished and the undulating stone serpents and the paneled terrace faces all were perfectly aligned and the whole majestic structure appeared as frosted silver against the velvet blue of the sky—then only did the master builder consider his work complete.

With the exception of the Snail-shell or Watch-tower, all of the Maya buildings are rectangular. None are lofty, all are massive. Yet in all respects they are excellent in their architecture, of appropriate dimensions, symmetrical, and well constructed. Stones are fitted with infinite pains. Many have even been drilled. It has been shown that sharpened bird bones twirled about on the stone were employed as drills. Stones having drilled holes of six inches or more in depth are not uncommon. Mortar, plaster stucco, and cement were as good as or better than similar materials of the present time and were expertly applied. The use of pigments as understood by these ancient artisans is a lost art and it is doubtful if we have any colors as durable and unfading.

Monolithic columns of great size, chiefly of serpent-head motif, are found everywhere. Built-up columns, both square and round, were used. Inlays, mosaics, and stone screens, bas-reliefs, full reliefs, murals, panels, cornices, balustrades, sills, lintels,—virtually the whole gamut of architectural design and embellishment known to the best of ancient or modern architecture,—were known and used by these builders isolated by two oceans from any foreign influence.

Lintels were made of stone and of sapote, that iron-hard wood of Yucatan which defies the wear and tear of time like the teak of the Orient.

In one respect Mayan architecture might be considered inexpert, from the standpoint of our present knowledge of building construction, and that is their method of roofing their structures and of building arches. Like the old Greeks, they did not know how to build an arch employing a keystone. Only by gradually receding courses of stone did they achieve an arch having a capstone instead of a keystone. The result, in the building of a roof, was a steep-pitched affair, comparatively low at the eaves and high at the peak. The vertical rise from eaves to peak was usually as great as the distance from floor to eaves. Being of stone, this roof was of great weight. Where a considerable expanse of roof was needed, the triple-vaulted arch was used. The Maya arch is not ungraceful, even though it is massive.

In the Nunnery, or Las Casas del Monjas, we see successive stages of building where a part of an edifice is filled in with rock to provide a foundation for a superstructure erected later. This, too, is a very common practice of the old builders and gives the impression that no very well-thought-out plans were employed. I think, however, that none of these buildings was built without a predetermined plan, which was probably drawn out upon some substance in great detail, so that priests and king as well as the builders knew the size and shape and mode of decoration before the building was started. Moreover, people so skilful at drawing and with so considerable a mathematical knowledge might surely have been able to produce in some simple form the plans of these structures. The stones are too well fitted, the dimensions of the buildings too well proportioned, the orientation too accurate to have been the result of chance. Everything bespeaks foreordination, careful planning carried through to completion.

In several of the other ancient cities are found curiously carved stelæ, monolithic slabs of stone resembling the totem-poles of Alaska. These are elaborately sculptured with human figures and glyphs. Many are carved with amazing skill. In his book John L. Stephens describes a number of these stelæ and his descriptions are accompanied by the faithful drawings of Catherwood, made directly from first-hand observation and often with great difficulty. Frequently a small altar is found before these monuments. There is considerable reason to believe, from legend and the ancient Chronicles, that they were the date-records erected every twenty years, and if we could but read the hieroglyphs we might learn the important happenings in each score of years.

From a close study of the architecture of the buildings and their decorations it is clear that there were several stages of culture. Mayan architecture and art followed the rise and fall of the nation, becoming more and more refined up to the golden age represented in the temples of old Chi-chen Itza, gradually deteriorating in the newer temples, improving again under the influence of the Nahuatl conquerors, and sinking into utter desuetude several hundred years before the coming of the Spaniards.

The story of the Mayas furnishes one more epic in the history of the human race; one more cycle of rise and fall; one more meteor flash of brilliancy followed by the darkness of oblivion. There have been in every part of the world similar instances of this groping toward knowledge and culture and their slow achievement, to be followed by decline and savagery, as though the life of a nation were a thing of nature which, like a tree or an animal, flourishes a brief while, then withers and dies.

Is the twentieth century an exception to the age-old rule? Have our ability to commit our knowledge to the printed page and our great advance in the science of transportation set at naught the old rule? Or will our civilization also crumble with the passing of the years?

CHAPTER XIII

STORY-TELLERS OF YUCATAN

IN wet weather the archæologist may take either a well-earned rest or he may busy himself with cataloguing and packing the trophies of his trusty pick and shovel.

"One day when the rain and the Evil Wind conspired to keep us indoors," says Don Eduardo, "I found it much more interesting to listen to the yarns of the Indians than to work at routine tasks. All I can say in self-defense is that in Yucatan the subtle contagion of 'mañana' does get into one's blood.

"My Indians are all very superstitious. They believe whole-heartedly in witches and elves, and if one digs deep enough he finds a good deal of veneration for several deities not mentioned in the Bible. One of these is Balam, the jaguar, known in ancient times as the lord and protector of the fields.

"These simple folk believe in ghosts which walk amid the ruins of the Sacred City, and they believe in all manner of fortune-telling and divination. They are particularly partial to crystal-gazing, using a crystal called *zaz-tun*.

"Among my Indians was Bat Buul, a little old fellow with twinkling eyes black as the seeds of the *jabin* fruit, and ears that actually wagged when he became excited in telling a story. His big thick-lipped, sensual mouth was ever ready to laugh heartily at a joke, even though the joke chanced to be on Bat Buul himself. Old as he was, he had still the supple quickness of a boy.

"Bat Buul, whose name means 'bean ax,' was a native of the neighboring village of Pisté and he was famous as a raconteur in a land where good tellers of stories are highly esteemed. More often than not he was the hero of the stories he told, and as he warmed up to the telling, he would become tremendously excited and his black eyes would snap and burn with the intensity of his narration.

"One of his best stories, that of the *xtabay* or forest lorelei, has the sweet flavor of those wonderful old Greek myths of nymphs and satyrs and of gods come down from Mount Olympus for a holiday.

"Often one sees glimmering gossamer flecks twisting, twirling as they scurry onward, aimlessly borne by a vagrant breeze. They look like a flock of diaphanous butterflies, but in reality they are the flying seeds of a climbing vine. The vine bears a slender, delicate, snowy flower and the seed-case is an olive-green oval pod filled with thousands of seeds. The seed mass is bisected within the pod by a light, silky membrane. As the ripening progresses the pod becomes chestnut in color and at last bursts open. The membrane with the seeds clinging to it falls out, but is brought up short in its descent by a thin filament that remains attached to the lower end of the pod. The fall detaches the seeds from the membrane, or they are soon blown clear, to be carried at the will of the wind. Each of the tiny seeds has a transparent wing or tissue.

"Curiously, the two halves of the dried seed-pod are perfect natural combs, which are much used by native women, who believe that use of these combs supplied by Nature herself preserves the natural color and luster of the hair. The natives far and wide speak of them as the combs of the *xtabay*—forest nymphs, dryads, or lorelei—and many, like Bat Buul, claim to have seen the nymphs combing their silken tresses. In the old days, also, the native belles used the combs, thinking thereby to capture some of the elusive beauty of the mythical forest maidens.

"Before I proceed with Bat Buul's story there is one other explanation necessary to a full understanding of the tale. Far in the hinterlands of Yucatan are Maya Indians still called the Unbaptized Ones and these natives wear always about their necks chains of gold and in their ears big hoops of gold wondrously adorned with filagree. The men, even more commonly than the women, wear these ornaments, which is strange, for among those natives who are at all civilized the men seldom wear ear-rings or neck-chains, though these adornments are popular with the women.

"But the belief is common over the whole peninsula that by wearing a gold chain with a sacred relic or crucifix pendent from it one will be protected from danger. Men engaged in hazardous occupations such as the making of fireworks for fiestas and religious celebrations; butchers, and those who work with mad white men digging in haunted cities will tell you that such a chain is a potent charm against evil and sudden danger. Gallants occasionally wear chains of this sort, as do goldsmiths —rather out of vanity than for defense against ill-fortune. Always, when worn by men, the neck chains are hidden under the shirt.

"Bat Buul, who, on his own admission, has tried his hand at almost everything, is a goldsmith by trade, a maker of rockets when and if these are required, and a beau gallant at all times. Naturally, then, he wears a solid-gold chain of extra length and weight, with a solid-gold cross at the end which has been blessed by the Archbishop of Yucatan in the cathedral of Mérida.

"On this rainy day Bat Buul was resting luxuriously, ensconced upon a *cauche* in the store of Monica, in his natal village of Pisté. As I entered the store after my three-mile ride in the rain from Chi-chen Itza, Bat Buul was holding forth to an eager group of listeners. In his hand was a thimble glass of that aromatic beverage *xtavantum* and evidently it was not his first. He nodded to me as I joined the audience, but did not pause in his talk. It was evident that he determined to outdo himself for my benefit, being reasonably certain that if pleased, I would do the gentlemanly thing in the way of refreshment for all hands. As we would say in Americanese, 'He was going strong.' I give you his story as nearly as I can in his own words:

" 'I, Bat Buul, am a man of great will-power. I say it—yes, and it is so. I am not large of body, but I am great of heart and very strong. There are those who have sought to prove my strength and they have found it to be so. I do not say these things boastfully, for only vain and cackling fools do that, and if I do say it, I am no fool. No man can deceive me long—no, and no woman, either. Many have tried, but few have succeeded, albeit most of those who have succeeded have been women.

" 'But it is not given to man that he should be hard of

heart and unbelieving toward women. No; many women have liked me; some have loved me, and because of this my heart is ever soft to all women; that is—' here Bat Buul swallowed an entire thimble tumblerful of the perfumed liquor and gazed at us benevolently—'that is, toward all *handsome* women.

" 'Well, sir, one day I started for the deepest part of the forest where I had some *chac-ti* logs that I had cut and left to dry for charcoal which I needed to make powder for my rockets. I had nearly reached the point on the road to Chi-chen Itza where one turns to enter the deep forest, when I noticed that I was beside the place where grow the ghost flowers which come up in the night and wither in a day. I stopped for a moment to look at them, for have I not told you many times that I love the beautiful things of the forest? Then it was I heard a soft, sweet sound like the notes of a bird very, very far away calling to its mate or like a reed flute played by one who is sad.'

"The old man paused and deliberately rolled and lighted a corn-husk cigarette. No one spoke. I have learned that it never pays to urge the native story-teller to get on with his narrative; story-telling is a rite which must be performed just so, and the artistic temperament resents any interruption not of its own making.

"At length Bat Buul resumed:

" 'I looked around me and saw a beautiful woman sitting under a tree. She was the most beautiful woman I have ever seen and she was crooning to herself, and all the while she was combing her long, shining black hair. Suddenly she looked up and saw me with her big, velvet eyes that held a brightness like some deep, cool forest pool upon which the sunlight falls between the leaves. But she said nothing and continued to sing softly in that sweet, far-away voice of hers, while her rounded arms slowly rose and fell as the comb slipped through her glorious hair, so soft and fine that the little breezes one could scarcely feel rippled and floated its tendrils.

" 'I went slowly closer to her and said quietly, in a way that I have of my own, "My handsome one, why are you out here so lonely and all by yourself?" I meant to say more, but she rose and moved a little away from me. Yet her eyes shone more brightly and she stopped singing and said ever so softly and sweetly, "Oh, Bat Buul!" Then she moved farther away. She was—how shall I say?—not thin, not fat, but plump like the wild partridge, and she moved as lightly as feather down. Yes, she seemed to float, so effortless was her retreat. Well, have I not said that my heart is soft toward a handsome woman? And so I followed her, even though she led me quite away from where my *chac-ti* logs were drying in the sun.

" 'She said nothing, but again began to hum a tiny, wistful, haunting melody and as she glided on she turned her head this way and that to glance at a plant or to inhale the perfume of a flower. And ever she kept an eye on me that seemed to invite me on and on.

" 'Farther and farther we went from my logs, and deeper and deeper into the forest, and she seemed to grow more lovely at each step. Suddenly I found that I had walked right into a thorny clump of *tynbins* and the *tynbin* ants were swarming over me with their stings like the pricking of red-hot needles, while she, on the other side, was as cool and fresh as though she had but stepped from her morning bath.

" 'And then I began to wonder, although the pain of the stings was very great. And when a man begins to wonder he is safe, for then he usually finds out why he is in trouble. "Ah," I thought, "when I first saw this lovely maid she was sitting under a tree, combing her hair, and she called to me." And I remembered it was a *benote,* the tree that the *xtabays* ever seek for shade as they sit and sing and comb their lovely hair and try to bring venturesome men to an awful death. "And so the Xtabay of Pisté has tried to play with Bat Buul this day. Poor thing! we shall see!" But all of this I said very softly to myself, for I am a wily man when dealing with women. Then, as if still unsuspecting, I worked my way out of the thicket. As she turned to elude me again, quick as lightning I slipped my long gold chain from my neck, hiding the crucifix in the palm of my hand. I know women and, after all, the *xtabay* is a woman, and a good-looking one at that.

" 'Then I stopped as if in surprise and said as I held up the chain, "I wonder who dropped this beautiful chain." The *xtabay* stopped singing and looked back at me. Just then a ray of sunlight touched the chain and made it glitter. And the sweet creature came up to me with unsuspecting curiosity and leaned close to look at the chain. Ah, I am the one who knows women! So quickly that she hardly saw the flash, I tossed the loop of the chain over her head so that it rested about her neck, and then held up the sacred cross so that she could see it. For a whole minute she stood perfectly still, then she began to tremble. Her eyes filled with big, glistening tears and she looked at me piteously and said with a sighing sob, "Oh, Bat Buul!"

" 'I felt sorry for her, for I am not heartless and she was one to melt even the hardest heart, *xtabay* or no *xtabay*. Yet I gave her only an unrelenting look and an answer that left her hopeless, for I said to her: "Things found by the roadside and unclaimed belong to him who finds them there. That is the law and the custom; and, pray, who is there to claim you from me?" She made no answer, but only bowed her head and cried the harder. Then I gave a little tug at the chain and said, "Come on home," and she followed without a word of protest and with great glistening tears dripping from her lovely eyes.

" 'And leading her in this fashion, I passed the big *tanauha* where all the animals of the forest drink their fill even in the driest season. I passed the rock where little Pol Mis was slain by Ek Balam, the jaguar—black pagan that he is! And we came to the *benote* tree with its green fruit like big arrow-heads standing sharp against the sky—the very tree where I first saw this entrancing nymph who now followed me like a dog on a leash. When we reached the tree she stopped and looked at me with pleading agony in her eyes, such a look as I never hope to see again upon the face of any woman and she said, "Oh, Bat Buul!" and then again, "Oh, Bat Buul!" and in her voice was the sound of strangled tears. A man does not like that sound, ever, for it either hardens his heart and makes him more cruel than he should be or it turns his heart to water and causes him to be more gentle than is just and right.

" 'So I stopped and looked at her. I did not want

to, but I could not help it; and as I looked I knew that she was more beautiful than any woman that ever lived, even though she were an *xtabay* and without a soul, as the priest tells us. She was marvelously formed—not thin, not fat. Her flesh was as soft as a child's, yet she was graceful and quick in her movements. She was all that a woman should be. She seemed like a bird just ready to fly. And, as I looked, I thought, "What will my friends say and what will the priest say and do?" Her eyes, filled with terror, pleaded with me more strongly than any words could have done.

" 'Ah, Señor, I have the big heart! I took off the chain of gold and covered the crucifix in the palm of my hand and released her. For a moment she did not move and I thought she hesitated and looked at me as though she were really sorry to be free. I was a young man then and not bad-looking, and even an *xtabay* may know what it is to love. She began to move slowly away, with light gliding steps. Then she stopped and said to me in the voice of the wood-dove talking to its mate, "Good-by, my Bat Buul."

" 'I could not move, but stood there spellbound and looked at her, and soon she reached the *benote* tree where the shadows now lay thick and dark. Here she paused and looked at me long and tenderly; and there was no longer terror in her eyes, but, it seemed to me, only regret at our parting. And the sun, which was just slipping beneath the horizon, cast for a long moment a spell of gold that gleamed upon her glossy hair like the sheen of light on polished ebony or the glint of many tiny bits of bright metal; and this is queer, for her hair was like my *chac-ti* wood after it has been burned very long.

" 'Deeper and longer grew the shadows, and at last I could no longer see her. I leaned a little forward and I was conscious that I was breathing hard as though I had run a long distance, and still I seemed to hear faintly the low, sweet song that she had crooned when first I saw her; and at last even that faded into stillness. I do not know how long I stood there, but it was almost dusk when I turned to retrace my steps. I was a long way from home. As I slowly turned about, I saw something at my feet that shone like dark metal. It was the seed-pod of the *xtabay* plant, which women sometimes use to comb their hair, and I was about to kick it carelessly aside when I heard a voice, "Oh, Bat Buul!" Just a whisper it was from far off in the forest. Then I knew it was *her* comb and I put it in my pocket, for she was a handsome woman and I could not throw the comb away. I have the comb to-day, although this happened long ago, when I was young and foolish.'

"Bat Buul paused and sat very still, his eyes seeming to look beyond us and back into the past. He did not touch the refilled glass beside him, even though he knew that the patron was paying for it and that by drinking it speedily he might quickly obtain another. At last he said, with a twinkle in his eye and more to himself than to his audience:

" 'I should like to see that *xtabay* again; perhaps I should act differently. And, then, perhaps I should act the same, for my heart is still kind to women, especially if they are handsome women.'

"As I have said before, one of the most interesting things I have encountered in Yucatan is the native custom of story-telling. Usually the teller of stories is an old man or an old woman with a wide repertoire of folk-lore. Ghosts, giants, fairies; mythical animals such as white jaguars; miraculous humans, and the ancient gods —all appear in these tales, which are told with amazing skill. A little group of Indians will gather about the story-teller almost anywhere, in the courtyard of a house or in the public square of a town, and they will sit by the hour as the speaker goes on without pause from one weird tale to another.

"I understand that in the near-by hamlet of Dzitas there is now a motion-picture theater and the telling of stories has been largely supplanted by the 'movies,' more 's the pity.

"The children are, of course, eager for stories, and nearly every village has some kindly old woman willing to entertain the children with oft-told tales. Such was X'Leut Cauich. X'Leut Cauich was old, very old, and yet, even though the outer wrappings, the casings of her mind and soul, were wrinkled with age, her mind and seemingly her soul remained undeniably very young.

" 'T is ever said that youth seeks youth as sparks fly upward, and the saying is a true one. Just so surely as old X'Leut seated herself comfortably before the *koben,* or three-stone fireplace, in her *na* (palm-thatched house) and started to make with colored threads and shining needle, on snow-white cotton cloth, the beautiful native embroidery *"xoc-bui-chui,"* just so surely would the children of the neighborhood spring up as if by magic from the very ground about her and beg for a story. And old X'Leut, because she was a born story-teller, never dreamed of denying them.

"Bit Euan; Phil Canul with his three brothers, all seemingly of an age; Pol Cocom with his big, soft eyes and harelip; Pablo Perez and his sister, white of skin, children of the Spanish storekeeper—all sat crouching, cross-legged, sprawling, each after the manner of his people, around old X'Leut, listening, motionless, with eager eyes and intent expression, to the words slowly spoken, clearly uttered, as they fell from her aged lips.

"For them, and for old X'Leut as well, the outer world—the prosaic world about the palm-thatched *na*— no longer existed—only the Wizard Potters as they worked, with swiftly moving hands and fingers, the magic clay, making the enchanted vessels of an ancient people.

"She told them of Aluxob 'The Little People,' how they searched in the deep-down caves for the *kat,* the *kut,* and the *ki,* the tiny crystals and the clays that the Wizard Potters used in the making of the ancient vessels. She talked with her eyes, her lips, and her hands. With agile feet alternately moving she showed how the ancient people revolved the shallow wooden disks as the potters of other lands work, with their hands, their revolving wheels. She told them of these vessels—vessels with magic worked into their very substance so that at night they changed into living things called Burro Kat and Hunab Pob; living things that tormented by their doings late night wanderers, thieves and drunkards; bad people generally; even children who, disobeying their parents, stayed out late at night or ran away from home.

"Then, as X'Leut finished, rolled up her *xoc-bui-chui,* poked the fire in the three-stone fireplace, and started the water to boiling in the earthen kettle, each man-child, introspectively brooding, hurried homeward to ask of his astonished mother if there was anything that he could do to put the house in order before night came. Ah! a guileful woman was old X'Leut, with her ever-young soul and nimble hand! A joy to the children and a solace to the tired mothers."

CHAPTER XIV

FORGOTTEN MICHAEL ANGELOS

AS I have said, the art of the Mayas, and of Chi-chen Itza particularly, represents several periods of culture. Some of the oldest examples of architecture, stone point-work, carvings, and murals, as well as temple ornaments and personal trinkets display the greatest artistry of design and craftsmanship.

Evidently art progressed until a golden age dawned, comparable in its way to the golden age of Greece. Just as Pericles and Praxiteles chiseled into stone a marvelous grace and beauty which later sculptors have never been able to excel, so these old Maya dreamers and creators have left behind them things more lovely than those of succeeding generations.

Gradually the golden Mayan age waned. Creative genius became more scarce. Sense of harmony and soaring imagination were dimmed. Technique itself became poorer.

And then came the renaissance—the period of Nahuatl influence when Chi-chen Itza probably reached its pinnacle of civic importance and new temples and palaces were built thick and fast. Art was encouraged and new genius arose, akin to that of the ancient masters, yet showing everywhere the influence of the Nahuatl invasion. But while the new art attained a high degree of excellence, it failed to reach the perfection of the older culture.

It is rather difficult to assign to a given period any building as a whole, or any piece of workmanship, because the older city was so frequently robbed of its art treasures in the construction of the newer city. Columns and cut stones and lintels were torn from the older and perhaps then nearly ruined buildings to be used in the newer edifices. As in the House of the Writing in the Dark, we see a lintel of such extraordinary beauty as compared with the rest of the structure that it cries aloud its story of ravishment from a nobler and older temple. Apparently the later builders cared nothing for the beauty of this stone, but took it simply because in size it was appropriate for their purpose.

In speaking of the three eras of Mayan culture in Chi-chen Itza, it is at least reasonable to suppose that the most ancient preceded the coming of the Itzas to the city; legend says there was a flourishing city here before the influx of the Itzas. The second period includes the rise and decline of art under the Itzas, ending with the Nahuatl-Aztec dominance. The third period approaches oblivion—the centuries following the decay of the Maya nations when "campers," as Don Eduardo calls them, inhabited sparsely the old cities, and these people built nothing of permanence and despoiled much of the old art, knowing nothing of the past history and grandeur of the walls which provided a better shelter than they could build. The little of artistic merit which they created—if indeed, they created anything—is crude and inferior to the work of their ancestors. "Campers" probably lived in the Sacred City for two or three centuries preceding the coming of Montejo and until his advent.

All that remains of the first period is the nearly obliter-

ated old Chi-chen Itza, where future exploration may
bring to light many treasures. Add to these the precious
carvings that have obviously been taken from the old
city for the building of the newer city.

The second period is represented by the many temples
and buildings, several in an almost perfect state of preservation, in the newer Chi-chen Itza, and the finds in the
Sacred Well.

The third period is represented only in the waste and
debris left by the "campers" in and about the structures
of the preceding periods.

One striking characteristic of Mayan art is the skill
of the ancient sculptor or painter in portraying the human
figure and especially the human physiognomy. The faces
in murals, friezes, and bas-reliefs are expressive, individual, full of character—the faces of men of intellect and
purpose. Nearly always these portraits in stone or
paint seem to have a sort of sublimity: an earnestness
of mien, an inscrutability, and withal an utter lack of
pompousness. None but great artists could so have
caught the real character of the person portrayed.
Mayan art is a decided step ahead of the art of the
Egyptians, and beside it the Buddhas of the Orient seem
insipid. There are, of course, grotesque figures and the
many hieroglyphs which, it must be remembered, are not
portraits but have been conventionalized into symbols
far in advance of the original and more primitive picture-
writing.

One of the most intriguing things is the constant
recurrence of the mask of Kukul Can, often conventionalized to fit the particular wall of a building, frieze, or
mural where it is used. And always it is shown with a

long upturned snout which some casual observer has called an elephant's trunk.

To go a bit afield, G. Elliot Smith's "Elephants and Ethnologists" takes up this subject of the elephant's head. He believes that several elaborately carved columns or stelæ in Copan, another Mayan city, possibly more ancient than Chi-chen Itza, present credible pictures of elephants' heads with the keepers or mahouts beside them. These carvings have caused considerable discussion; some stoutly maintain that they portray the elephant and others say the motif is derived from the tapir or from the head of the blue macaw. At any rate, the appearance is that of an elephant, but very likely is intended for the mask and nose of the great Maya hero-god Kukul Can.

Of the many murals in the Sacred City, those in the Temple of the Tigers are the most interesting. On the opposite page is a reproduction of the scene on the west wall; it is from a tracing done twenty-five years ago by Teoberto Maler, of whom I shall later give further account. Much of the lower part of the mural has since been defaced by vandals or has chipped away through natural causes. The colors are vivid and the battle action enthralling. Of the many human figures no two are in the same pose. At the upper right is the Itza king or ruler, protected by his king of serpents spitting fire and venom at the enemy. A little lower down, and in front, is the chief Itza general with his protecting serpent, and all about are warriors armed with *hul-ches*, darts, and shields. At the extreme left is the opposing general with his king of serpents and his warriors.[1] Near the bottom at the left are the Itza notables holding a consultation, and at the bottom, center, is the time-keeper with his calendar wheel.

Facing page 221 is an enlarged view of just a bit of this scene which, because of its larger size, gives a better idea of the technique of the painter.

Another part of the battle scene, covering the east wall, depicts the invading army coming over the mountains to attack the Itzas. At the left in the picture is an Itza general or ruler, supported as usual by his beneficent Ahau Can or king of serpents. He is identified as belonging to the Itzas by his typical Itzan costume. The figure with the symbolized protecting serpent is similar to many others to be seen elsewhere in Chi-chen Itza, in paintings and bas-reliefs. A little lower down is his commanding general, also with a protecting serpent, and all about are the Itza warriors, now, due to mutilation, indicated only by the heads of their spears, pointing upward toward the enemy. In the upper right-hand corner of the painting is an Itzan horn-blower, standing upon a temple. His nationality is evidenced by the knee-protectors he wears.

The invaders wear an entirely different style of clothing and their armament is not like that of the Itzas. For example, although they use the *hul-che,* their shields are rectangular—a shape never seen in Chi-chen Itza nor in the whole Maya area. Still more striking is the peculiarity of their head-dresses of three blue feathers with yellow

[1] The protecting serpent does not necessarily indicate that the invaders were Mayas or believers in the cult of Kukul Can; it merely points out the "big man" or leader.

tips surmounting the regular feathered head-gear. It is significant that Don Eduardo, some years ago in the excavation of a temple, uncovered a gigantic painted head having a head-dress of three blue feathers with yellow tips. The stone containing the picture of the head was found upside down, and from the situation in which it was discovered it had evidently been so placed originally and had not fallen or been displaced. The reversed position of the head was the Maya method of conveying the information that this foe was conquered.

Evidently the painting in the Tiger Temple was executed to commemorate the victory over the invaders of the blue feathers, and the other temple which Don Eduardo excavated also was decorated with murals that indicated victory.

On each of the shields of the invaders is shown a curious red symbol which indirectly gives a clue to the nationality of these foreigners. In the central part of the state of Vera Cruz are found the remains of a highly cultured people, the Totanacs. The descendants of this ancient clan still reside in the neighborhood and their language contains many Mayan words. Because of the peculiarity of the design, as shown on the engraving of a clay Totanac facing page 225, there can be no doubt that it is the same identically as appears on the shields in the Tiger Temple. The same peculiar design occurs frequently upon the ancient Totanac sculptures and pottery.

The Totanacs are neighbors to another tribe just to the north, the Huastecas, who spoke the pure Maya language and were a part of the Maya brotherhood. It seems probable either that they were left behind in the

great Maya migration from the west or that their country
was originally the home of those Mayas who later emigrated to Yucatan under the leadership of the mighty
Kukul Can.

Either supposition might be correct, for it was in this
locality that the now famous Tuxtla statuette was found
which bears the earliest date ever discovered in this part
of the world—113 B. C. The earliest date-stone in
Chi-chen Itza is the one found by Don Eduardo and
its date is more than seven hundred years later. During
the interval between the two, or even before, the emi-
gration to Yucatan from the west might have occurred.

Another curious thing in the Tiger Temple painting
is the fact that the invaders are shown coming over
mountains. Northern Yucatan contains no mountains,
not even a high hill. But in the state of Vera Cruz there
are mountains. There is little to substantiate any theory
that the people of the Sacred City invaded Vera Cruz
and it is much more probable that the Totanacs were the
invaders.

In passing, another hypothesis of the ethnology of the
Mayas is that they were descendants of the Toltecas, a
peaceful and cultured people who inhabited Mexico
proper before they were driven southward by the
Nahuatl or Aztec tribes. In various places in Mexico,
Toltecan remains have been found similar in construction
and design to those in the Maya areas. Yucatan may
have been the final stopping-place of these people, but
as they moved ever southward, bands dropped out along
the road, and settled.

It is known that many years later Aztec soldiers
marched clear around the rim of the Gulf of Mexico

and through the jungles to Chi-chen Itza, which was their final destination. Their influence is very evident in the buildings in newer Chi-chen Itza.

Because many of the murals in the Sacred City have reached the critical point of deterioration in the last decade or so, I have made a point of photographing as many of them as possible. Much of the photography has employed the color-separation process. All told, I have taken upward of a thousand photographs, and in addition I have made a large number of drawings or tracings where it was impossible to use the camera. A number of murals which were clear and perfect during my earlier trips to Yucatan, some eighteen years ago, are now entirely faded or chipped off.

From a minute study of the paintings I am reasonably sure that the artists of this past age waited until the walls of a building were completed and the inner surface had been covered wtih a thin, hard stucco, then they painted the whole wall-surface to an even tone of color, usually a light olive green. Upon this the outlines of their pictures were sketched, either with red chalk or some soft red stone. The outlines were then intensified with a brush dipped in red pigment. From the character of the brush-marks I judge the brushes to have been made of hair or feathers. The next step was the laying in of the colors, the pigment being mixed with some sort of varnish that dried and permitted other colors to be superimposed.

For example, take the figure of a man. After the outline was completed, the whole figure was painted flesh color. When this was dry, further outlining within the figure was done. Then another color was laid over the shield, clothing, and other portions. Some details of the shield might then be ornamented with still another color, and another would be laid on the bosses of the shield and perhaps several colors put into the head-dress. Wherever the red outlines were painted over, yet were needed for completion of the work, new red outlines were painted in.

Facing page 220 is the reproduction of a tracing I have made of a red outline, showing as faithfully as possible the beginning and ending of each brush-mark. It is in the same free-hand style used by the modern painter.

Bas-relief work was much used in the Sacred City and for this type of art the cracks between the stone-work were filled in with stucco to give an even surface and then the whole surface was polished. The artist cut his designs into both stone and stucco. I cannot say how this work was laid out, but it is reasonable to suppose that it was outlined in red chalk and pigment much as murals were. The incised work is from a quarter to half an inch deep and the figures stand out boldly, especially when the direction of the light is from a particularly favorable angle.

The projecting part of each relief was painted in identically the same manner as murals, one color after another being superimposed. A notable example of this type of art is found in the Temple of Bas-Reliefs, which is just back of the mound of the Tiger Temple, and is unique in the fact that it is situated upon level ground and not upon a pyramid.

Of this building there is still standing the right wall, nearly all the back wall, a fragment of the left wall, and about a fourth of the ceiling. The colors upon the bas-reliefs, with which walls and ceiling are covered, are quite clear except upon the left wall, where for some reason they are much faded but still distinguishable. On the ceiling the colors are remarkably distinct, especially several tones of blue. I recollect that my uncle, who painted the "Spirit of Seventy-Six," once told me that blue is a fugitive color and that there is no such thing as permanent blue, which, he jokingly remarked, is the reason why painters use a pigment called "permanent blue." The prevailing shade of blue used in these bas-reliefs is what artists of to-day would term indigo blue in various tones.

Appropriate coloring has been used throughout. The flesh is flesh-colored; garments, war-gear, everything is properly colored. In these as in nearly all the bas-reliefs, the incisions or background are colored a deep red, origi-nally, I judge, as brilliant as Chinese vermilion but now mostly faded to a brick red.

These walls represent the very pinnacle of Maya art. There is nothing of antiquarian interest upon the Ameri-can continents that excels or even approaches them. The figures are not stiff and unlifelike as are Egyptian figures. On the contrary, they are uncannily faithful portrayals of men in action. They are about three feet high, and on these walls are more than eighty figures of kings, gods, priests, and warriors. Many, particularly the priests, are clad in most wonderful and elaborate vestments. The warriors are more simply clothed and all carry *hul-ches* such as were actually found in the Sacred Well. Upon the back of each fighting man is a quiver holding five darts. Each dart bears the individual mark of its owner, so that if retrieved it might be returned to him.

The bas-reliefs depict six different scenes, and each runs completely about the room. Separating each scene from the one above it is the conventionalized body of a great serpent.

In all of this work I have discovered but one female figure. Below this figure is an ornamental border about eight inches high on which are engraved flowers and small human figures in curious acrobatic postures.

The front portion of the roof is now fallen in, but I surmise that originally the illumination of the building was such as to bring out the relief work most prominently.

At present one gets a much better impression of this work at about ten o'clock in the morning than at any other period of the day.

In the National Museum at Washington, there is a reproduction of these bas-reliefs, but this modern work has scarcely caught the spirit of the old Maya artists. It should be the immediate aim of archæologists to preserve or duplicate the bas-reliefs in the most faithful manner, for the sake of posterity, for I doubt if we shall ever uncover anything finer in American antiquity.

Teoberto Maler spent a great deal of time in making photographs, drawings, and tracings of the old Maya murals and reliefs, and the world owes him a debt of gratitude for the minute care he took and the faithfulness of his reproductions. Maler, who is now deceased, was no mean antiquarian. He was also an artist and a man of most peculiar personality.

For several years his more or less undirected explor-

ation was done for the Peabody Museum, and then he
fell out with the heads of that institution and thereafter worked as a free-lance. For years his livelihood
was derived by selling information, photographs, and
drawings to dilettant antiquarians. So many of these
failed to pay him for such services that the poor fellow
became suspicious of virtually every one who attempted
to be friendly with him. I called on him four times before I could even get him to talk about archæology.
But I always took several bottles of beer with me, so he
became more cordial; and as I was especially careful
not to question him in any way to indicate an interest
in his work, he finally thawed out completely.

An Austrian by birth, he had accompanied the ill-fated
Maximilian to Mexico and had finally drifted southward into Yucatan, where he centered his interest on
archæology.

One day he presented me with about twenty photographs from his collection, which I was happy to have,
although some were discards. Seeing the sincerity of my
gratitude, he offered to show me some things which he
said had never been seen by any one else. Among these
treasures was his excellent tracing of the battle scene in
the Tiger Temple. The next day I asked him with some
trepidation if I might make a copy of the tracing. He
was quite willing and when I suggested that I would
travel to Mérida to get some tracing-paper for the purpose he produced a whole roll of it. I spent an entire
week making this tracing and several others, Maler working beside me and helping for several hours each day.

I tried to pay him when the work was completed, but
he would never accept a penny, saying I was the only

man who had ever come to him without trying to get something for nothing, and he repeated this remark, I have been told, to other people. He told me he trusted only two men in the world. Naturally, I was very glad to have won his regard.

One day, some years later, he showed me several golden ornaments which I afterward found had come in some devious way from the Sacred Well. I fortunately made some photographs and drawings of them, for the next year, when I asked to see them again, Maler no longer had them. Some he had evidently sold to a museum abroad and the remainder he had disposed of otherwise.

Maler had a foolish hatred for Don Eduardo and called him "falsifier Thompson," but the latter had no such feeling toward Maler; in fact, one can scarcely imagine Don Eduardo's hating anybody.

During one of my visits Maler promised me that the following year we should make a two weeks' journey into the interior of Yucatan, where he had discovered a temple unknown to the world which contained some marvelous murals. He said that he had discovered an underground extrance to the temple and when he left he had covered up the entrance and planted shrubbery over it so that it would remain hidden from archæologists. At that time I made a tracing of one of his drawings, showing a wall of this temple on which is depicted a water scene, with a volcano spouting fire and smoke, buildings falling into the water, people drowning, and a figure dressed like a warrior, paddling away from the scene, in a boat. Maler was a firm believer in the Lost Atlantis theory and contended that this picture represented the destruction of Atlantis. It was an obsession with him that nothing from this secret temple should come into the possession of what he termed "that infamous museum."

I shall always regret that Maler died before I was able to make the intended trip with him to this hidden temple, as the knowledge of its location died with him.

Teoberto Maler, soldier of fortune, artist, archæologist, and eccentric misanthrope, yet at heart kindly and lovable, died of a fever three years ago, in his adopted land of Yucatan. All of his personal belongings were taken over by the Austrian consul, and I am told that except for his numerous photographs and drawings there was nothing among them of value.

Among the modern inventions which the antiquarian has to be thankful for, place first in the list the camera, which makes possible faithful reproductions, frequently under most unfavorable conditions. Compare modern photography with the difficulties that beset Catherwood, who made the exceptionally fine engravings with which Stephens's books are illustrated. Catherwood did his work nearly eighty years ago, using a "camera obscura," a rather clumsy device which projects an image on a screen so that it may be traced. In making a single tracing Catherwood worked for hours at a stretch in the tropic heat, beset by insect pests, whereas to-day a few moments with a camera would be sufficient.

One of the interesting things shown in the old murals and bas-reliefs is the diversity of costumes. The dress of the figures varies from the simple wide belt, with flaps hanging down front and back, to the very elaborate vestments of the priests. To the belt might be fastened armor of heavy quilted cotton or of wood or even of metal.

The costume of the warrior always included an ornate feathered head-dress and there was wide variation in these head-ornaments. In some cases they were made of wood in the shape of a bird or other animal and the surface was covered with a thin layer of metal such as beaten copper or gold or with well-tanned deerskin or of finely woven cotton fabric embroidered with feather-work. From the top of the head-dress, feathers sometimes descended in graceful curves clear to the ground. The entire head, wings, and tail of a bird were often a part of the head-gear. The head-gear of kings and nobles was decorated with the feathers of the sacred quetzel, or bird of paradise. On a few of the pictured head-ornaments, one or more serpents' heads are seen, and these may have been a symbol of rank or the coat of arms, so to speak, of a certain family. In other cases the front of the head-piece shows the face or mask of some deity, often the face of Kukul Can.

Fastened about the warrior's neck is often a cape of cotton fabric so heavily embroidered with feathers that it appears to consist of feathers alone. Some of these capes or tunics are covered with metal scales to ward off the thrust of spear or dart. The Maya love of finery is indicated by the ubiquitous string of jade beads about the neck, ending in a heavy jade pendant or medallion. Such beads are worn by many of the pictured figures.

Around the warrior's waist is a wide, embroidered belt supporting an ornamented apron. Protectors of feather-work surround the knees, and upon the wrists are curious wristlets. Sandals are made of deerskin or heavy felt and are decorated with geometrical figures; they are laced in front and frequently have high sides like a shoe. Both deerskin and felt sandals have been found in the Sacred Well. A band is worn around each ankle, with feathers projecting from the front. This band is purely decorative and has no connection with the sandal.

Usually the fighting-man is shown either holding five darts in his left hand or having that number of darts in a quiver on his back. In his right hand he grasps the *hul-che*.

Some of the figures have their arms almost entirely obscured by bands covered with feathers. Other figures wear cloaks or mantles fastened at the throat and reaching nearly to the ground. These are generally embroidered heavily with the feather-work so dear to the ancient Mayas.

Figures are also shown wielding the formidable spear tipped with flint. Some of the spear-heads taken from the Sacred Well are from eight to nine inches long and two to three inches wide, and razor-edged. Spears were usually gaily decorated with feathers attached to the shaft where it joined the head. In the bas-reliefs is shown, also, a spear-head with serrated edges. For fighting at close quarters the battle-ax was used. It consisted of one or several stones or of a metal blade fitted into a wooden helve.

In addition to the armor worn there were shields. Some of the shields were built to fit closely the back and sides of the warrior and were fastened to the broad band of his belt. Other shields, carried in the usual manner, were made and ornamented in several different ways. Usually the base was wood, embossed with metal, studded

with jewels or ornamented with feathers. I was fortunate enough to be with Don Eduardo at one time during
the dredging of the well and had the thrill of picking
from the muck of the dredge the golden section of a
shield-front, which had been a large round ornamented
disk of considerable size, embellished with carvings of
flowers and scrolls.

The net also was used in battle and, as shown in the
bas-reliefs, was carried by the spear-thrower, in his left
hand. Very likely it was effective in stopping the thrust
of a spear. Or—who knows?—it may have been used
to entangle the enemy in the manner of the Roman gladi-
ator armed with net and trident.

The warriors went into battle to the resounding blare
of horns, and trumpets were used to signal troops in
action. There were whole companies of horn-blowers,
each man provided with a horn nearly as tall as himself.
Horns and horn-blowers are clearly shown in the murals
of a second-story room in La Casa del Monjas.

Our information obtained from a study of the bas-
reliefs and murals and from the articles retrieved from
the Sacred Well and other finds checks with remarkable
closeness the writings of Landa, whose sources of knowledge were chiefly legend and the old Maya writings.
Landa says:

They had for their defense round shields which they made of
split reeds woven round and adorned with deer-skins. They had
jackets padded with cotton and filled with salt. These were of
two thicknesses or layers of padding and extremely strong.

Some of the chiefs and captains had helmets of wood. They
went to war with plumage and tiger and jaguar skins on—those
that had them. They always had two captains, one hereditary

and perpetual, the other selected with much ceremony for a term of three years.

On the roads and passes they erected defenses of twigs and wood and sometimes of stone for their archers.[1]   If they captured some distinguished man, they sacrificed him, because they did not want to leave alive anyone who might later harm them.

They had hatchets of certain metal which they fastened into handles of wood and these served them as arms and also as instruments to cut wood.   These they sharpened by pounding with a stone to harden them as the metal was virginally soft.   They had small, short lances with points of hard flint.

In their earth there was not discovered until now any kind of metal with which they might make implements with which to work on their numerous edifices.   However, not having metals, they found in the earth flint with which they made materials for their lances which they used in their wars; and the knives for sacrifice were made from flint which the priests had selected.[2]

They had a certain kind of white brass with admixture of gold from which they made their hatchets for different functions and also hawk-shells and a certain kind of small chisel with which they made their idols.   The brass and other plates of metal and hard copper plates they used to barter for things from Tabasco for their idols, trading back and forth.

In the illustration following page 232 may be seen the more elaborate costume of the priests.   This illustration of a small section of the back wall of the Temple of the Bas-Reliefs represents a religious ceremony.   The whole wall is covered with figures of priests and warriors paying devotion to Ahau Can, the king of serpents.

The Great Serpent looms majestically over and about

---

[1] By "archers" Landa doubtless meant fighting-men armed with the *hul-che*.

[2] Several sacrificial knives were found in the Sacred Well.

the high priest, who is decked in gorgeous apparel. Mask and helmet cover his face and head, and from his body intricate scrolls extend in all directions, denoting the words or chant to which he is giving voice. In his hand he holds a shield over the surface of which the body of the protecting serpent undulates. From the mouth of the Great Serpent issue scrolls of red and yellow, which may be words or venom.

Perhaps one may realize from this sculpture how keen was the decorative sense of these ancient people. It was ever seeking an outlet for expression. The undecorated space on wall or ceiling must have seemed to the Maya artist an inartistic space. He crowded his areas with ornamentation, yet with so nice a balance, so true a harmony that he achieved a perfect result without giving an impression of congestion.

Other figures show the use of ear- and nose-ornaments and of labrets made of thin disks of gold and of highly polished jade.

Finally, there are the wonderfully worked ornaments of fine flint, flawless and shaped curiously like the parts of a bishop's crozier.

In the Tiger Temple is a frieze near the top of the wall, extending clear around the four sides, which shows a procession of jaguars. It is a thing of sheer beauty, for the artist has caught in his paintings the very nature of the beast. There he is, in all his slinking, lithe, feline ferocity, conventionalized but losing nothing of his character.

Above and below the row of jaguars is an ornamentation of conventionalized serpent motif which is graceful, accentuating the litheness and grace of the huge cats. The whole frieze is done on a surface of stone polished to such smoothness that it conveys the idea of white marble worked by the hand of an old Italian master.

Another remarkable mural was upon a stone which was found by Sylvanus Morley in the debris of a partially ruined temple in old Chi-chen Itza which he named the Temple of the Owls. It is so named from the fact that many of the fallen columns bear sculptures of owls. For a number of reasons I believe that this is one of the earlier temples, built when Maya art was at its best, and I was thrilled at the quality of workmanship on the stone. The colors were much faded and the entire picture too faint for the camera. I found first, in cleaning the corners or unimportant parts by washing in water, that the paint would stand almost any sort of gentle rubbing. In fact, the only way it could be destroyed was by scraping it off with an edged tool. Washing showed that the colors were somewhat more vivid when the stone was wet and it occurred to me that it could be treated in much the same manner as an old oil painting, which may be greatly revivified by cleaning and then applying a coat of varnish.

Acting on this assumption, I first cleaned the stone with a weak solution of hydrochloric acid, which had no effect on the pigments but did remove much dirt. The next question was varnish. I had some turpentine and a few other chemicals but no varnish. And then I thought of the copal incense that Don Eduardo had taken from the Sacred Well. I took a ball of this and scraped off the calcined outer surface. The remainder of the copal I broke up and placed in an earthen bowl which also

came from the well. Then I added a little turpentine
and heated the mixture over a slow fire until the copal
was melted. Finally I strained the liquid through
a piece of cloth and had an excellent transparent copal
varnish. I tried it out on several unimportant stones
and found that it gave a fine surface gloss. I then applied it very carefully to the painted stone I had discovered, first to the blue border and then to the whole
surface. I was overjoyed, when the varnish had dried,
to find the colors magically restored, several of them
being nearly as bright, I think, as when originally applied,
perhaps a thousand years before.

It was now a simple matter to obtain excellent photographs and I took several, both in black and white and
with color separations.

This stone, which I named the Stone of Kukul Can,
told a complete story. It represented the long-nosed
god, the particular deity of the Sacred City, emerging
from the mouth of a serpent, just as shown in the old
Maya books and in many other places. In other words,
it depicted the birth of Kukul Can, the feathered-serpent
god. Below the serpent and the figure of the god was
shown the bowl of the earth, or the archaic representation of the earth. Here and there were cacao pods,
from which was obtained chocolate—then as now an important article of food, a highly prized delicacy among
the Mayas and other races. Cacao is one of the fruits
the Mayas thought to have been brought them by Kukul
Can.

The god held in his hands emblems of life and generation. Above were the celestial heaven and the zodiac.
At right and left were the hieroglyphs of the sun and

planets. On the upper margin was an inscription. The whole was majestic and exquisitely done. It indicated all of the good things of life,—prosperity and plenty,— bestowed upon his people by the mighty god Kukul Can, born of a serpent.

When I had finished photographing and studying this extraordinary stone, I wrapped it carefully and stored it in Don Eduardo's hacienda, where it was later ruined when the hacienda was burned by unruly Indians.

This lost stone was an excellent example of the older and finer Maya art and a careful comparison of it, as photographed, with the pages of the Perez Codex, one of the few remaining ancient Maya books (now in the National Library in Paris), shows its similarity to the work therein displayed. The portraits of Kukul Can are identical. The hieroglyphs have the same peculiarities of shading, due to the stroke of the brush being heavier on one side than on the other. If the artist who painted the Stone of Kukul Can did not also illuminate some of the Maya books, he at least belonged to the same peroid and the same school of artists. I am sure that the great work of Mr. Morley of the Carnegie Foundation, which is now going on at Chi-chen Itza, will uncover many more stones similar to this one and it will be demonstrated that many of the Maya books were produced in the ancient city.

Very frequently in the murals or the bas-reliefs, where figures of men are shown, the glyph representing the man's name appears above his portrait. Thus we have "Mr. Can," or, in English, "Mr. Snake," as in the second cut opposite page 112. Above him is the carving of a serpent. This gentleman has the conventional nose- and ear-ornaments and over his head is the double feather of a warrior. From his mouth issues a scroll representing speech. Other figures are "Mr. Duck," "Mr. Phallus," etc.

In one of the Codices is shown an eclipse of the sun. It is remarkably well drawn in colors.[1] At the top of the page is what may be called the text, which we are not able to read although we know many of the characters. Directly below is the celestial band, representing sun, moon, and planets. Dependent from this band are three hieroglyphs of the sun in the heavens. The central figure is the sun, and wings at left and right mean movement of that body, or day and night. Under each of these figures is a bird in the act of devouring the sun. The word for eclipse in Maya is *chi-bal-kin*, literally "mouth-action sun," or "bitten sun," and it was the ancient belief, which persisted until fairly recent times, that at the time of an eclipse the sun was bitten by a serpent or by birds or other creatures.

Beneath each picture representing the devouring of the sun are the date-glyphs.

An interesting colored mural from the ceiling of La Casa del Monjas shows a warrior standing upon a pyramidal structure. In his left hand is the *hul-che* and in his right a shield and battle-ax. He has just shot two lances to which are fastened firebrands, which have passed over a walled inclosure and are intended to set fire to the buildings within. In one corner of this picture is a building representing the Iglesia (one of the annexes of the Nunnery) or a similar structure, as denoted by the mask of Kukul Can sticking out from the wall of the building. In the foreground, at the left, is a mammoth head-dress,

[1] Shown on page 39.

which may be explained by the fact that it was not uncommon for the Maya artist to make a picture and then to introduce into the foreground large figures entirely out of proportion to the remainder of the picture.

As for full-relief carving, one need only see the serpent columns of El Castillo or the Tiger Temple, and the serpent balustrades, to know that the Maya artists were fully as skilful at such work as in producing bas-relief and murals.

Among the pottery, incense-burners, and funerary urns discovered at Chi-chen Itza are frequently exceptionally fine examples of ceramic art. A vase of a substance like alabaster found by Don Eduardo is a thing of matchless beauty.

Of metal-work in gold and copper there are many pieces indicating great skill and artistry. Jade ornaments such as beads and plaques are exquisitely worked and perfectly polished.

Of stone point-work, heads of darts and spears, and blades of battle-axes, as well as cutting-tools and weapons, nothing has been found in America which can compare to the Maya work. The sacrificial knives found in the well are peerless in their artistry.

The art of the Mayas shows the greatest variety in media, style, and technique. Even casual observation of that in the Sacred City shows that many different painters and sculptors were employed; yet everywhere painted or carved figures are natural, true to life, the proportions perfect. The best are comparable to those of ancient Greece; the worst, though crude, are never stiff and mechanical like those of Egyptian art.

Unfortunately there are no statues like the Memnon

of Thebes nor the Apollo Belvidere, for the Mayas did not produce statuary or monolithic carving, with the few rare exceptions of Chac Mool figures and serpent columns. Rather their effort was toward detail and precision of figure and design. Some of the carvings are so minute that they are hard to see easily without a magnifying-glass. We can only wonder at the exceptional ability of this ancient people to originate, imitate, and express in stone or pigment or by the goldsmith's or the lapidary's art.

CHAPTER XV

THE TOMB OF THE HIGH PRIEST

JOSÉ ALVARADO, once a common mine laborer, an ordinary peon, became the Silver King of Mexico, so fabulously rich that he offered to pay off the whole national debt of Mexico. His offer was declined by Porfirio Diaz, then President of Mexico. Alvarado inherited from a hard-working father a meager silver-mine and he took up the arduous working of this mine upon the decease of his parent, gaining from his toil scarcely enough to pay for his scant frijoles, chiles, and tortillas, until chance led him aside and caused him to strike his crowbar into an obscure cliff, a mountain of virgin silver.

"Some of my finds in the Sacred City," says Don Eduardo, "have been as much a matter of sheer chance as that of José Alvarado. And if the truth be told, I fancy a good many pioneer operations, scientific or otherwise, depend largely on Dame Fortune—or Lady Luck, as I understand she is now called in the States.

"Earlier in life I gave rather less credit to chance and more to scientific deduction, and once I made a discovery in the Sacred City which followed so closely my calculated prediction that I concluded I had evolved a formula which, so far as this special class of work was concerned, would eliminate chance entirely. I went at the work of excavation with a new vim and mounting enthusiasm. It was hard, back-breaking toil for me, digging and heavy lifting, yet I was sure of my diagnosis, certain of final triumph. I kept on digging,—endlessly, so it seemed, but with hope unflagging,—until suddenly I brought up against a solid ledge of living rock. It could not be explained away. To me it seemed to say, 'Well, here I am and here I have always been, and your wise deductions, your clever calculations—where are they now?' And to prove to me further that I must not ignore the little gods of chance, as I returned dejected and crestfallen along the deep trench, my crowbar accidentally struck a projecting limestone fragment which fell to the bottom of the trench, disclosing a dark cavity, within which were a rich find of pottery and a most interesting skeleton. But for the chance dislodgment of the stone, I should have missed the object of my search.

"While I was engaged in some excavation in the building called Chich-an-chob (literally, "The Strong, Clean House," called now the Red House) a small but unusually high mound to the southwest of the building was often in my line of vision. Although I could only guess at its outline through the thick growth of tall trees and matted vines that covered its sides, the little I could make out of its peculiar form excited my interest and kept it in my thoughts.

"Eventually the progress of the work brought me to it and I had the opportunity to obtain at least an approximate idea of its structure. I found it to have been originally a small but well-built shrine or temple crowning a steep-terraced pyramid, but now converted by time and disintegration into a mere conical mound. The greatest factor in the decomposition of the shrine, as in the case of many others, was not wind and weather but

the wrenching apart of the stone-work by the growing
roots of trees.

"The temple itself was similar in plan to the great
edifice which towers above Chi-chen Itza. In fact, it was
El Castillo in miniature but differing in several important
details, among which were corner and lateral stelæ or
carved stone monuments, the rear ones bearing inscriptions which seemed to place the shrine in a different
category from any of the other buildings I had examined
in the Sacred City. Like huge El Castillo, this miniature
temple has a main stairway facing the northeast, and
similarly the approach is guarded by twin serpent-heads,
each a finely carved monolith. Protruding from the massive heads are forked tongues extending for some little
distance. The serpent bodies, conventionalized into
wide, flat bands, serve as balustrades, extending one on
each side of the wide, steep stairway, clear to the temple
platform. The big blocks of stone and masonry, fallen
from the temple level, had rolled down these stairs and
carried away most of the stairway, leaving just enough
of the handsome, carefully cut steps and balustrade to
indicate what had once been a perfect thing. Indeed, the
stairway is no longer usable, although a few of the steps
remain in place, and the difficult ascent is made by grasping projecting roots of trees and stone fragments and
treading in the gashes left in the mound by the avalanche
of rock masses from above.

"Gaining the crown of the pyramid, we found there
massive serpent columns corresponding to those encountered on the plain below. Well carved, artistic, they
were half buried in the fallen walls of the temple, while
one of the impressive capitals of the now-famous serpent

columns, consisting of the conventionalized rattles of the rattlesnake, lay precariously balanced on the very edge of the platform. Its twin companion had long since crashed down the steep incline and its great bulk lay amid the debris and matted growth at the base of the mound.

"In clearing away the forest growth and surface accumulations on the top of the mound, we uncovered the capstones of four large square columns which had once supported the triple-vaulted arched roof of the inner chamber. These capstones indicated by the almost effaced carvings on them that the columns beneath probably were covered with carvings. Believing these to be of real importance, as well as a safe guide to follow in the work of excavation, we began carefully to clear the space about them, and as fast as the column faces were cleared and cleansed I made plaster casts or molds of their wonderfully carved surfaces. When we at last reached the floor-surface of the chamber, we gave these ancient columns an opportunity to dry out thoroughly, after their centuries of accumulated dampness, before we continued work in their vicinity.

"Being a dyed-in-the-wool New England Yankee as well as an antiquarian, I have, naturally, evolved some mechanical aids for my particular line of work in the thirty years I have been at it. Among these contrivances is an instrument which has proved most useful in detecting subterranean cavities near the surface. The device consists of an octagonal bar of steel with a tuning-fork at one end. The other end flares out into a protuberance like the bulb of an onion. By tapping with this crude instrument, using it as long experience has taught me, I have often been able to locate burial vaults and other cavities which I might otherwise have overlooked.

"After the floor of the shrine had been cleared I sounded the whole area with my steel stethoscope and it indicated a large, deep cavity about midway between the first line of columns.

"The floor was made of heavy cut stones, smoothly joined, and with our simple tools it was something of an undertaking to loosen and remove one of these large blocks. But at last we did raise it and found, beneath, a square cavity about four feet wide. At first the depth could not be determined, because the cavity was completely filled with crisscrossed roots. None was thicker than a pencil and most were thread-like, but all were so intertwined that they virtually formed a solid mass. My helpers looked doubtfully at this yellow, spongy mass of unknown depth. 'Who knows what strange underground poisonous creatures may be hidden in this sickly mass of yellow and brown?' they asked.

"A stout pole was laid across the cavity and a rope tied to it so that it dangled down into the hole. Finally two of my bravest workers were persuaded to descend the rope, each clinging to it and wielding a dexterous machete with his free hand, hacking away at the spongy mesh of roots. Hardly had they warmed to the work when one of them, in heaving up a root mass, found himself covered with large red scorpions. Angry at being so rudely ejected from their habitation, they crawled over him with upraised, menacing tails, and several did sting him. Both men came popping out of the hole in record time and I at once administered antidotes, from my medicine case, to the man who had been stung and

A sculpture in bas-relief showing a warrior-priest in ceremonial attire, representing the Maya hero-god Kukul Can, the plumed serpent.

A religious ceremony depicted in the Temple of Bas-Reliefs. This is but a small section from the interior walls, which contain more than eighty figures.

sent him back to the plantation house for the remainder of the day. Another man took his place and the work proceeded, but more cautiously.

"We had just about finished getting out the root masses when there came from the cavity two terrified yells and two even more terrified men. When they had quieted down enough to talk intelligently they said that after cutting away a root mass, the last one on the bottom, and tying it to the rope so that those above might raise it, they had perched on a projecting ledge and lighted cigarettes, waiting for the rope to be lowered again. As it came down between them and rested on what they supposed was the bottom of the pit below them, they saw the bottom heave into a writhing mass and out of it rose the head of a big snake with shining eyes and jaws that yawned at them wickedly. As one man they climbed the rope and scrambled into the open. I think they would have rolled down the side of the mound and kept rolling right up to the plantation house if I had not grabbed and held them. Eventually their fright subsided and was replaced by curiosity and they stayed on willingly enough.

"Nobody seemed particularly anxious to go down into the pit, so I thought it might be just as well to make some long-range observations before starting any hand-to-hand encounter with whatever was down there. A reflecting mirror threw a shaft of clear, strong sunlight into the well or shaft and my field binoculars, adjusted to a short-distance focus, revealed to me the coiled body of an amazingly large snake. As the shaft of light played about, the big fellow raised his head, waved it uncertainly, and then dropped it again. To judge from the size of the head and the shape of the body, the snake evidently was not a crotalid, or rattler, but rather some species of boa. Boas are not very difficult to handle, especially if you would just as soon have your boa dead. This particular representative of the boa family was, apparently, sleeping off a hearty meal and was still rather torpid, and it was no trick at all to kill him.

"When brought to the surface, the deceased proved to be a *chaib,* a kind of boa noted for its beautiful skin, handsomely marked with large mottles—greenish yellow and chocolate brown. Our victim was fourteen feet long and had a maximum diameter of eight inches. From his skin, native tanners made me a money-belt and a very comfortable pair of slippers. The *chaib* is not poisonous and I have never heard of a case where a human being has been attacked by one as South American and African boas are said to attack. Nevertheless this snake bears an evil reputation among the Mayas, who believe that a nursing mother crossing its path becomes powerless in its coils and that the reptile sucks the milk from her breasts, though it does not otherwise harm her.

"After disposing of the snake we resumed operations in the shaft. We discovered that some emanation of a gaseous nature or perhaps a fine dust from the roots produced a violent headache, much like that caused by the fumes of dynamite. I remembered that quarrymen find relief from dynamite-fume headaches by drinking strong, hot coffee, and similarly we found this beverage an effective remedy for our headaches.

"Cleared of invading roots, the cavity was now really

a cavity. Descending hand over hand by the rope a full twelve feet from the level floor of the temple, I found myself standing on what seemed to be an accumulation of little stones and plaster, intermixed with small bones which I took to be those of animals that had been the prey of the *chaib*. There was a good deal of parchment-like material lying about, which I thought at first was cast-off skin of the big boa, but which was actually an epidermal root-covering sifted down from above. Standing at the bottom of the square shaft and looking up at the vertical walls, I saw that each wall-surface was built up of a myriad of small cut blocks of tan-colored limestone, so smoothly polished as to suggest marble. It was unlike any ancient wall-surface I had ever seen. The stones were not inserted in mortar like Florentine wall mosaics; neither were they built up into high relief, like the famous walls of tombs and chambers at Mitla. Rather, each tier of small stones was cut to a bevel, with the upper or horizontal surface projecting some two inches beyond the face of the tier above.

"As nearly as I can describe it, the effect was like the siding, or clapboards, on a house, supposing that the siding were put on upside down, thick side uppermost. The stones were cut with exceeding niceness, and each wall section, though simple, combined with the others to form a most artistic whole. At the four corners, where the lateral bands would have met, they were intercepted by vertical stone bands about four inches wide, running from bottom to top of the shaft.

"At the time I could spare only a passing interest in these walls, for in the debris beneath my feet were fragments of pottery and a projecting human jaw-bone. We painstakingly removed the stone fragments and mortar-dust. Working with trowel, spatula, and whisk-broom, I found that the chamber contained the disordered remains of two graves.

"Evidently one grave had originally been superimposed on the other, and the contents of the two had been thrown together by the force of falling debris from above. The two graves, I think, were once square and separated by stone slabs. Here I found fragments of pottery and splintered human bones, brittle with age and gnawed by rodents. Reconstructing the scene from the fragments, I surmise that each grave contained, besides its human remains, a small, shallow tripod vessel, the outer surface of which was burnished with red pigment, and a deeper gourd-like vessel. I believe that the shallow dish contained food and that the deeper one was filled with drink of some sort—very likely *sacca* or *bal-che,* both of which the ancient Mayas believed were acceptable to the soul of the departed and to the gods.

"The skeletons were so broken and disturbed that beyond the fact that they were two in number and that the bones were so old they were fragile as pipe-stems, nothing else was casually to be noticed. The finding of skeletal remains and of funerary urns made it clear beyond dispute that this building was a mausoleum, a tomb of kings or of priests.

"I carefully collected all of this fragmentary material and sent it aloft to be preserved for future study. Then I made measurements of the chamber and jotted them down in my note-book. This being done, I turned my attention to the stone floor of the tomb. My steel stethoscope indicated that below there was a still deeper cavity. With much careful effort we pried up the stone floor-slabs, disclosing another grave. Apparently this burial-vault had suffered but slightly from the concussions and disturbances which had all but destroyed the two upper graves. The walls and bottom were lined with thin slabs of stone covered with mortar. Much of the mortar had flecked off and lay spread out unevenly over the various objects in the grave, but no serious harm had been done either to the skeletal remains or to the funerary vessels. The bones, however, had been gnawed and dragged out of place by rodents.

"A shallow earthen vessel was found in the grave, of the customary small tripod type, painted red, with a blue line around the rim. A bowl-shaped vessel, gray-colored and smooth, was placed at the right of the skeleton, and both vessels were half filled with sifted mortar. Even though the bones were somewhat disarranged, it was plain that the human remains had been buried with the knees drawn up to the chin, and the arms placed over them, with hands clasped. I found the hunched-up remains reclining upon their right side. Whether the body had been so buried or had been buried in a sitting position and had later toppled over, is a matter for conjecture. If this grave or the others had ever held anything of perishable nature it had completely disappeared.

"When the vault had been cleared, I resorted once more to my crude stethoscope, which left no doubt of a still further cavity. Raising the floor-slabs, we discovered a grave similar to grave Number Three, but the contents were interesting variations. The usual tripod vessel was there and also the bowl-shaped container, but the bottom inner surface of the tripodal receptacle was cross-hatched with deep-cut lines, and beside it was a large tripod vessel containing a caking of hard material that proved to be copal incense of finest quality. It was so altered by time that it was crystallized, almost fossilized, but when a small portion was burned it gave off the familiar copal fragrance.

"In one corner of the vault, almost hidden under mortar-dust, was a little heap of verdigris. This proved to be a number of copper bells, like our sleigh-bells in shape but very much smaller, like the bells brought up from the Sacred Well. The outer bells in the heap were so oxidized that they simply flaked away when we tried to clean them, but the inner ones retained their shape and finish even after they were washed and cleaned. Copper bells played an important part in the rituals and in the economic life of the ancient Mayas and of their successors, even down to almost modern times. That old and faithful chronicler Padre Cogolludo says of the olden people: 'The monies they used were copper bells and valuable according to their size.' But the probable reason for the presence of bells in this tomb is the fact that in still older history bells were a part of the regalia of Ah Puch, the God of Death, and were attached as anklets to his person. He is so shown in the many hieroglyphs of him.

"The skeletal remains in this grave seemed to point to a re-burial. Either the bones were taken from another tomb and re-interred here or else they were cleared of their integuments and flesh prior to burial. I say this because they were found in a queer bundle-like heap, with no reference to their relative anatomical positions.

"In all of these graves were found traces of wood-ashes, but no signs of burned or calcined bones to bear out any theory of cremation.

"Once again the steel stethoscope was put to use and again it told us that we had not struck bottom. The floor of the fourth opened up into a fifth grave, deeper than any of the preceding ones and more free from accumulations. It contained pottery and a mingled heap of bones, as the grave above had done. But in one corner, just where we had found copper bells in the grave above, we discovered what looked like a dusty pile of glass, which proved to be a handful of beautifully polished and glistening rock-crystal beads some of which were handsomely fluted. This find was the first recorded one of rock-crystal beads or pendants in Yucatan. And amid the dust and debris on the floor we recovered a dozen or more perfectly cut and artfully shaped jade beads of small size. They were found either just above the surface or buried in a fine ash deposit which may have destroyed somewhat their original luster. Even so, they are valuable specimens, especially because of the surroundings.

"The floor of this fifth and last of the several graves was on a level with the base of the pyramid, and I concluded, therefore, that it rested upon ledge-rock formation and that we had now reached the end of our search. In fact, I had noted an upward tilt in the ledge rock and had wondered why we had not already encountered it in the shaft. The ancient builders very wisely took advantage of these rises and outcroppings of ledge rock, in placing their buildings, so as to save filling-material and the labor otherwise required to give the structures a solid foundation.

"Judge of my surprise, despite my silent prediction, when the tuning-fork device again signaled, 'Good-sized cavity below'! It took more than a casual glance to find the seams in the floor of the crypt, so closely were the stones fitted, and we had considerable difficulty in dislodging and raising them. Instead of a sixth and similar tomb we encountered a flight of steps hewn out of the living rock.

"We had spent many days of constant back-breaking labor in the excavation of the five graves, the noting of data, the preparation of the specimens, and the packing of them in cases. Incidentally, the deeper we went, the greater was our danger of cracked skulls from falling stones and we had all taken to wearing stiff, high-crowned, wide-brimmed Mexican sombreros. The high crowns we stuffed with *pochote* (tree-cotton). We covered our shoulders with thick pads of gunny-sack, worn like a cape. When not working we threw the flaps back over our shoulders. Occasionally a stone did fall, striking harmlessly upon our improvised helmets and padded shoulders. If, however, it chanced to hit a naked leg there was a howl of mingled pain and rage, followed by words of unmingled Maya expletive. Such accidents happened but rarely and the whole undertaking went through without a single serious mishap.

"Each day, as the work progressed and we went farther and farther down, the light from above became more and more feeble, except when the sun was at the zenith, and much of our work had to be done by candle-light. When we came to the flight of steps we found it so choked with ashes, lime-dust, small bits of stone, potsherds, and charcoal, each in quantity in the order indicated, that at first we could obtain no idea of the dimensions of the chamber below. From the contour of the roof-stones I judged it was not large, but it was so filled with debris that I had to enter it feet foremost and lie upon my side to fill the wicker baskets with material and pass them back to one of my helpers, who in turn passed them on. Thus from one to another they passed, until they could be hoisted up to daylight, where trusted hands and experienced eyes separated the dross and placed the remainder in field safety-boxes for my later inspection.

"In this manner, an endless chain of filled baskets went up and empty ones came down to one man in the mysterious vault, lying on his back, half naked, dripping with sweat, and plastered with grime, but now and then smiling seraphically as he caught the gleam of a shining jade jewel or a finely worked bit of flint. He could not see clearly for more than an instant at a time, for when he was not blinded by sweat the alkaline ash-dust smote his eyes, and the two at times combined to make him fairly writhe. And he would not have changed places with a king, for every once in a while he came upon something more precious to him than kingly possessions.

"At first this work progressed very slowly for, perforce, I was the only worker in the heaped-up chamber, my head and shoulders in the flickering light of wild wax-candles while the rest of my body was buried in the darkness of unknown centuries, my high-booted feet crowding against who knows what noxious cave creatures.

"The mass of material, though hard-packed by time, was mostly wood-ashes; and once these were loosened, a heavy booted foot or even a sandaled one might injure some priceless museum specimen. And so for a while I preferred to work alone in the confined space. At last I had cleared away the accumulation above the second step of the stairway, and I worked a clear space about the third step, using only my bare hands, a sculptor's spatula, and a whisk-broom. Even the trowel was tabooed. Finally a sufficient space was cleared for my two most trusted aides, Manuel and Pedro, to work beside me and then the work progressed more rapidly.

"For several days things went along in this manner, with our interest and curiosity mounting hourly, so that all who worked with me, down to the last peon, grew feverishly excited and food and drink became mere irritating interruptions. And each day added to our hoard of potsherds, human bones, and shining jade.

"To this day I cannot think of that strange chamber without wonder. Neither can I account for the presence of the material which so nearly filled it. That it was a depository for the contents of previous burial-places, is, I think, a fact beyond a doubt. Ashes, half-burned fragments, even pieces of smooth wall-finish foreign to this particular chamber, potsherds and jade ornaments— all lead to this conclusion. At first I thought that the place had been a crematory, but I was soon convinced that this could not have been so.

"As the work went forward the outline of the chamber became well defined. The opening was relatively high and wide and I could stand there almost erect. The passage, however, narrowed quickly like a funnel, ending in a dead wall. The week was drawing to a close and with it, so it appeared, our task. The work within that deep-down, badly ventilated shaft was not too pleasant.

The air was close; the place was frightfully hot, and the big wax candles, dim and smoky, did not tend to make the place more comfortable.

"We three—Manuel, Pedro, and I—were stripped to the waist and looked more like chimney-sweeps than delvers after scientific lore. The work seemed so nearly at an end that we kept doggedly on, the boys digging and sifting while I stopped frequently to make notes. Late in the day, all seemed finished except for a few isolated ash-heaps and a big flat stone that leaned again the very end of the wall.

"Heaving a sigh of relief and wiping away the layer of grime and sweat from my eyes, I said, 'Well, boys, there's nothing left but to haul away that big flat stone and sweep up the ashes behind it on the chance that there are some beads or small objects in the mess; then we'll take a few measurements and call the job finished.' I grasped the stone slab with both hands and pulled it toward me. It yielded so suddenly that I fell back with it; and my companions likewise fell back, for, instead of uncovering a pile of ashes, it disclosed a big, circular, pitch-black hole and from that unsuspected, terrible hole came a long, soughing rush of cold, damp wind. Our candles went out at once, leaving us in inky blackness. The cold wind chilled our overheated bodies. I was left with an insecure foothold too near the opening to dare a movement in the dark. The two natives were simply glued to their places in sheer terror.

"Finally Pedro spoke. 'It is the mouth of hell,' he said, and I heard his teeth chatter as he said it. Even then, with my feet so placed on the sloping wall-space and my body so inclined on the sloping floor that it seemed

as if an incautious move might slide me smoothly into
that black hole and through it into Eternity, I felt a
pleased interest in Pedro's statement, for to the ancient
Mayas, hell, called by them Metnal, was not a burning
pit of fire and brimstone but a dank, cold place where
lost souls, benumbed with chill, struggled forever in thick,
dark mud. The words of Pedro, coming so spontane-
ously from the heart and coinciding so nearly with the
ancient belief, the belief of his ancestors, caused me to
wonder.

"For the moment, however, it suited my purpose to
have the more Christian idea prevail and I did some rapid
missionary work, saying reprovingly in the native tongue,
'Ehen, Pedro! What did Padre Ortiz say about the hot
flames of an ever-burning hell? It is a cold wind and not
a hot flame that comes from this hole.' My logic evidently appealed to them and freed them of a superstitious fear and they became once more calm and
resourceful.

"Working slowly and carefully in the utter darkness,
we managed to block up the hole with our wide-brimmed
hats and we held them in place by toppling the big flat
stone against them. I was then able to get to my feet
and relight our candles. By long experience in subterranean work, cave explorations, and descents into ancient
cisterns, I have learned to take certain basic precautions.
As one of these, I wear about my neck, hanging from a
stout cord of deerskin, an air-tight metal case within
which are a glass vial of proof alcohol and some wax
matches. By this means I am freed of the vexation of
damp matches and a futile blue line of phosphorescence
when a light is quickly and urgently needed. I also carry

invariably in such work a small Davy lamp and a hundred-foot steel tape.

"The lamp is a safeguard against possible gas explosions. Lighting it, I once more uncovered the hole, and once more the rush of cold air began. I waited until the air-currents had balanced themselves as nearly as they were likely to do and then proceeded to a further examination of the hole. The orifice was about thirty inches in diameter and after piercing the rock for about two feet it opened into a cavity of unknown size and depth. I could, of course, have dropped a stone into the cavity and timed its fall, gaining at least some idea of the depth. But I wanted to take no chance of breaking anything of antiquarian interest which might be there. Instead, I fastened the lantern to the end of the steel tape and slowly lowered it into the hole, but the thickness of the two-foot wall between me and the perpendicular descent prevented me from seeing what was discovered by the lantern as it went down. So I had the two boys hold tight to my legs while I squirmed through the orifice until, head down, I could sway freely above the pit. The convulsive hold on my legs assured me that I should not drop down the hole suddenly if the boys could prevent it, so I turned my entire attention to the void beneath me.

"By feeling the tape nicks as the lantern rested on the bottom of the pit I found the depth was almost exactly fifty feet. By swinging my body and the tape with the lantern at the end like a pendulum I ascertained that the cavity was bottle-shaped and about twenty feet wide at the bottom. I also ascertained that it was quite dry, the air pure in it and the ventilation perfect. This seemed to be all of the data necessary for the moment, so I had the boys pull me back to terra firma and then cautioned them to say nothing whatever about our latest discovery. And so we returned to the upper air and the scent of orchids and to a hearty supper.

"That night, when I knew the men were resting and chatting before taking to their guitars and their hammocks, I sent for Manuel—wise, level-headed, dependable, my trusted companion through long years of this sort of work. I said to him, 'Manuel, to-morrow is going to be a very interesting day even for old-timers like you and me and we shall not often see and handle that which I hope we shall discover to-morrow. Now, I want you to see Juan Cancio, Mathildé Uh, and José Uh. I will see Pedro and his brother. Tell Juan, Mathildé, and José to meet us here at five o'clock in the morning with their machetes, with their water-gourds filled and with dinner in the *sabucan*. And, Manuel, tell each of them that a shut mouth catches no flies. We may find something and we may find nothing but piled earth, and if the latter we do not want the other men laughing at us behind our backs.'

"Early the next morning we hastened toward the mound and with us went stout ropes, block and tackle, shovels, and all the necessary tools for six men. We slid down the rope into the shaft and then made our way down the stairway into the funnel-shaped chamber. Here we fixed a strong post and attached to it a double block and tackle, with the several necessary ropes, so that all of us could safely descend and ascend the fifty-foot bottle beyond the small, dark orifice. With a lighted miner's lamp on my head and my Davy lamp preceding me by ten feet, I placed my foot in a noose in one of the ropes, swung myself through the orifice, and hung over the pit. Between my teeth was my sharp hunting knife which I always carry in this fashion in entering a subterranean reservoir.

"My plans were well made and it was my intention to be lowered slowly that I might study these grim walls as I descended. I had gone down less than half the distance when I began to turn and whirl in the air like a dancing dervish, with the difference that the dervish whirls on solid ground, to the prayerful cries of his brethren, and he can stop when he wishes, while I whirled in mid-air in darkness and silence, like some dead celestial sphere and as powerless to stop. In our haste we had forgotten to take the kinks out of the new ropes we were using and my rope was avenging itself by beginning to unkink as my weight was felt on its twisted strands. For a few seconds I could do nothing but hang on dizzily. Meanwhile the rapidly twisting rope had caught and jammed in the block, serving as a brake and had entirely checked my downward progress.

"Suddenly a coil of rope from above fell loosely on my shoulders and aroused me to my danger. The men above, not knowing what was going on below in the darkness, were steadily paying out the rope and if the choked block became suddenly free, there was nothing to prevent my falling headlong through that terrible blackness to whatever was below. Hurriedly looping the rope as best I could, to insure my present safety, I yelled to the men above, and a voice came down to me, sounding thick and flat in that black space.

" 'What is it, Master?' the voice said.

" 'Listen,' I replied, as steadily as I could. 'Do exactly as I tell you, for my life is at stake!'

" 'We will do it, Master,' answered the voice.

" 'Haul up the slack of the rope until I tell you to stop.'

" 'I hear you, Master,' and the snake-like coils began to recede, to grow small, and finally to disappear. The slack had been taken up. 'What now, Master?' came the voice and I knew from the tension in it that the sight of the slack rope had told its own story.

" 'Send me down Manuel and José.' (They were the lightest and most agile of the men.) I had no more than spoken before they came sliding down the other ropes and shortly I was descending as slowly and carefully as I had planned to do, until the pilot light of the lamp touched ground beneath me, standing as firmly erect as though placed by unseen hands. I glanced at the two men beside me on the ropes and we all nodded our heads approvingly.

"Below, clearly seen in the light of the lamp, was a pure-white vessel which had fallen apart, and from it streamed gleaming, shining objects. We landed as carefully as though stepping on a mound of eggs. Before taking our feet from the nooses we called to the men above to make the ropes fast and to be ready for our signals. Leaving the lantern standing as it was and no longer troubled by air-currents, we lit our candles. Directly in the center of the pit was a large mound and crowning it was the white vase, made of translucent material like alabaster, carved from a solid block and engraved with a leaf design in highly conventionalized meanders, combined with geometrical designs around the rim and sides. It was broken into several pieces, but these were large and the whole was quickly and easily fitted together into the original shape.

"The vase, which had a capacity of about a quart, contained a quantity of exquisite jade beads and pendants, a large plaque with surfaces richly carved and representing conventionalized human figures with religious regalia, a polished jade globe over an inch in diameter and shining clear in spite of the ages of dust, oblong pendants, and thin, minutely carved ear-ornaments. This was but a tenth of what the vessel had once held. The rest we found later in the heaped-up material beneath it.

"At a signal anxiously expected, the other men came swirling down the ropes like firemen sliding down a brass pole to answer an alarm. Then we all went to work. Each of the men had had long experience in similar labors under my supervision. Occasionally was heard a swift intake of breath and a man would hold up some interesting find and then settle back to his task. While they worked I made notes, numbered the specimens, and helped to pack them in the safety-boxes. Thus the work went on. Occasionally we had to stop to kill a *tzeentum*, a big, flat, crab-like spider. *Tzeentum* spiders can give an ugly sting producing a fever hard to subdue, and at times they seem to swarm out of hidden crevices. By reason of their flat bodies and quick movements, killing them is not always easy.

"We found temple vases, incense-burners, tripod vessels, cylindrical urns, some of which are perfect, others marred, and many broken. We obtained fragments of large, hard-baked earthen vessels of complicated design. Unbroken, these must have been at least thirty-six inches high. We secured, also, chipped flints of fine workmanship and of unknown use. All these and many other finds came to us from this mound, and after it had been gone over carefully by hand and had then been screened we decided we had left nothing of value and as with one mind we began to think of supper. Pedro swarmed up one of the ropes hand over hand, followed by his brother, and they hoisted the specimen cases and tools. The rest of the workers followed one by one. I was the last to leave the mysterious burial-chamber, which seemed to name itself by occult suggestion 'The Sepulcher of the High Priest.' And as I left its dark depths behind me, the mysterious atmosphere, which no one, probably, will ever be able to dissipate, seemed to cling to me.

"When we arrived at the top of the square-walled shaft it was eleven o'clock at night and all the people of the plantation were there, anxiously awaiting us. The families of the men who accompanied me were in a hysterical state. Ropes had been brought and an attempt was about to be made at our rescue. With our specimen cases held aloft and in the midst of a rejoicing crowd we returned to the plantation house and soon the noise died away and we all slept.

"I am asked why I call this shrine upon the mound with the crypt beneath it the Temple of the High Priest. That is a fair question.

"I believe there comes to most sentient beings, after protracted periods of intense observation and deep interest in a given subject, a certain mental domination over the subject beyond a mere recognition of the facts which have been encountered. One becomes possessed of a clarity of vision not psychic but reaching farther than cold logic. Call it intuition or what not; it so frequently arrives at the right answer, spanning the gap that cannot be spanned by the chain of facts, that I have great respect for it when it is honest, genuine, and strongly felt.

"As I left behind me the black depths of the pit, its haunting mystery seemed to permeate me. I had had the same strange feeling come over me before, in research work among the burial-places of Labna and also during and after my discovery of the ruined city of Xkickmook. Never had it been so potent, so definite as when I ascended this wonderful old burial-shaft and came into the moonlight of the living world.

"The feeling, impressive beyond words, was undoubtedly intensified by the vision of the treasures I had so recently seen and handled: the beautiful alabaster-like vase above all comparison with anything of its kind hitherto found in the whole Maya area; the remarkable terra-cotta votive urns nearly three feet high, each bearing the mask of a god surrounded with sacred ornaments; the elaborate incense-burners and other extraordinary pottery; the big, polished, globular beads of jade; the carved jade plaque; the labrets, ear- and nose-ornaments; the tubular rosettes; the thin disks of polished jade; the wonderfully worked, flawless ornaments of flint, shaped like the parts of the crozier of a bishop.

"And linked with these in my mind's eye were the deeply paneled surfaces of walls and columns, everywhere in the Sacred City, depicting god-like personages with all the regalia of exhalted priesthood: neck-chains of big globular beads, breast-plaques of finely carved design, ear- and nose-ornaments, and, grasped in the hand of these dignitaries, a staff crowned with an object resembling the crozier of a bishop.

"To me these pictures and the finds we had just made dovetailed perfectly. Beyond dispute, too, is that fact that many ancient races placed at the side of the departed those things which were most used in life and which they would, presumably, want first in the hereafter. The old Phœnicians, the Egyptians, the Scythians, the Norsemen, the Eskimos, the redskins of the North and West, the Pueblos and the Nahuatls, and the Incas and pre-Incas— all followed this custom. And I know at first hand that the Mayas were no exception, for I have found well-defined graves, never previously disturbed—graves containing child skeletons with toys beside them; graves of women in which were bone needles and spinning-whorls of terra cotta or worked stone; graves where beside the thick bones of once-powerful men were found flint lance-heads and heads of darts for the *hul-che* and knife-points of obsidian.

"Beyond question I had uncovered the last resting-place of a priest obviously of very high rank. Reason and logic and facts carry us thus far. But those five hidden graves, each guarding the one below and blocking the way to the deep secret passage and the pit at its end wherein lay the sacred relics of the arch-priest —how may these be explained? It is here that the mysterious assurance came to me—the sure intuition, if you will—that this was not merely the tomb of a great priest but the tomb of *the* great priest, the tomb of the great leader, the tomb of the hero-god, Kukul Can, he whose symbol was the Feathered Serpent. Evidence is lacking, I can offer no scientific proof, and yet I am certain that ultimately further discoveries in the Sacred City will bear out my intuitive belief."

CHAPTER XVI

THE LEGEND OF THE SACRIFICIAL PILGRIMAGE

WITHIN the province of Mani the water-holes, the *satenejas*, were dry. For many weeks no rain had fallen and the growing corn had withered and died. The people were perishing of hunger and thirst and Ah Pula Xia, overlord of the province, saw that something must be done and swiftly or the tribe of Mani would be no more.

And so he caused the great summons to be sounded, the command to every man, women, and child in the whole province to appear before him—the command that had not been heard for twenty years. The *uliche*, drumsticks with heads of rubber, striking upon the *tunkul*, caused the earth to tremble with the loud booming of the summons, while swift-footed *holpopes*, or runners, carried the message to the most distant parts of the nation.

At the appointed time Ah Pula ascended to his kingly seat under the spreading shade of the great *yax-che*, the sacred tree of the Mayas, and grouped around him were his councilors and chiefs; the *ah-kin*, the high priest, the *kulel*, the aged prime minister, the *nacon*, chief of the warriors. Behind each of their leaders were grouped the officers of lesser grades, each clad in his richest vestments and holding the badge of his office. And flanking these nobles were the *tupiles*, or guardians of the law, in long lines; and each bore the white wand, insignia of their authority. Beyond, as far as the eye could see, clear to the horizon where the level plain met the forest, were massed the commoners, the whole nation of Mani.

Slowly Ah Pula, the *batab,* rose from his throne, and as he rose the tall lances, the great battle-swords, and the *hul-ches* clashed together in one mighty salutation like the sound of giant trees crashing to earth in a hurricane.

The gaze of the *batab* roved over the assembled multitude and with one hand upraised he commanded silence.

"O friends and councilors, sons and brothers! Those armed for war and ever ready to defend the province! Priests of the Sun, who bring to us the words of our gods and transmit to them our prayers! Listen to my words and listen closely, that your answering thoughts may be well chosen and weighty, light-bringing and life-giving. Thus and thus only may we survive the calamity that threatens.

"Five times have the seasons come and gone. Five times have we planted our fields of corn since the strange white men came to our land. We did not invite them nor seek them. They sought us, these strange white men coming in strange craft from a far land. They came and we did not welcome them as did the Cheles and the Peches, nor did we meet them as enemies when the Cupules, the Cochuahes, and the Cocomes fought against them. Three times while they were here we planted and gathered abundant harvests. Three times have we planted our fields since their departure. Twice we have failed to gather enough even for seed for the following season and the last planting, the third one, is now parched and dying.

"How, then, shall we feed our people? How shall we fill the breasts of the nursing mothers and warm the cooling blood of the aged and feeble? In this time of need even the wisest and strongest require the wisdom and counsel of their brothers."

Ah Pula Xia the king sat once more upon his throne, that ancient seat of authority shaped in the form of a jaguar. Turning, he said to the *ah-kin,* the high priest, in measured words, "O Father of the Temple, Brother of the Sun, tell us from the store of thy sacred knowledge and from thy god-given wisdom, why have the gods been deaf to our prayers? What have we done that they have forsaken us and left us to be scourged so sorely?"

The pontiff, tall, spare, and lined of feature, with eyes burning bright in their deep sockets, rose from his seat and faced the king. His words came forth so clear and simply that even the youngest and the dullest of his hearers could not fail to hear and, hearing, understand:

"O Batab, ruler! O Halach Uinic, father of thy people, hear what the outraged gods say through my lips to thee and thy people:

" 'Unknown beings from a strange land and worshiping pagan gods have polluted this earth with their tread, have deafened our ears with their foreign tongue and defiled our temples with prayers to other gods. They have entered as guests into your towns and villages and you have received them. They have lived in your homes and you have suffered it. Your servants, at your command, have given them food and drink.

" 'The gods of our fathers are slow to wrath. They

waited in patience your repentance, but you repented not. Then did the gods turn against you their wrath. With quarrels and dissensions they divided the evil white men. With pestilence and strange diseases they decimated them. Smitten by enemies, harassed by insects, and poisoned by reptiles, these white men faded in strength and numbers, until the few that still lived returned to the unknown land whence they came.

" 'All this was by the command of your gods, the gods that now you have forgotten. But though the serpent passes, his trail still remains. Because of these things that you have done the gods are punishing you. They have forbidden the clouds to form and they have forbidden the rain to fall. They have forbidden the grain to germinate and the roots to sprout in forest or field. They have caused hosts of insects to devastate your stores and eat up your substance. They have brought upon you terrible diseases that your wise men and physicians cannot cure.'

"You ask what can be done to appease the anger of the gods. Now, the knowledge has come to me, through the ancient records and writings handed down from high priest to high priest since time began, that once before in the history of our people was the wrath of the gods, and especially the wrath of Yum Chac, the Rain God, kindled against us when we forgot his precepts and disobeyed his teachings.

"In that olden time beautiful maidens were sent to him as messengers, to plead for his forgiveness and to carry with them rich offerings of viands, flowers, and precious jewels. Thus was his ire appeased and fecundity restored to this unhappy land.

"My words are these: 'Let us follow the ancient example. Let us go in solemn procession with maidens as chaste and lovely as the opening buds of the white pitahaya, to carry our plea to the god, and with our prayers let us send food and drink in fine vessels, the ripest fruit, the fattest grain, and our richest jewels. Thus may we hope to avert the divine wrath and restore to life our starving nation.' "

The *kulel,* the prime minister, then stepped forward. His form was bent, his hair gray, and his face seamed with lines of deep thought. His voice, though low and calm, was heard distinctly amid the crowding ranks of the common people.

Said he, "O Batab, ruler of the people, we have listened to the words of our pontiff and his words befit his high office. We listen to them with the respect due him as high priest and as the mouthpiece of the gods. To hear these words and the command they convey, is to obey without question.

"He who is ordered by those above to go upon a journey, surely goes if he is faithful. But he who goes upon such a journey without due preparation is not a good servant, for, by reason of his unpreparedness, he may be delayed, led astray, or otherwise impeded in carrying out the will of his master.

"Therefore let us think what this act of expiation requires us to do, and then consider how to do it with the least delay and without waste of life and effort. What we seek to gain is evident, for we all feel the pangs of hunger and have seen our nearest and dearest fade away and die. We have seen the grain and the fruit wither. We have seen our scant stores devoured by clouds of insects.

We have seen our people wander into the deep forest seeking food and they have never returned.

"What we most desire is to appease the dread anger of our gods, that we may have once again food and health and happiness.

"We are all agreed that we must make sacrifice at the Sacred Well, the Chen Ku of Chi-chen Itza. The question is, then, how shall we reach the Sacred Well and how shall we make our sacrifice? The way is long, full of thorns, and covered with sharp stones. The thorns are the lance-points and the stones the pointed darts of the Cocomes, the Cochuahes, and the Cupules, our ancient enemies, through whom we must pass to reach the well. Either we must gain their permission to pass in peace and friendship or we must push our way through them by force of arms.

"My voice is for peace with these our lifelong enemies. I have said."

Then came the *nacon*, the chief of all the fighting men, powerful, thick-set and sturdy. As he arose the warriors clashed their weapons in a deafening roar and then all were silent, awaiting his words.

"O Batab, ruler," he said, "we have listened with reverence to the words of our high priest, with awe and submission to the words of our gods that came from his lips. We have heard with respect the measured, temperate wisdom of our aged *kulel*. He has said that we must not delay our sacrifice and yet his voice is for peace.

"I, too, say that we must not delay, but why need we who are among the greatest and strongest in the land, ask of any one permission to sacrifice and worship? Who gave the Cocomes the right to say who may worship in the temples or make sacrifice at the Sacred Well? Is not Chi-chen Itza the holy city of the gods, our gods as well as theirs?

"Let us open wide the path to and from the Sacred City and keep it open with the points of our spears, the keen edges of our swords, and the swift terror of our *hul-ches*. I have spoken."

The *batab,* with the *ah-kin,* the *kulel,* and the *nacon* turned toward the assembled people and the *batab* cried in tones that rolled over the thickly packed mass and beyond into the trees of the forest:

"What is your voice? What is the word of my people?"

With a noise like thunder came the mighty chorus:

"We want food! We are dying. We go into the forest to dig for roots to fill our empty stomachs and we find none. The land is accursed and even the birds no longer fly over it and the snakes even no longer burrow within it."

The *batab* pondered deeply and long, then raised his head and said:

"This we will do: We will first ask of the Cocomes that they allow our people to pass to make sacrifice at the Sacred Well. If they consent we will make a great pilgrimage and a sacrifice that shall be remembered through the ages to come, for it will be the seal of friendship and of peace between old and bitter enemies. If they refuse us their permission to pass freely and to make our sacrifice, we will then take that right, as they of old took it, by force, and by force we will hold it for all time.

"Now, this very night we will send the message to

the Cocomes, so that we may know without delay what course to follow. Until then let each of you in his own way so prepare that whatever comes we shall be ready.

"At once, summon the swiftest runners to take the message to Nachi Cocom, Batab of Zotuta, and through him to his allies, the Cupules and the Cochuahes!"

Nachi Cocom, Batab of Zotuta, King of the Cocomes and leader of allied provinces, sat in his great council chamber. About him were his chiefs and nobles and those of his allies, the Cupules and the Cochuahes. Upon the high walls of the council chamber were war-banners and trophies of many hard-won battles. On broad wooden platforms, one at each end of the building, were heaped the captured weapons, war-masks, and armor of those who had fought against the Cocomes or their allies and lost.

Gathered around the entrance were keen-eyed warriors armed with lances and swords and *hul-ches*. Lounging but watchful, they first gave the warning, high-pitched and long, that echoed through the city and carried even to the houses nestled in the fringe of the forest: *"Hek-utal le macoboo!* Here come strangers!"* Down the winding path came the messengers from the Batab of Mani, carrying his word to Nachi Cocom, Batab of Zotuta.

The messengers were three brothers, picked men, *holpopes* all three; good men to look upon and worthy of their office. For Mayas they were tall but well pro-portioned and lithe, as supple as young jaguars. Wide of brow and clear-eyed they were. None could doubt their fitness to be the messengers of the king. Striding up to where the Batab of Zotuta and those of his council sat, each fearlessly and proudly made his obeisance and gave his salute—the sign of a *holpope* bringing a message.   To the chief *holpope,* the eldest and tallest of the three brothers, the *batab* said, "Welcome, *holpope,* and those with you.   Speak!"

Said the chief *holpope:*

"To thee, O Batab of Zotuta, I bring a message from the Batab of Mani and thus runs the message:

" 'To the Batab of Zotuta and its provinces I, Batab of Mani and its provinces, send greeting.

" 'We are brothers, in that we were both born and are nourished from the same earth-mother, this land of Mayab.   Therefore I, Ah Pula Xia, Batab of Mani, do now and by these my chosen messengers send to you, Nachi Cocom, Batab of Zotuta, this brotherly greeting and with it a brother's request:

" 'The gods have smitten us sorely for our sins, you and me and all our people.   I, Batab of Mani, with my people desire to make peace with our god by a pilgrimage of atonement and solemn rites of sacrifice, that we may once more receive the blessing of the Rain God, your god and ours.

" 'We have had our brothers' quarrels, but the quarrels of brothers can be forgotten.   We have had our hard-fought battles, but wars that have been fought are things of the past, things to forget.   To-day we are scourged together, you and I and all our people.   Let us, then, forget the past with its bitter memories and come together like brothers, forgiving and forgiven.   Let us unite in a great and solemn pilgrimage of atonement and sacrifice to the angered god, in his temple at the Sacred Well of Chi-chen Itza.   Thus will his wrath be appeased.

The rains will follow the clouds in the heavens and fecundity will come once more to the earth, now sterile, baked, and dead.

" 'For this we ask your word and your promise that my people may pass undisturbed and unharmed to pray in the temples and to make sacrifice to the Rain God in the Sacred Well at Chi-chen Itza. I and my people await your answer."

Nachi Cocom sat motionless in thought, neither asking nor receiving counsel from those about him; and such was their fear and awe of this indomitable and cruel ruler that none dared speak as he sat with crafty eyes staring at the ground before him. At last he raised his head and fixed the messengers with his inscrutable gaze and said:

"Messengers from the Batab of Mani, listen closely and carefully that your words to him be my words to you.

" 'From the Batab of Zotuta to the Batab of Mani, greetings! You say that we are brothers, in that this land of Mayab is our common mother. You say that we are together and alike scourged by an outraged god. These things are true. The land, our common mother, has felt the curse of the white man's tread. By this act was she violated and we, her sons, permitted it—you by acquiescence, I by impotence.

" 'But all this is past, you say, and we must now find means to avert the disaster which threatens to overwhelm us both—a calamity that can be avoided only by a pilgrimage and sacrifice to Noh-och Yum Chac at the Sacred Well of Chi-chen Itza.

" '*Be wale!*—so let it be!

" 'You say that brothers quarrel and then forgive; that the war that is ended may be forgotten.'

"Now," and here he bent forward and spoke in deep earnestness, while about his thin lips wreathed a twisted smile that made those who knew him well recoil in terror, "tell my brother, Ah Pula, Batab of Mani, to send his pilgrims, the maiden messengers, the sacrificial offerings, and the priests, when and how he wishes. When they come they will find me and my people ready and waiting to give them warm welcome. No spear shall be cast, no weapon raised against them. We will guard the pilgrims and send them on their way to worship and to make sacrifice to that god with whom they so urgently wish to make peace—to your god and our god, for are we not the offspring of a common mother?

"They will need to bring neither food nor arms, for I, Nachi Cocom, and my people will provide these things. Thus can your people come on more quickly to ask the forgiveness of the god for traitorous acts, snakelike deceptions, and cowardly submission to strange white men.

"I have spoken. Messengers of Mani, eat, drink, rest, and then speed back the word of Nachi Cocom to—" and here again he smiled sardonically— "to his brother Ah Pula Xia."

Thereupon the *batab* rose and departed, and his councilors likewise left the chamber.

But the chief councilor spoke in a whisper to his brother, leader of the warriors, and said:

"No man may know but the *batab* himself what thoughts are deep buried in his mind, but I know and fear that thin-lipped smile, and as he spoke to the messengers of Mani a strange feeling came over me like *ek muyal,* the black cloud. I had a fear of something, intangible but terrible; something he is planning that will bring down upon us the annihilating wrath of the gods.

"Brother," his companion answered, "do not voice such thoughts nor even think them. I have forgotten that you spoke. Remember that the will of the *batab* is supreme. We may not question it. I also felt your fear, but say no more!"

Swiftly, tirelessly the messengers of Mani sped on their homeward journey; over sunlit plains, threaded by the smooth worn paths of the jaguar and the wild boar; through cool forests whose shade beckoned enticingly; past wells of crystal-clear water where thirst cried to be quenched. But they stopped not at all until, as the sun sank slowly down into the west, they passed between the great parched corn-fields of Mani and at last reached the palace of the *batab.*

So quickly had the *holpopes* returned that the *batab* said of them, "They are birds, not men."

And the *nacon* answered: "If they are birds, then are they eagles, for these three *holpopes* in the battle with the Uitzes killed three warriors and took three prisoners."

The *batab* cast an approving glance at the deep-chested, thin-flanked young *holpopes* and said:

"Let it be proclaimed from the temple that for their services in time of peace and for their brave acts in battle these three brothers shall henceforth be of the eagles and shall bear the regalia and wear the mask of the eagle in the sacred rites." And so it was from that time on. The three brothers, known as the Three Eagles, wore the feathers and mask of the eagle in the sacred festivals and until after the coming of the later white men the figures of the Three Eagles were to be seen carved upon the walls of a temple in Mani.

Great was the enthusiasm and greater the joy at the message sent by the Batab of Zotuta to the Batab of Mani and the tale of the warm welcome given to the *holpopes* and the warmer one promised to the pilgrims.

Ah! could they but have seen the venomous look and the twisted smile that was hidden behind the unctuous softness of those pleasant-sounding words!

In the province of the Cocomes great preparation was made for the expected guests. At frequent intervals along their destined path from one village to another were placed arches made of saplings tied together and bent to the ground. Those at the entrance of each village were adorned with fresh vines and bright flowers until the curve of the arch was a solid mass of green leaves and fragrant blossoms. There were scarlet clusters of *cutz-pol,* or turkey-head, white *sac-nute* blooms, the frail blue jungle morning-glory, and the golden trumpets of the *xkan-tol* flower.

As the pilgrims reached each new village the head men and the most beautiful maids of the district came to meet and welcome them, the head men with the symbols of their authority and the maidens with gourds of cool *sacca* to quench the thirst of the travelers. And with songs of welcome they invited the tired but happy pilgrims to rest and then to feast in the village. As they neared Zotuta, where dwelt the *batab,* he and his councilors came forth to welcome them. The whole city, even to its most distant outskirts, was seething with the hum of preparation. Wild turkeys, wild pigs, green corn, big tubers, white, flaky, and succulent—all were being cooked underground with heated stones and surrounded with fragrant herbs after the manner and custom handed down from ancient times.

On came the pilgrims, heralded by groups of children and women singing and chanting words of welcome. At the feet of the pilgrims were strewn clusters of flowers and along the way were bowls of incense, so that the fragrant smoke pleased their nostrils. First came the priests and the nobles. Then came the lovely maidens chosen to be the messengers to the great god at the bottom of the Sacred Well, and these girl brides of the god were carried upon litters richly adorned and smoothly transported by trained bands of bearers. After them came the devotees, their arms filled with rich offerings. And last came captive warriors, men of fighting renown, esteemed for their valor to be worthy of sacrifice to the Rain God.

Thus with solemn joy and chanted welcome the pilgrims entered Zotuta, not only as pilgrims on a sacred mission but as an embassy bearing offerings of peace and good-will between brothers long estranged but now reconciled and reunited by the god to whom they would soon offer prayer and joint sacrifice at the Sacred Well.

Soon came the feasting, the religious games, and at last the solemn ritual of the Sacred Dance. The hours passed too pleasantly and sweetly to be heeded, until drooping lids could no longer stay open and the pilgrims were conducted to the group of houses that had been set aside for their use.

In the cool darkness that precedes the first gleam of dawn, that time when the whole world sleeps, the Cocomes in the houses beyond the palm-thatched dwellings where the pilgrims lay and the pilgrims themselves —all were buried deep and sound in slumber. Then silent, shadowy forms swiftly surrounded the quiet houses where the pilgrims rested in fancied security.

Red tongues of flame, smokeless because of the dry materials upon which they fed, shot up from each house corner and like snakes crawled along the thatched roofs. Before the sleepers could arouse to their danger the big structures were roaring and crackling, each a huge funeral pyre.

Shrill shrieks of women, hoarse cries of men, choking, gasping moans, frenzied prayers, imprecations, and inarticulate sounds filled the morning air and the barred doors and burning roof-poles were shaken furiously.

The voice of Nachi Cocom of the crafty eyes and the thin-lipped cruel smile was heard above the crackling of the flames and the shrieks of the dying pilgrims. His black eyes glittered venomously, like the eyes of a deadly serpent when it strikes home its fangs, but his voice was smooth and oily as he said:

"*Ehen!* pilgrims, brothers, brothers of a common mother! How fares it? It would seem to me, standing here and looking on, that you have changed your minds and that you are making sacrifice to Yum Kax, god of fire, and not to Yum Chac, god of rain! But what does it matter, brothers of a common mother? Both are gods and both are worshiped by brothers that spring from a common mother. You are now saved the trouble of visiting the Sacred Well."

As he said these words, as if by a common signal, the blazing roofs sank slowly in, the cries of agony ceased, and shortly all was still.

Once again the *batab* spoke and the twisted smile was on his lips as he said:

"Rest now in peace, brothers. This is the warm welcome that I promised you. Long years ago, I promised you such a welcome, but you had forgotten. And Nachi Cocom never forgets."

The *batab* turned and strode from the place, the baleful glitter still in his eyes, but the populace—people of Zotuta and those from distant villages, drawn by the pilgrimage and the feasting—fled from the city, and many rushed into the jungles and were never seen again. Only the soldiers of the *batab,* with callous obedience to their orders, remained to watch over the smoldering funeral pyres.

It is said that the Rain God, incensed at this act, deserted the Sacred Well with all his court and, leaving the land and the people to their fate, made his home in a far distant and unknown region. The people, abandoned by their god, ended by fighting with one another like rabid animals. The shrine on the brink of the Sacred Well was no longer carefully tended, and it fell gradually into ruins, piece by piece. The beautiful carved cornices and roof-stones were wedged apart by the growing roots of trees and toppled into the still, dark waters below. When, in after years, the white men came again they found a few miserable Mayas living in carelessly made huts under the shadow of the great ruined city, and these natives shunned the Sacred Well and believed it to be haunted.

Thus passed the power and majesty of mighty chieftains and thus died the Maya nations.

CHAPTER XVII

THIRTY YEARS OF DIGGING

RIGHT here in America, only a short journey from the United States and closer to them than our Panama Canal, are the remains of at least sixty ancient ruined cities—marvelous places about which we know almost nothing, nor of the people who built them.

We know infinitely more of the ancient Egyptians—of their buildings, their customs, their beliefs, their history, and their writings. Virtually every hieroglyphed surface left by them which has been uncovered has been pored over by many archæologists and its meaning deciphered beyond question.

For a hundred years antiquarians from every civilized land have spent their lives in studying the ancient empire of the Nile. Millions of dollars have been expended in scientific, minutely careful exploration. No slightest clue to further knowledge has been ignored, and tons of books, written in every language, have been printed, so that the man on the street anywhere may go to his nearest library and, if he will, read all there is to know on the subject.

And here at our very door, on our own continent, are the remains of an early culture not one whit less interesting than the Valley of the Kings. Possibly it is not so old, but on the other hand it is more steeped in mystery because of our profound ignorance. We know next to

278

nothing about it: who were its builders; where they came from; their history, creeds, or customs. We can read but a few scraps of the writings of which they left such an abundance—enough, in all probability, to fill in many of the empty spaces in our knowledge if we but had the power to decipher them and extract their meaning. Even our hard-won and sadly limited information concerning this culture has never been given to the general public. To get it one must read Spanish and French and German, as well as English, and the average public library contains possibly three or four books on the subject.

Until last year no well-planned, completely equipped exploration backed by ample finances had ever been undertaken. Archæologists have delved in many of the ancient Maya cities—puny expeditions pressed for time and cash. The work backed by the Peabody Museum has been the most consistent, but even that has suffered often from lack of finances, and much of Don Eduardo's work has been done at his own expense.

Happily, I think the American public and American antiquarians are waking up to the neglected opportunity. The expedition sent out by the Carnegie Foundation is most promising. It has well-laid plans; it is under the leadership of Sylvanus G. Morley, a thorough-going archæologist and one of the foremost in knowledge of the ancient Maya culture. He has made the study of the subject his life-work and has achieved fame through his finds in the Maya area. He has uncovered many important date-stones and is the most eminent authority in this specialized activity.

The new exploration is being carried on at Chi-chen

Itza on a big scale and most methodically; and, best of all, it is prepared to continue twenty years if necessary, to the ultimate completion of its work.   Fallen temples will be rebuilt, stone by stone.   Every scrap of knowledge that can be extracted from the excavations and study of what is already uncovered will be noted and correlated. There can be no question that this work will add very largely to antiquarian lore.

I await with eagerness the delving into what Don Eduardo calls "old Chi-chen Itza," the completely ruined and tree-covered part of the ancient city, which lies to the south of the newer and less damaged buildings, for it is there that the most ancient architecture and the noblest carvings are to be found and, with them, other remains of the highest Maya culture—the relics of that earlier golden age which had already fallen to decay before the Nahuatl dominance resulted in the buildings of a lower order in the newer city.

The Spanish conquerors discovered many of the ancient cities and wrote about them in their annals; and the world promptly forgot about them for two hundred years. Then vague stories about them began to drift back to civilization, carried by adventurous wanderers who had seen or heard of them.   At the end of two hundred years we knew considerably less about early Mayan culture than was known by Landa and Cogolludo and the other Spanish padres who followed in the wake of the conquering Spanish flag.   It remained for Stephens to lead the way once again and show us the wonder and mystery of the old cities.   The great Von Humboldt came and was deeply impressed.   Le Plongeon labored like ten men for years and tragically broke under the strain, leaving

little to advance the world's knowledge from the much
that he discovered. Then came Maler and knowledge
of a hidden city—knowledge lost to the world when he
died.

To Don Eduardo must be given credit for bringing
to light in the past thirty years the things which gave a
real forward impetus to this particular phase of American
archæology. Many of his finds, consigned to the Peabody
Museum, are not yet accessible to the general public,
having been held in reserve by that institution, doubtless
for sound reasons which are unknown to me. For thirty
years Don Eduardo has followed unswervingly the ambi-
tious, adventurous dream of his boyhood. Literally, he
has followed the rainbow to its end and unearthed the
pot of gold. His dream was to make the Sacred Well
yield up its treasures. That he has done and more.

Edward Thompson—or Don Eduardo, as I have
called him through these pages, because that is the name
by which I have known him so long and well—is no
richer in a material sense than if he had never raised
the fabulous treasure from the great Sacred Well of
Chi-chen Itza. But he has had what money cannot buy:
a life of notable achievement; a cherished dream realized
to the full; a thousand gorgeous memories, each packed
with such adventure and thrill as we less favored folk
have never experienced.

He has made the well of sacrifice yield its secrets. The
skeletons of the girl brides of the Rain God; the bones
of sacrificed warriors; the copal incense and the religious
vessels; the jade ornaments and objects of gold; the
hul-ches; the sacrificial knives—each is a link in the chain
of evidence which makes fact out of legend. His finds

prove the existence of the ancient belief in the Rain God and the fact that sacrifices were made to him. They prove that this great water-pit actually was the Sacred Well. They make plausible the legend that Chi-chen Itza was the Sacred City, the center of the cult of Kukul Can.

The finding of the date-stone, by Don Eduardo, may, to the casual reader, seem insignificant, but from the scientific point of view it is tremendously important, for it gives us one more indisputable fact. From it we know that the city existed in the seventh century, A. D. We do not know how much older than that it is actually or how long it flourished thereafter. There remains the incontrovertible date from which we may, in time, proceed forward or back to a further knowledge.

His discovery and excavation of the Tomb of the High Priest is a brilliant achievement. It lays bare more facts and opens up new avenues for speculation. Time alone can prove whether it is, as Don Eduardo so sincerely believes, the tomb of the hero-god, the great leader, Kukul Can, around whom all Mayan theology revolves.

And now Don Eduardo is no longer in his first youth. He is still far from decrepit, but the time has come when it is fitting for him to step aside from the active and strenuous work of exploration and he has leased all his holdings, including the Casa Real, to the Carnegie expedition. I know that he takes a profound pleasure in the feeling that this expedition is going to finish thoroughly and completely what he has so ably started and carried on under handicaps that will not beset the newer work.

To the layman Don Eduardo's achievements may seem

small as against thirty years of ceaseless endeavor, but do not forget the days and weeks and months of profitless effort that must be spent in this sort of work. It does not move forward like the building of a railroad, the manufacture of goods, or the planting and reaping of fields.

Thirty years are well spent if their labor helps in the least to shed even a feeble ray on the nearly obliterated pages of the past. And each rising sun brings fresh the hope that to-day will be the day of a great discovery, the finding of a key that will unlock the door to knowledge concerning a wonderful people whose monuments are to us as a few torn pages of some master manuscript without beginning or end, but still of such absorbing interest that one cannot rest until the missing pages are found.

As antiquarian thirst grows—as it surely must, for few things in the world contain a deeper human interest than antiquity—attention will certainly turn more and more to the still unsolved mystery of ancient American and, particularly, Mayan culture. Instead of one great scientific exploration there will be scores. Each of the ruined cities is worthy of research. There are magnificent temples to be restored; priceless finds to be bared; and that vexing riddle to be completely solved—the clear reading of the Maya glyphs.

And with all of this must come inevitably the tourist to a new and delightful land, and through him will grow a new and keener appreciation of America.

APPENDIX

List of More Important Gold and Jade Objects Found in the Sacred Well

One basin of fine gold, twelve inches in diameter with shallow rounding bottom. About a pound in weight.

Four other basins, bowls or cups, smaller in size, uncarved, but of massive material and very artistic in contour.

None of the above basins were twisted, cut or broken.

Seven gold disks, embossed or beaten, about ten inches in diameter.

Eight gold disks, embossed or beaten, about eight inches in diameter.

Seventeen gold disks, embossed or beaten, about six inches in diameter.

Ten gold disks, embossed or beaten, small sizes.

One handsome *penache,* forehead band or tiara, over eight inches long by four inches wide, of beautiful openwork, the design being entwined serpents with plumed head-dress.

This is the finest piece of gold work ever found in the Maya area.

Eleven reptile and animal figures, probably brooches and similar ornaments; all massive gold and finely worked. Frogs, bat-like figures and monkey-like objects, most of them cast (not beaten work), massive and of pure gold.

Fourteen small gold objects shaped like candlesticks.

Ten human or monkey-like figures of gold.

Twenty gold rings, mostly of thin but pure gold.

Sixty other objects of unknown use but of gold material.

One hundred bells of various sizes but all gold, even to the clappers.

Forty other unclassified objects, either of pure gold or of gold and bronze; sandals, disks, ferrule-like objects, pieces and strips evidently portions of shields and regalia ornaments.

Forty gold washers or scales, one and a quarter inches in diameter, with holes in the center.

One solid-gold mask seven inches in diameter, the eyes closed as if in sleep or in death and over the right eyelid the same kind of slanting cross that we often see carved on the so-called elephants' trunks.

One gold *hul-che* (throwing-stick) of entwined serpents.

Seven jade plaques or tablets, broken but restored, three inches by four inches.

Nine jade tablets, two inches by four inches by one quarter inch thick. The jade tablets were evidently broken intentionally before being thrown into the well.

One hundred sixty beautifully carved large jade beads and pendants of large size, virtually perfect.

Seventy carved jade ear-ornaments, nose- and labret ornaments, from two inches in diameter down to one half inch, all finely cut and polished.

Fourteen jade globes, one and a half inches in diameter, all very finely polished and several finely carved with well-executed figures and other designs.

One small but very finely worked and polished jade figurine, four inches wide and four inches high. It represents a seated figure of the Palenquin type with elaborate head-dress. It is perfect and is one of the finest, if not the finest figure found in the Maya area.

Many hundreds of small jade beads of all sizes and shapes, all polished; many of them artistically carved and shaped.

One flint-bladed sacrificial knife with the handle formed of golden entwined serpents. It is the only perfect one taken from the Sacred Well and probably the only authentic and perfect knife of this kind in any museum on the American continents. At least it is the only one in the Peabody Museum.

Several parts of other knives, such as handles, flint blades, etc.

Many beautiful flint spear-heads worth many times their weight in gold, worked down to the thickness of a steel spear-head with edges as sharp as a razor, the finest ever found anywhere in the world.

A thousand other articles of great value to archæology.

INDEX

Agriculture in Yucatan, 6

Aguilar, Gerónimo de, first of the Spanish conquerors, 166, 167, 170

Akab Tzib, or House of the Writing in the Dark, 62, 63, 64

Alphabet of Landa for employing Maya glyphs to denote Spanish letters, 41, 42

Alvarado, José, Silver King of Mexico, 235

Ancient cities, condition of at time of Spanish Conquest, 43, 44

Animal figures and carvings recovered from Sacred Well, 135, 137

Annexes, unnamed temples near Nunnery, 69, 70

Arches, Maya, 195

Atlantean figures, 78, 79, 85, 86

Atlantis theory of Mayan ethnology, 36

Bal-che, an ancient intoxicating beverage, 115, 137, 244

Balustrades with serpent motif, 77, 78, 80, 238

Bas-reliefs and full-relief works, 79, 80, 81, 82, 219, 220, 221, 224, 225, 226, 227, 228, 229, 230, 232, 233, 234.

Bas-Reliefs, Temple of, 81, 82, 219, 220, 221, 228, 229, 230

Beams, sapote, 78

Bells of copper from High Priest's Tomb, 246

Bells of copper and gold recovered from Sacred Well, 131, 132

Boa-constrictors, 95, 96, 182, 241, 242

Bolshevism among natives, 17

Bowls and disks of gold recovered from Sacred Well, 133, 134

Brooches recovered from Sacred Well, 135

Caluacs or ceremonial wands, 135, 143

Caracol, or Snail-shell, 71, 72, 73

Carnegie Expedition in Chi-chen Itza, 87, 279, 280

Casa Real, home and estate of Don Eduardo,

Ancient gateway, 55, 56, 57

First view by Don Eduardo, 55, 56

Looting by unruly natives, 17

Size of estate, 60

Caves, 33, 97, 139

Cenotes (see Wells), 135, 143

Chac Mool figures, 82, 182

Chich-an Chob, Red House, or Strong, Clean House, 73, 74, 75

Chilan Balam, Maya writings in Spanish characters, 37, 38, 40

Chi-chen Itza,

Arrangement of buildings, 60, 61

Distinction between old and new cities, 47, 60, 280

Lack of streets, 60, 61

Location and how to get there, 3, 5

Montejo's military headquarters, 172, 173

Retreat of Spaniards from, 70, 71, 173

Chisels,

Recovered from Sacred Well, 132, 133

Of nephrite found near Great Pyramid, 192, 193